POWERS

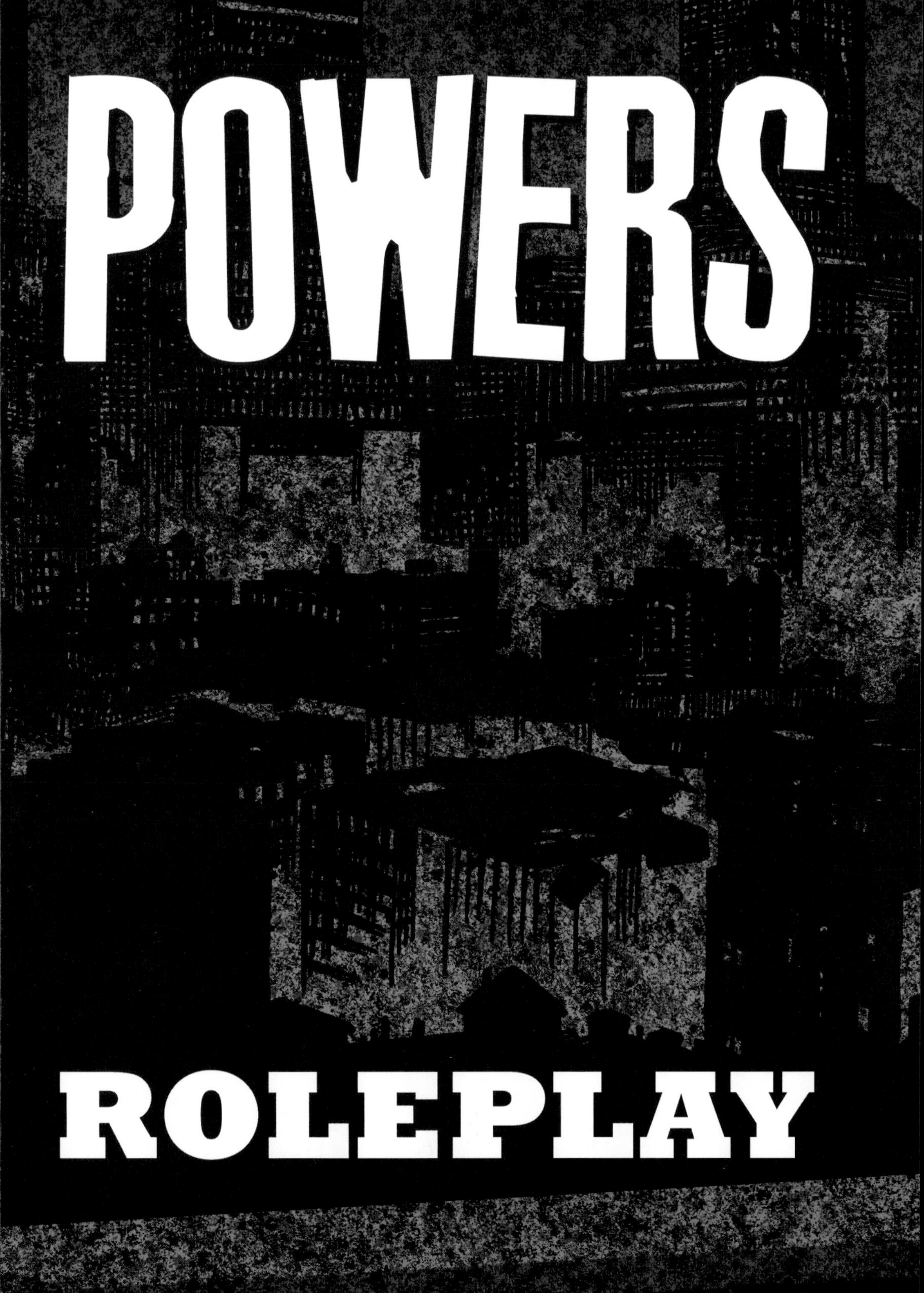

ROLEPLAY

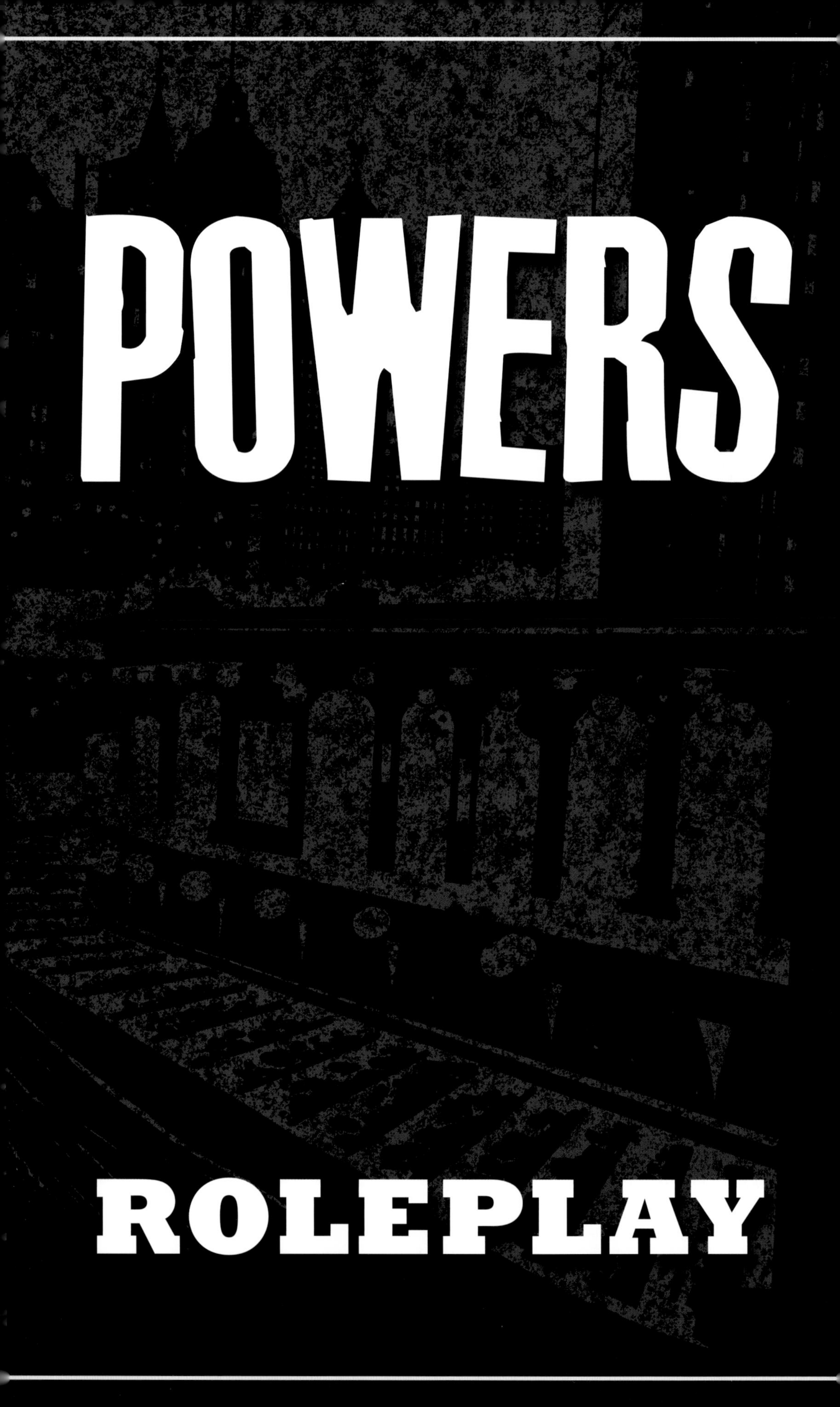
POWERS
ROLEPLAY

Created and Produced by

BRIAN
MICHAEL
BENDIS
&
MICHAEL
AVON
OEMING

Color Art: **PAT GARRAHY**

Separation Assists: **OJO CALIENTE STUDIOS**

Letters: **PAT GARRAHY**

& BRIAN MICHAEL BENDIS

Editor: **K.C. McCRORY**

Collection Editor: **JENNIFER GRÜNWALD**

Book Design: **PATRICK McGRATH**

Cover Design: **TIM DANIEL**

Business Affairs: **ALISA BENDIS**

POWERS VOL. 2: ROLEPLAY. Contains material originally published in magazine form as POWERS VOL. 1 #8-11. First printing 2011. ISBN# 978-0-7851-5983-4. Published by MARVEL WORLDWIDE, INC., a subsidiary of MARVEL ENTERTAINMENT, LLC. OFFICE OF PUBLICATION: 135 West 50th Street, New York, NY 10020. Copyright © 2000 and 2011 Jinxworld, Inc. All rights reserved. Powers, its logo design, and all characters featured in or on this issue and the distinctive names and likenesses thereof, and all related indicia are trademarks of Jinxworld, Inc. ICON and its logos are TM & © Marvel Characters, Inc. No similarity between any of the names, characters, persons, and/or institutions in this magazine with those of any living or dead person or institution is intended, and any such similarity that may exist is purely coincidental. $19.99 per copy in the U.S. and $21.99 in Canada (GST #R127032852); Canadian Agreement #40668537. **Printed in the U.S.A.**

10 9 8 7 6 5 4 3 2 1

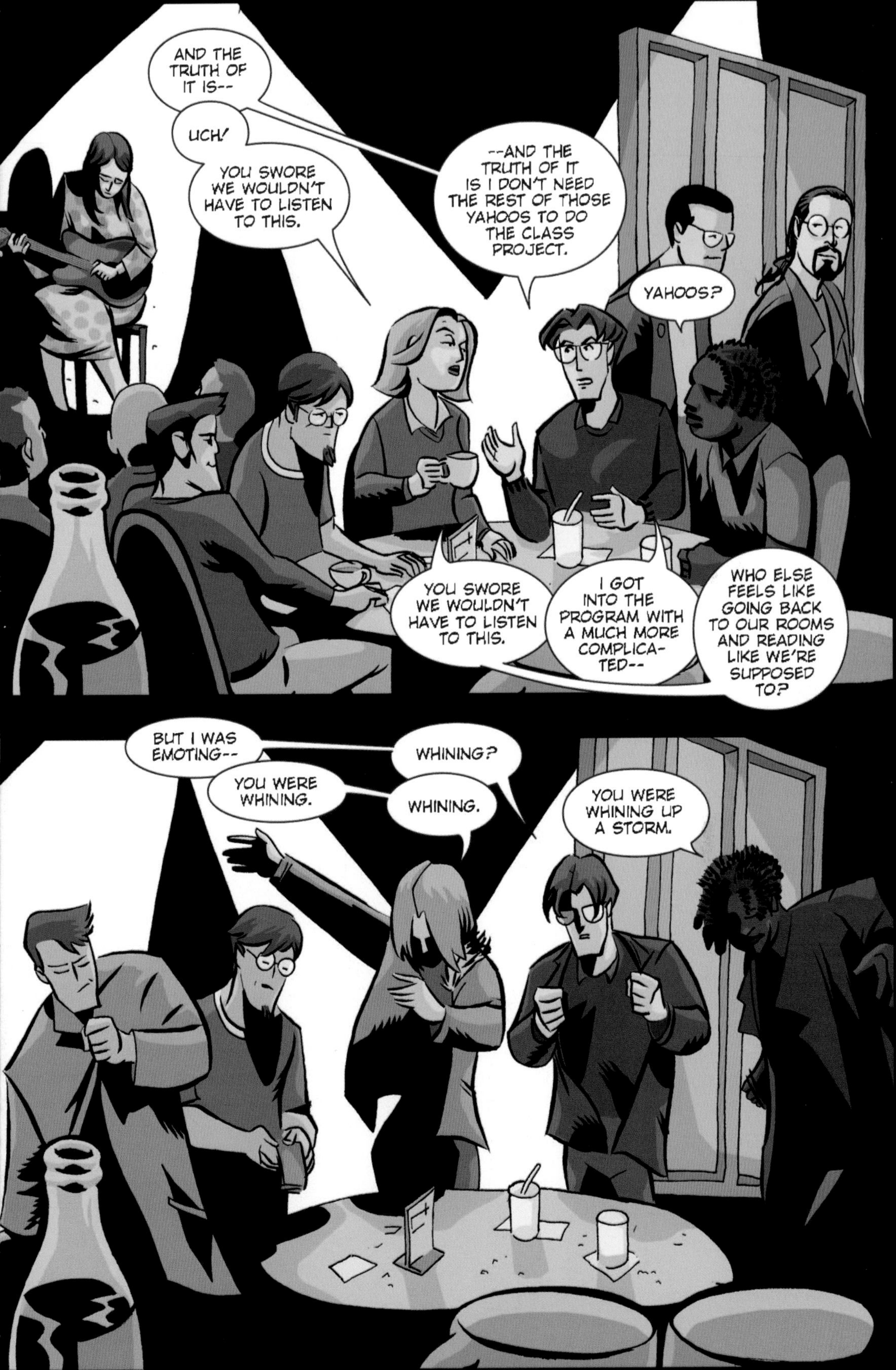
AND THE TRUTH OF IT IS--
UCH!
YOU SWORE WE WOULDN'T HAVE TO LISTEN TO THIS.
--AND THE TRUTH OF IT IS I DON'T NEED THE REST OF THOSE YAHOOS TO DO THE CLASS PROJECT.
YAHOOS?
YOU SWORE WE WOULDN'T HAVE TO LISTEN TO THIS.
I GOT INTO THE PROGRAM WITH A MUCH MORE COMPLICA-TED--
WHO ELSE FEELS LIKE GOING BACK TO OUR ROOMS AND READING LIKE WE'RE SUPPOSED TO?
BUT I WAS EMOTING--
WHINING?
YOU WERE WHINING.
WHINING.
YOU WERE WHINING UP A STORM.

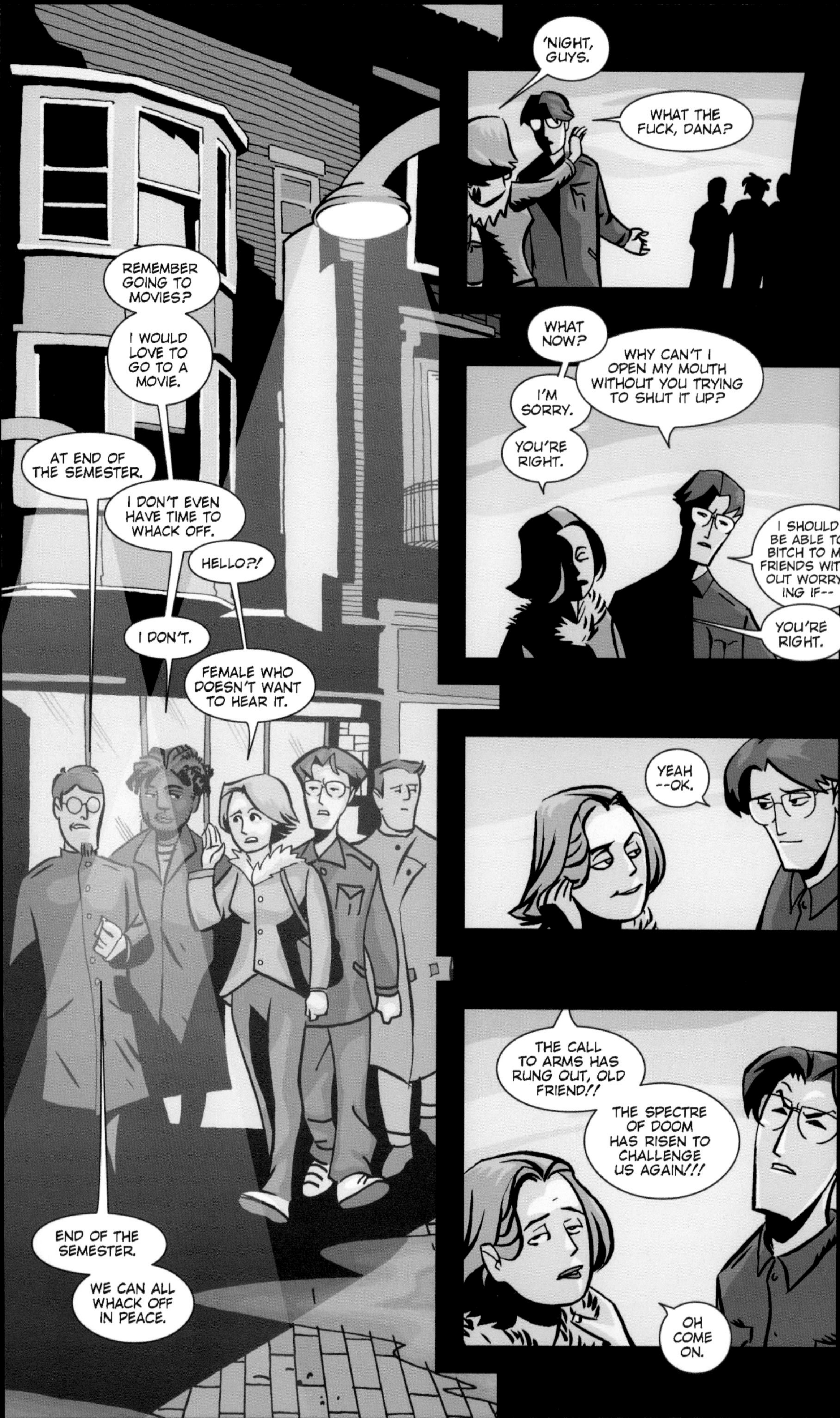
REMEMBER GOING TO MOVIES?
I WOULD LOVE TO GO TO A MOVIE.
AT END OF THE SEMESTER.
I DON'T EVEN HAVE TIME TO WHACK OFF.
HELLO?!
I DON'T.
FEMALE WHO DOESN'T WANT TO HEAR IT.
END OF THE SEMESTER.
WE CAN ALL WHACK OFF IN PEACE.
'NIGHT, GUYS.
WHAT THE FUCK, DANA?
WHAT NOW?
WHY CAN'T I OPEN MY MOUTH WITHOUT YOU TRYING TO SHUT IT UP?
I'M SORRY.
YOU'RE RIGHT.
YOU'RE RIGHT.
YEAH --OK.
THE CALL TO ARMS HAS RUNG OUT, OLD FRIEND!!
THE SPECTRE OF DOOM HAS RISEN TO CHALLENGE US AGAIN!!!
OH COME ON.

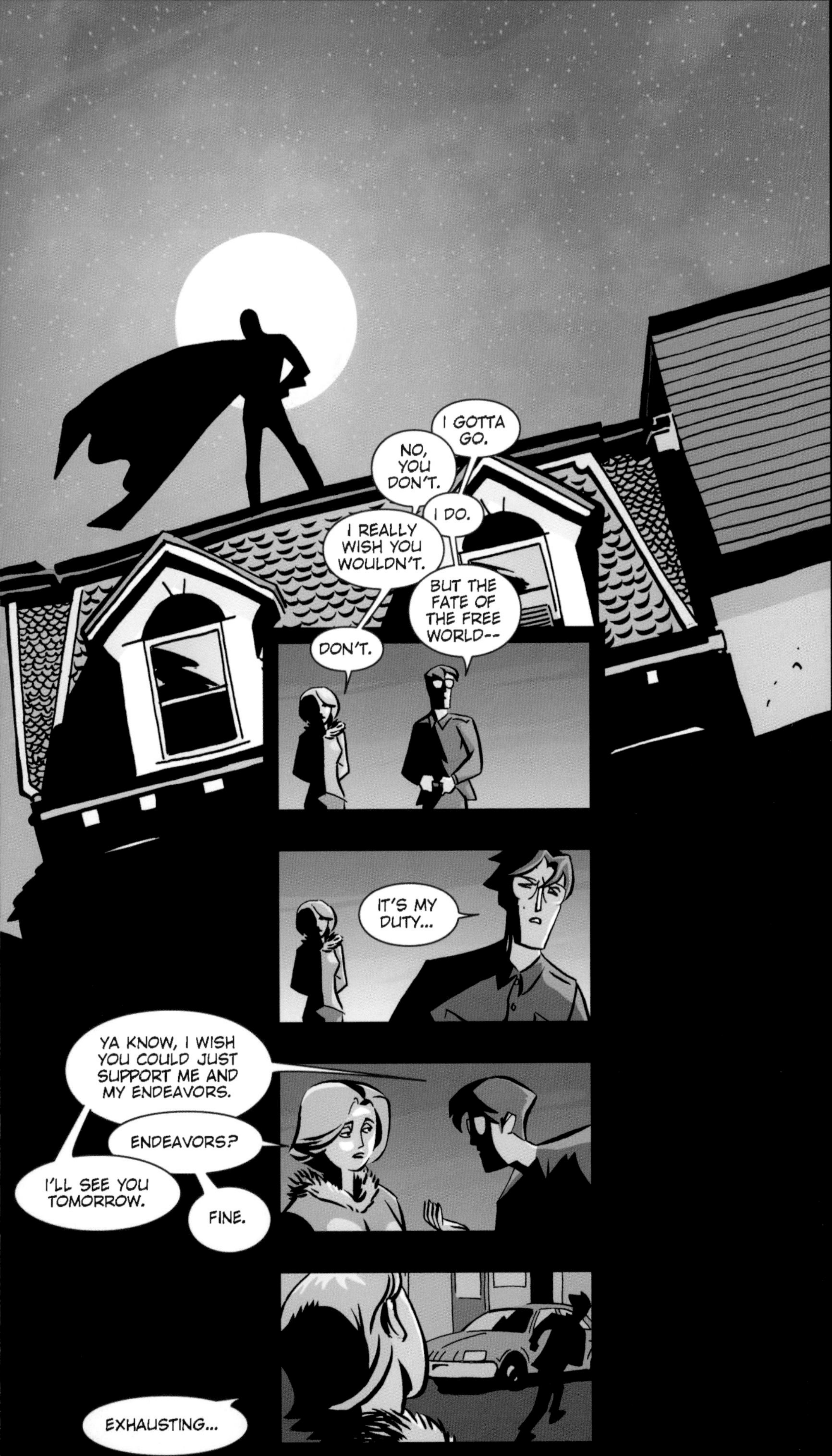
I GOTTA GO.
NO, YOU DON'T.
I DO.
I REALLY WISH YOU WOULDN'T.
BUT THE FATE OF THE FREE WORLD--
DON'T.
IT'S MY DUTY...
YA KNOW, I WISH YOU COULD JUST SUPPORT ME AND MY ENDEAVORS.
ENDEAVORS?
I'LL SEE YOU TOMORROW.
FINE.
EXHAUSTING...

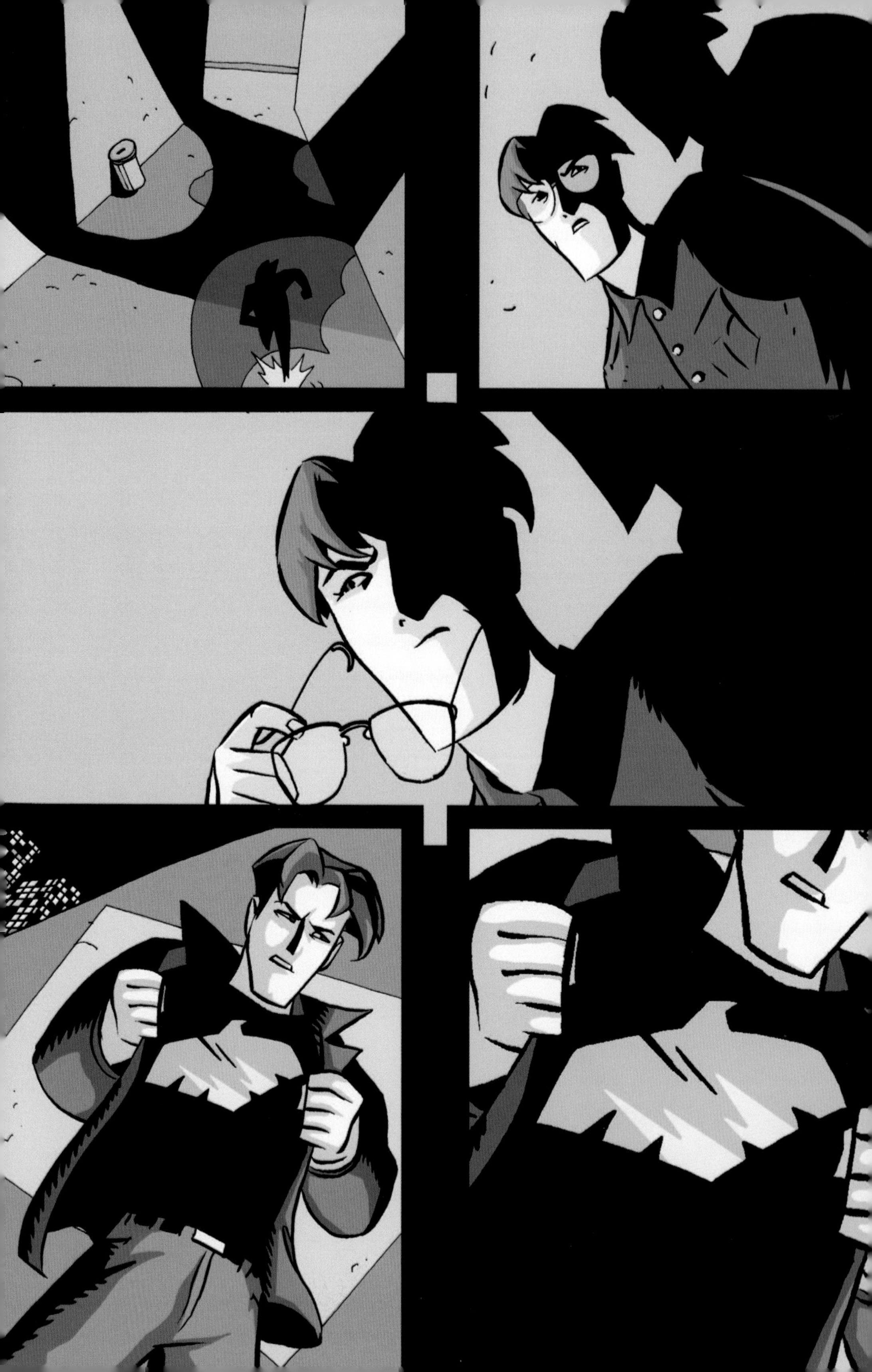

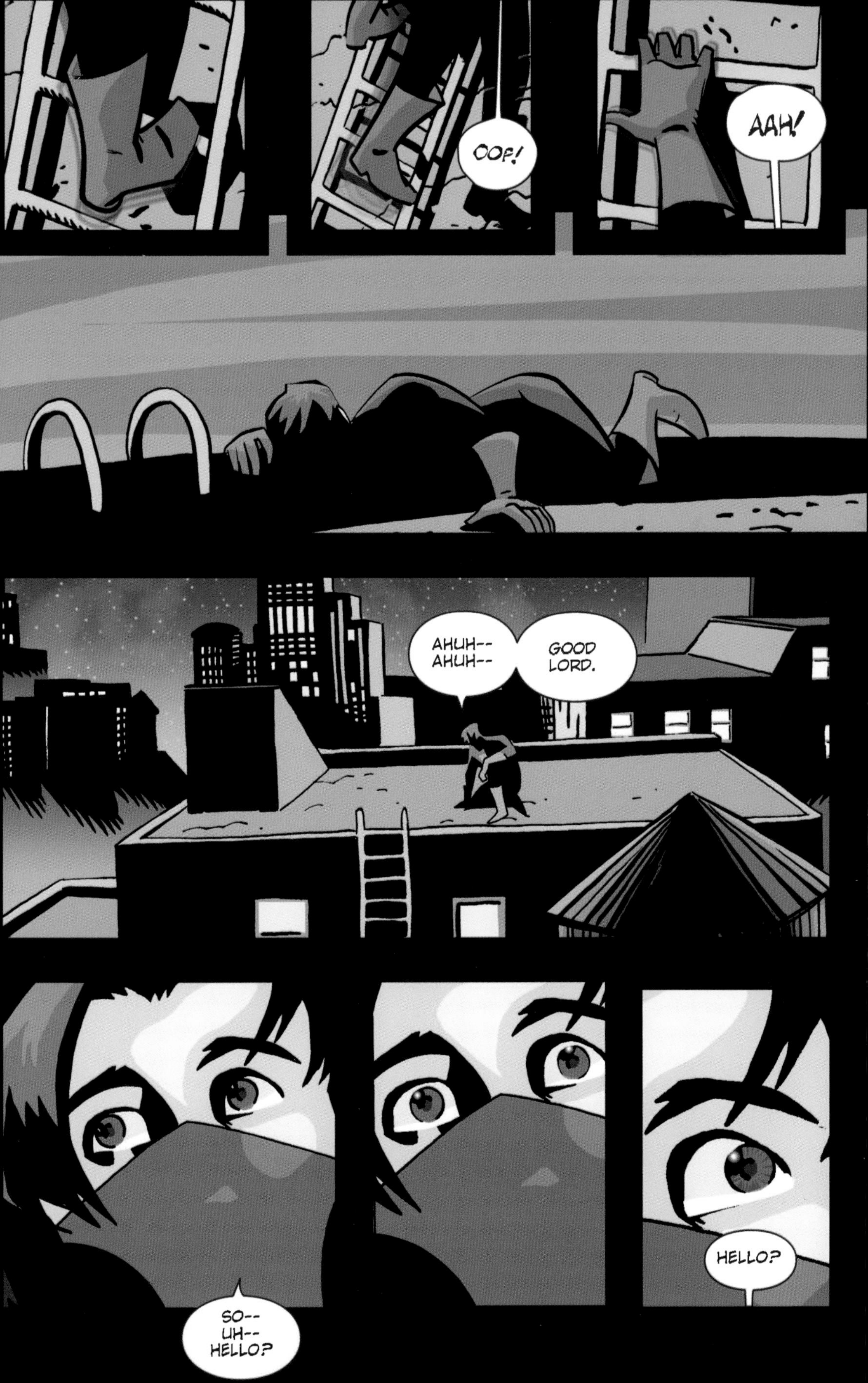
OOF!
AAH!
AHUH-- AHUH--
GOOD LORD.
SO-- UH-- HELLO?
HELLO?

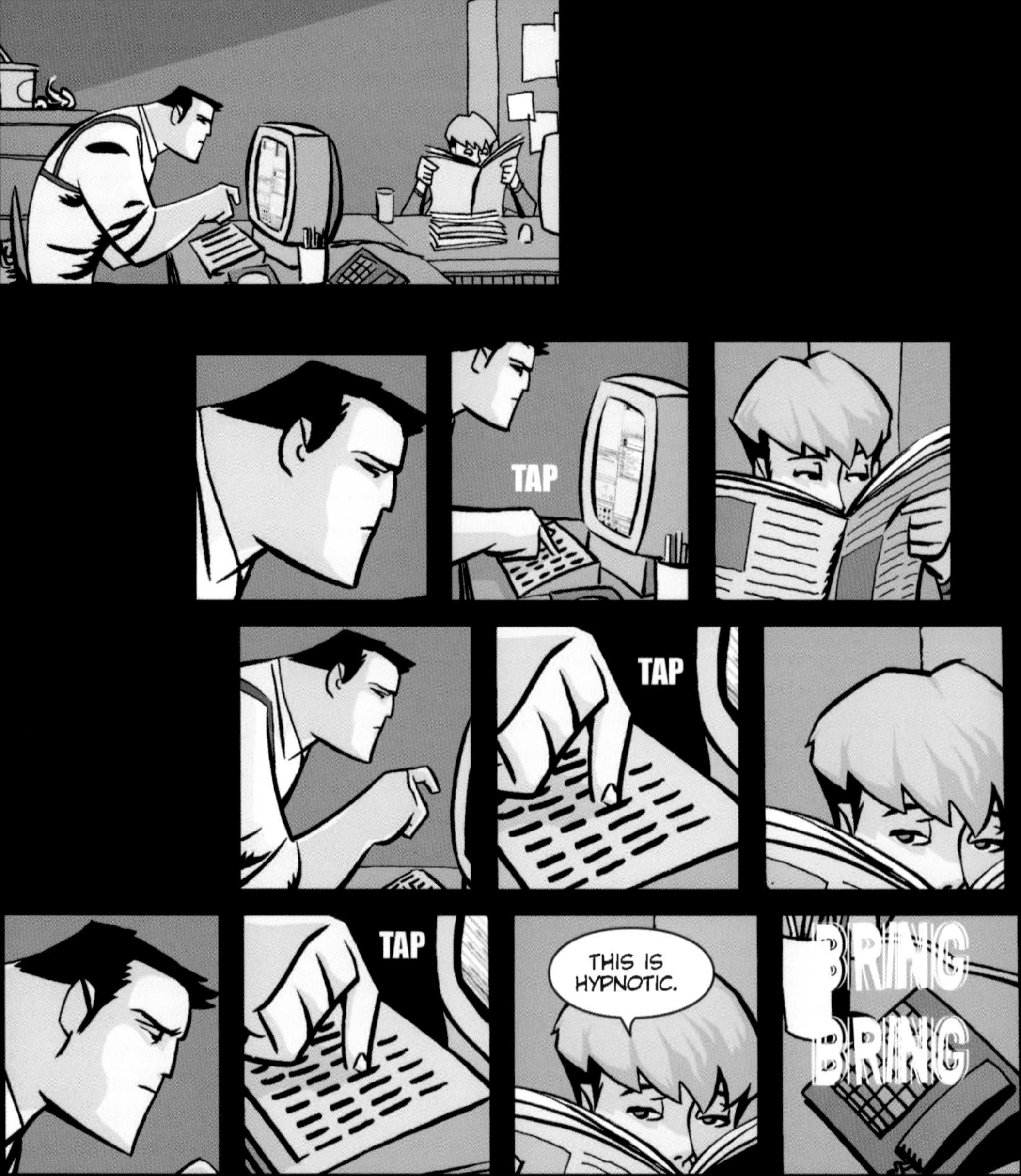
TAP
TAP
TAP
THIS IS HYPNOTIC.
BRING BRING

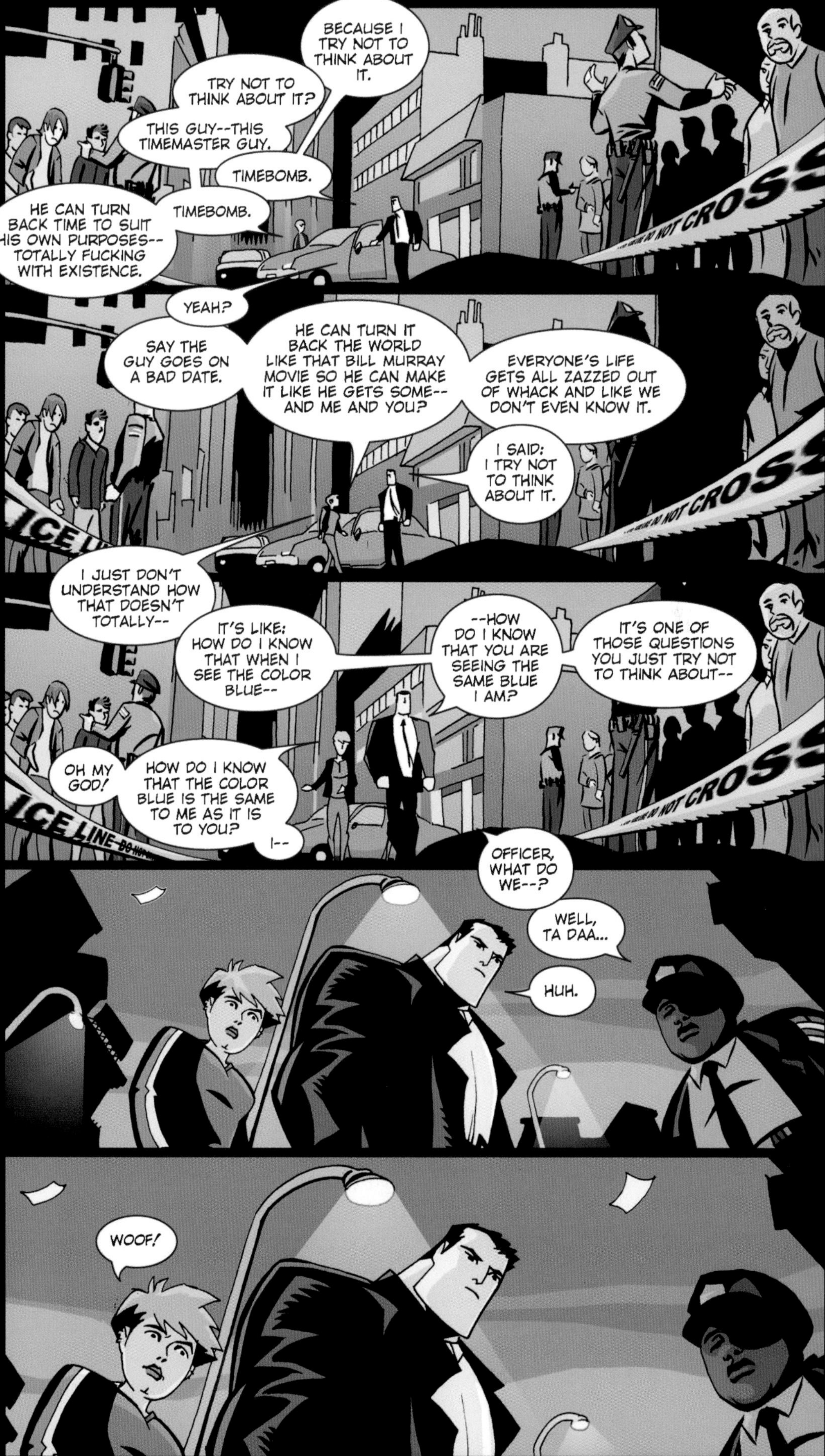

BECAUSE I TRY NOT TO THINK ABOUT IT.
TRY NOT TO THINK ABOUT IT?
THIS GUY--THIS TIMEMASTER GUY.
TIMEBOMB.
TIMEBOMB.
HE CAN TURN BACK TIME TO SUIT HIS OWN PURPOSES-- TOTALLY FUCKING WITH EXISTENCE.
YEAH?
SAY THE GUY GOES ON A BAD DATE.
HE CAN TURN IT BACK THE WORLD LIKE THAT BILL MURRAY MOVIE SO HE CAN MAKE IT LIKE HE GETS SOME-- AND ME AND YOU?
EVERYONE'S LIFE GETS ALL ZAZZED OUT OF WHACK AND LIKE WE DON'T EVEN KNOW IT.
I SAID: I TRY NOT TO THINK ABOUT IT.
I JUST DON'T UNDERSTAND HOW THAT DOESN'T TOTALLY--
IT'S LIKE: HOW DO I KNOW THAT WHEN I SEE THE COLOR BLUE--
--HOW DO I KNOW THAT YOU ARE SEEING THE SAME BLUE I AM?
IT'S ONE OF THOSE QUESTIONS YOU JUST TRY NOT TO THINK ABOUT--
OH MY GOD!
HOW DO I KNOW THAT THE COLOR BLUE IS THE SAME TO ME AS IT IS TO YOU?
I--
OFFICER, WHAT DO WE--?
WELL, TA DAA...
HUH.
WOOF!

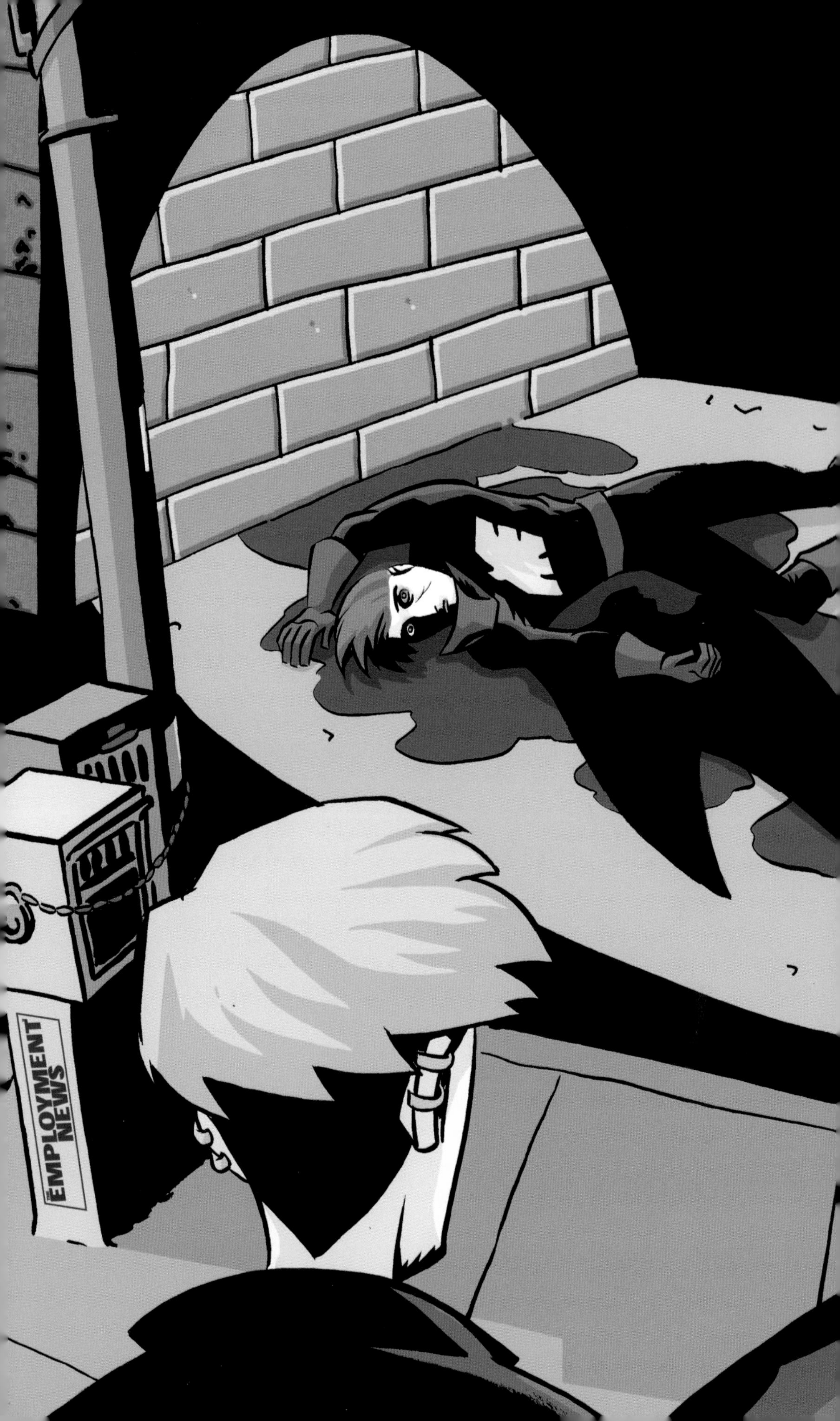
THE EMPLOYMENT NEWS

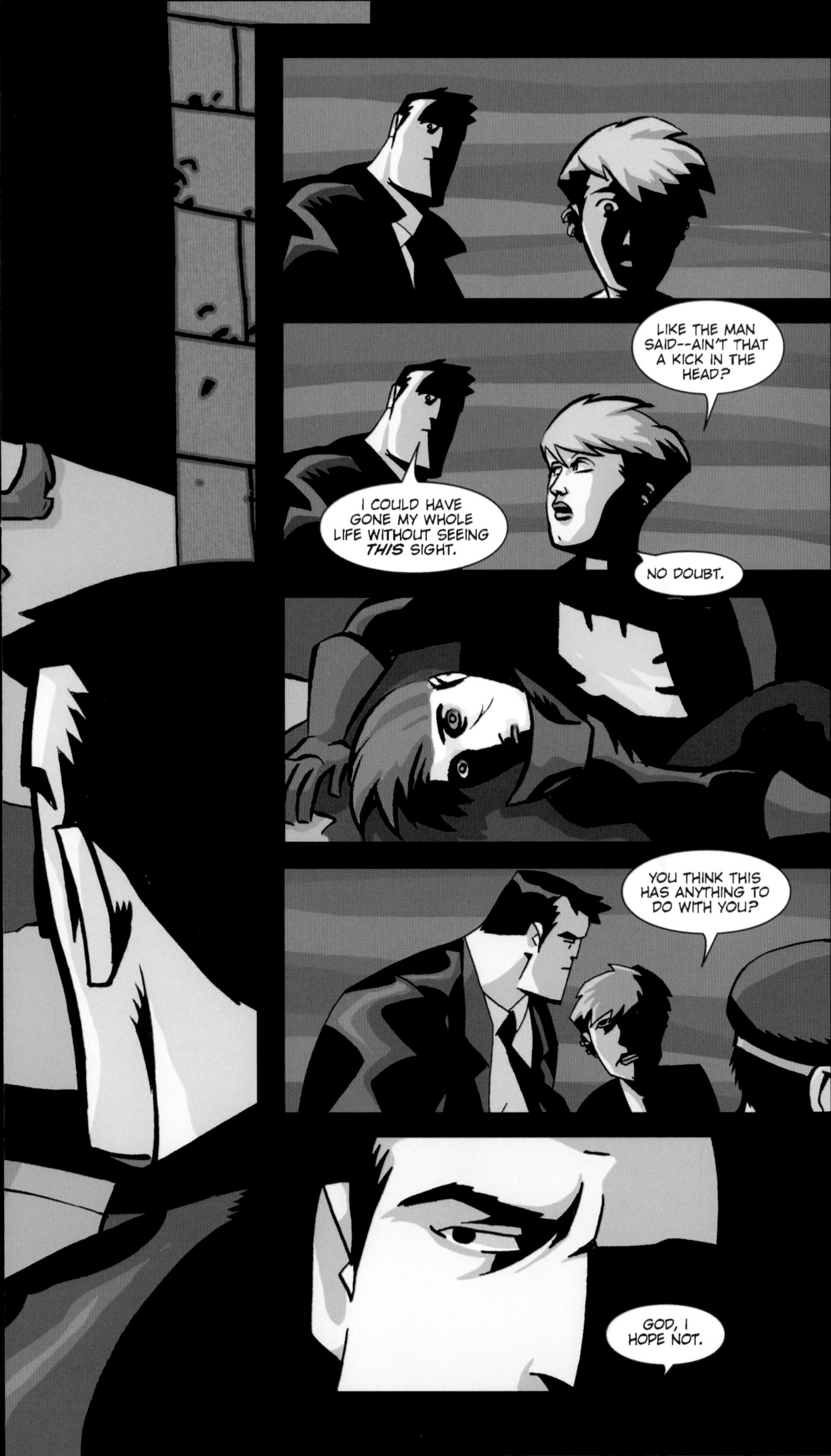
LIKE THE MAN SAID--AIN'T THAT A KICK IN THE HEAD?
I COULD HAVE GONE MY WHOLE LIFE WITHOUT SEEING *THIS* SIGHT.
NO DOUBT.
YOU THINK THIS HAS ANYTHING TO DO WITH YOU?
GOD, I HOPE NOT.

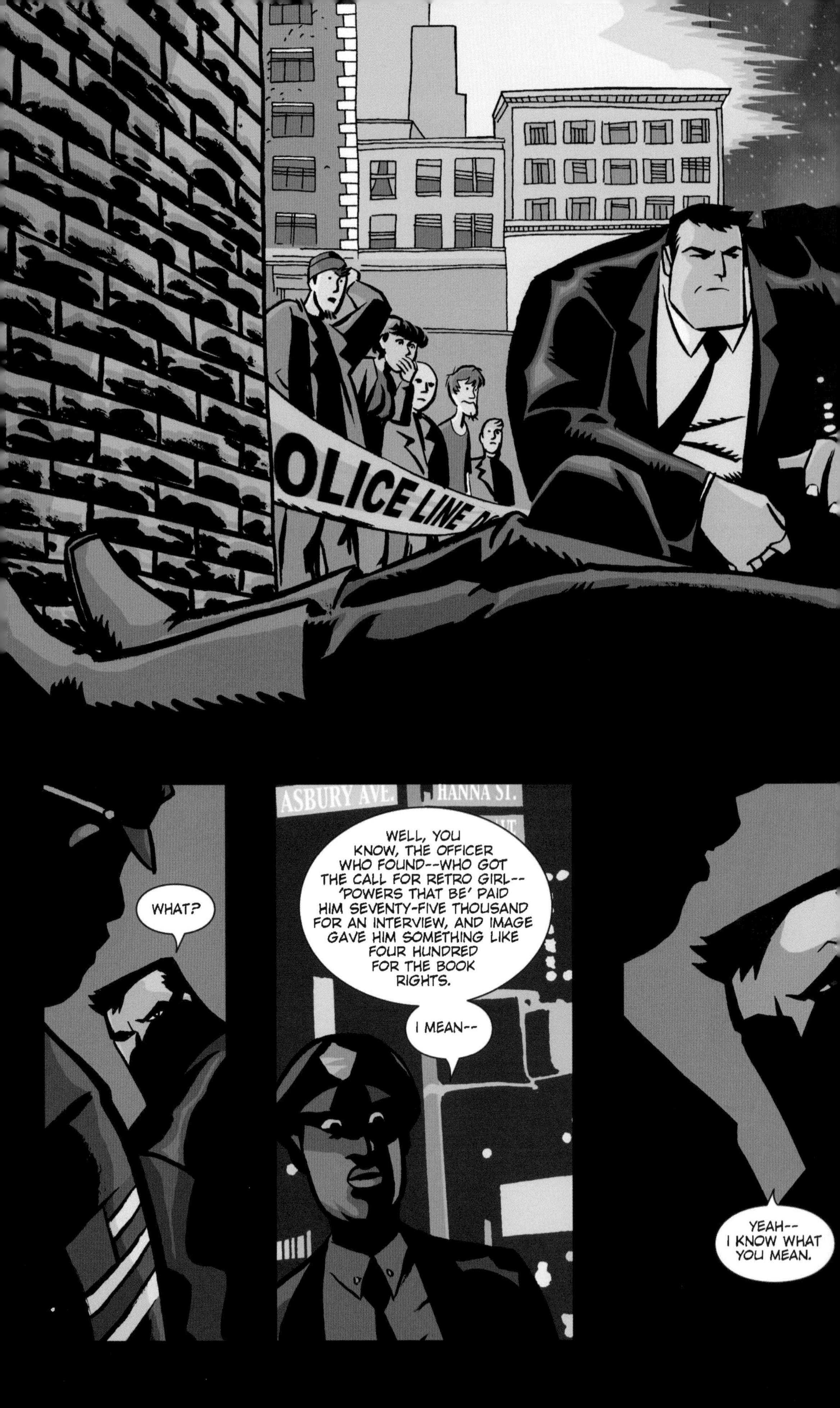
OLICE LINE D
ASBURY AVE.
HANNA ST.
WHAT?
WELL, YOU KNOW, THE OFFICER WHO FOUND--WHO GOT THE CALL FOR RETRO GIRL-- 'POWERS THAT BE' PAID HIM SEVENTY-FIVE THOUSAND FOR AN INTERVIEW, AND IMAGE GAVE HIM SOMETHING LIKE FOUR HUNDRED FOR THE BOOK RIGHTS.
I MEAN--
YEAH-- I KNOW WHAT YOU MEAN.

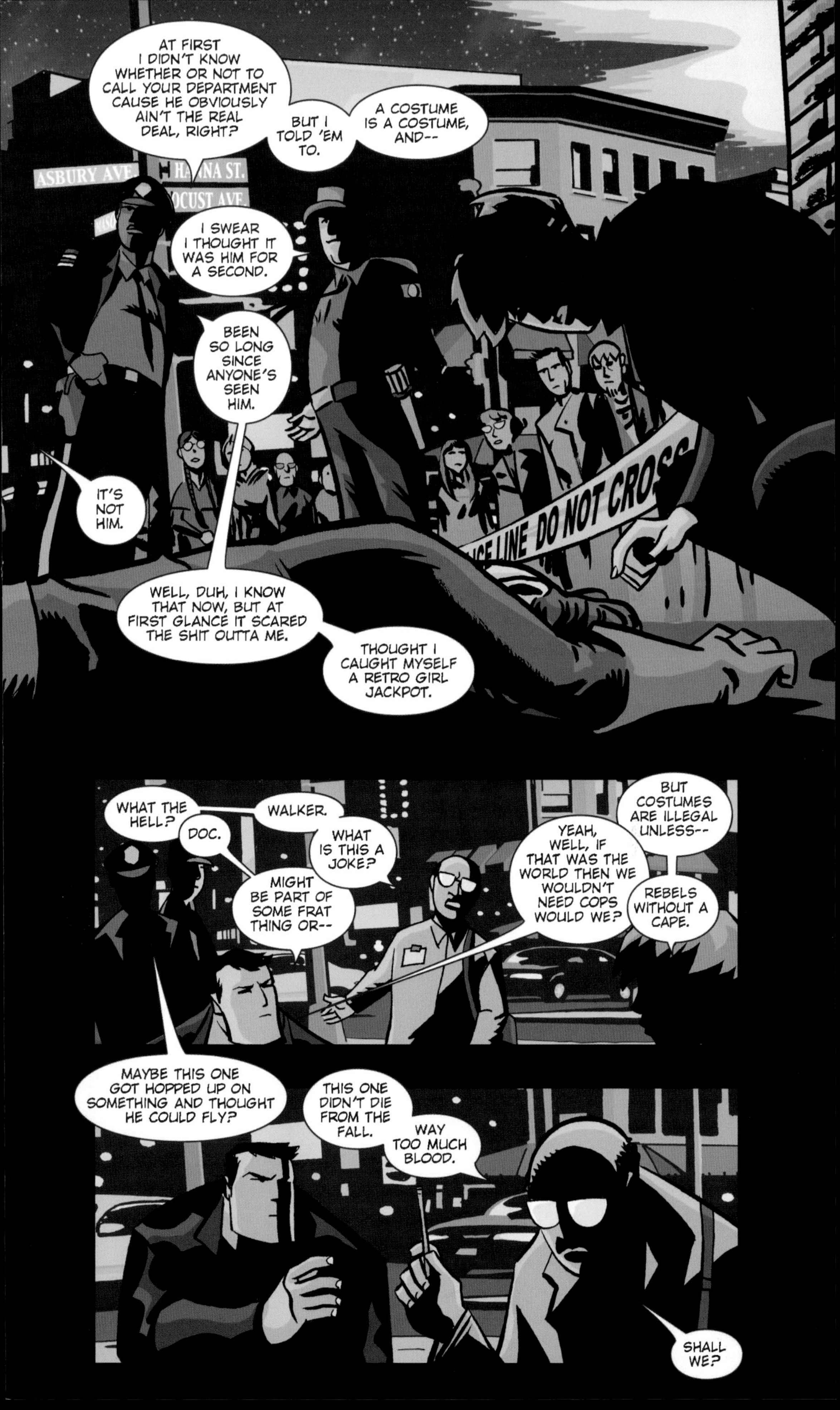
AT FIRST I DIDN'T KNOW WHETHER OR NOT TO CALL YOUR DEPARTMENT CAUSE HE OBVIOUSLY AIN'T THE REAL DEAL, RIGHT?
BUT I TOLD 'EM TO.
A COSTUME IS A COSTUME, AND--
ASBURY AVE.
HANNA ST.
LOCUST AVE.
I SWEAR I THOUGHT IT WAS HIM FOR A SECOND.
BEEN SO LONG SINCE ANYONE'S SEEN HIM.
IT'S NOT HIM.
DO NOT CROSS
WELL, DUH, I KNOW THAT NOW, BUT AT FIRST GLANCE IT SCARED THE SHIT OUTTA ME.
THOUGHT I CAUGHT MYSELF A RETRO GIRL JACKPOT.
WHAT THE HELL?
WALKER.
DOC.
WHAT IS THIS A JOKE?
MIGHT BE PART OF SOME FRAT THING OR--
YEAH, WELL, IF THAT WAS THE WORLD THEN WE WOULDN'T NEED COPS WOULD WE?
BUT COSTUMES ARE ILLEGAL UNLESS--
REBELS WITHOUT A CAPE.
MAYBE THIS ONE GOT HOPPED UP ON SOMETHING AND THOUGHT HE COULD FLY?
THIS ONE DIDN'T DIE FROM THE FALL.
WAY TOO MUCH BLOOD.
SHALL WE?

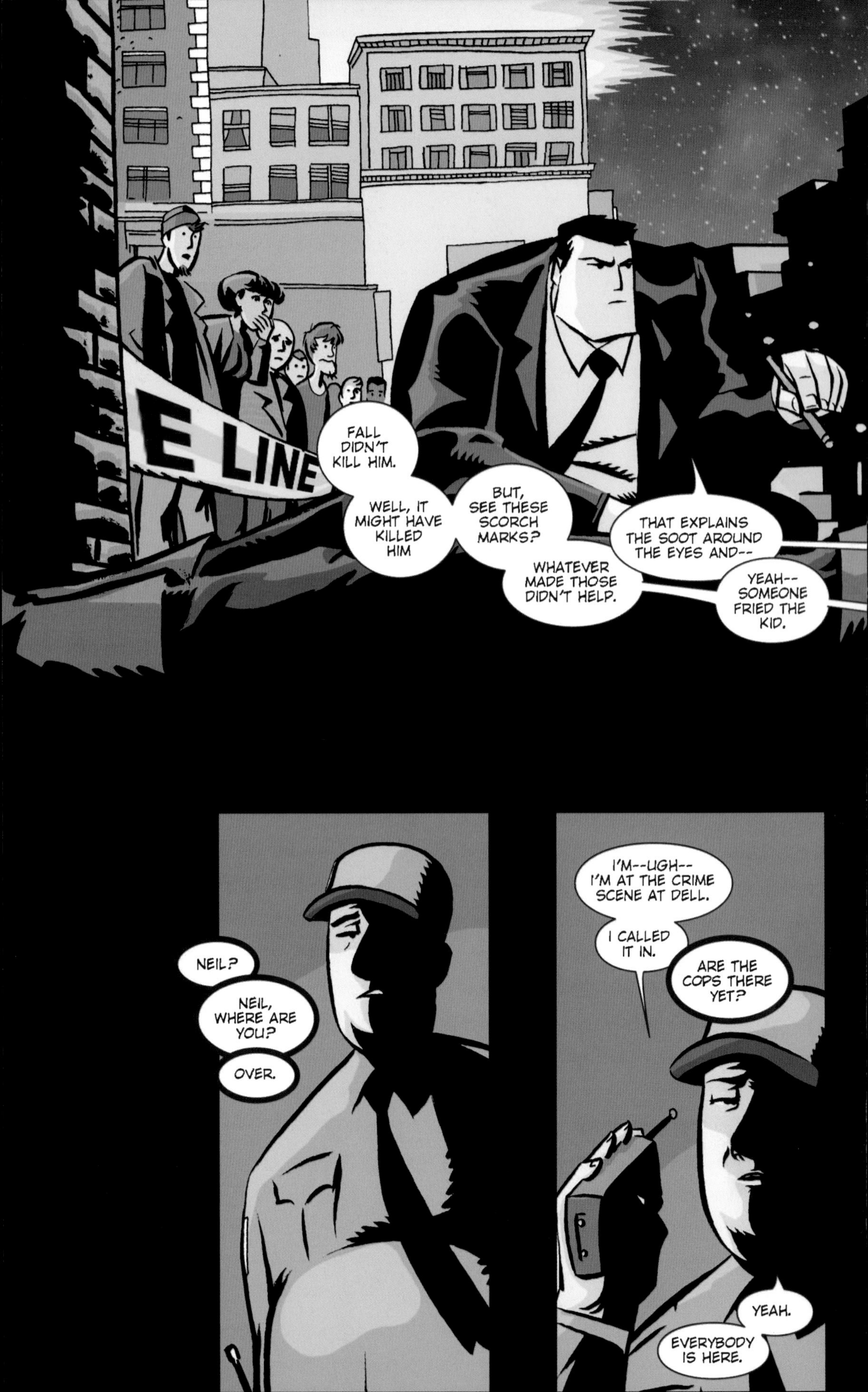
E LINE
FALL DIDN'T KILL HIM.
WELL, IT MIGHT HAVE KILLED HIM
BUT, SEE THESE SCORCH MARKS?
WHATEVER MADE THOSE DIDN'T HELP.
THAT EXPLAINS THE SOOT AROUND THE EYES AND--
YEAH-- SOMEONE FRIED THE KID.
NEIL?
NEIL, WHERE ARE YOU?
OVER.
I'M--UGH-- I'M AT THE CRIME SCENE AT DELL.
I CALLED IT IN.
ARE THE COPS THERE YET?
YEAH.
EVERYBODY IS HERE.

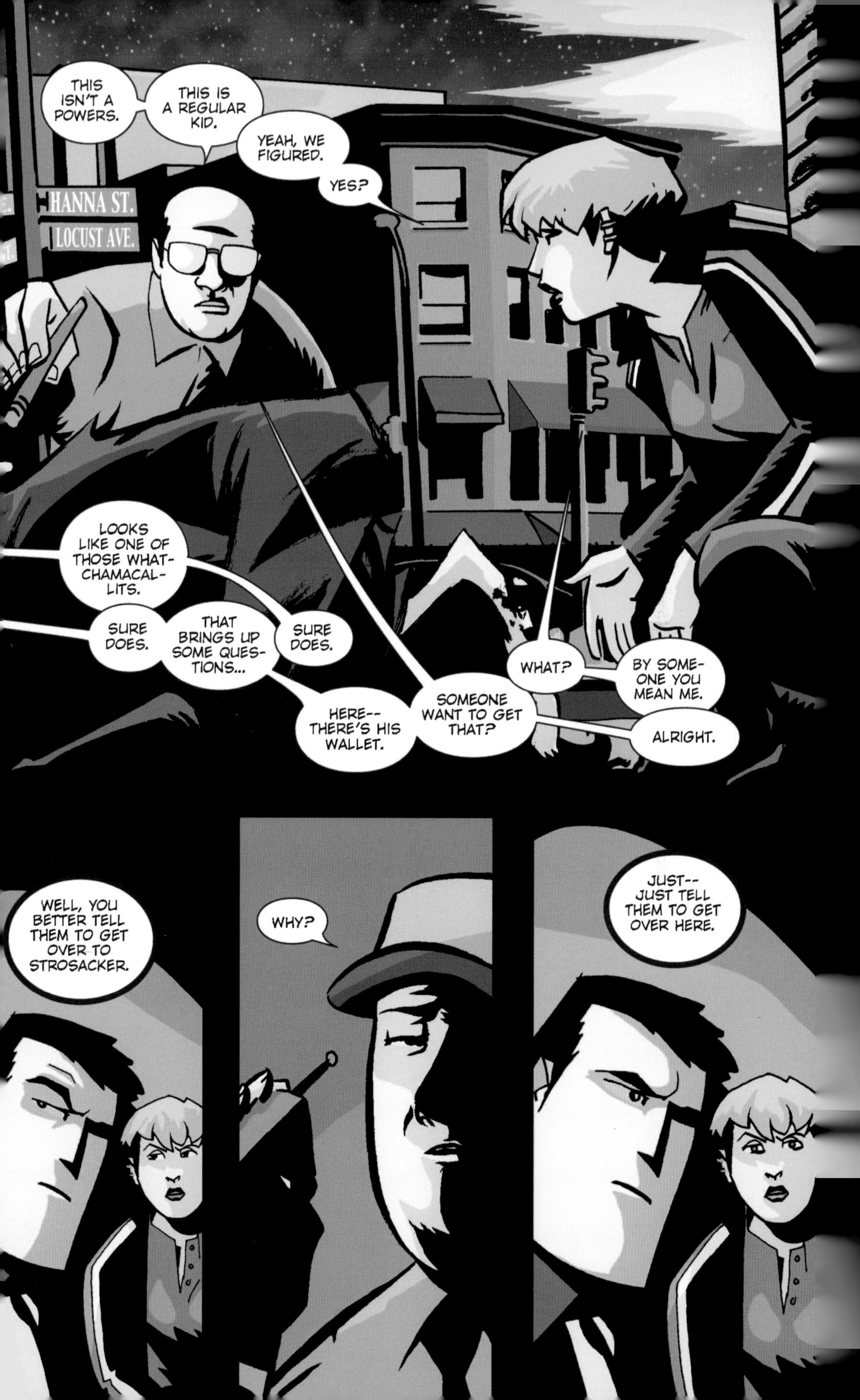

HANNA ST.
LOCUST AVE.
THIS ISN'T A POWERS.
THIS IS A REGULAR KID.
YEAH, WE FIGURED.
YES?
LOOKS LIKE ONE OF THOSE WHAT-CHAMACAL-LITS.
SURE DOES.
SURE DOES.
THAT BRINGS UP SOME QUES-TIONS...
HERE-- THERE'S HIS WALLET.
SOMEONE WANT TO GET THAT?
WHAT?
BY SOME-ONE YOU MEAN ME.
ALRIGHT.
WELL, YOU BETTER TELL THEM TO GET OVER TO STROSACKER.
WHY?
JUST-- JUST TELL THEM TO GET OVER HERE.

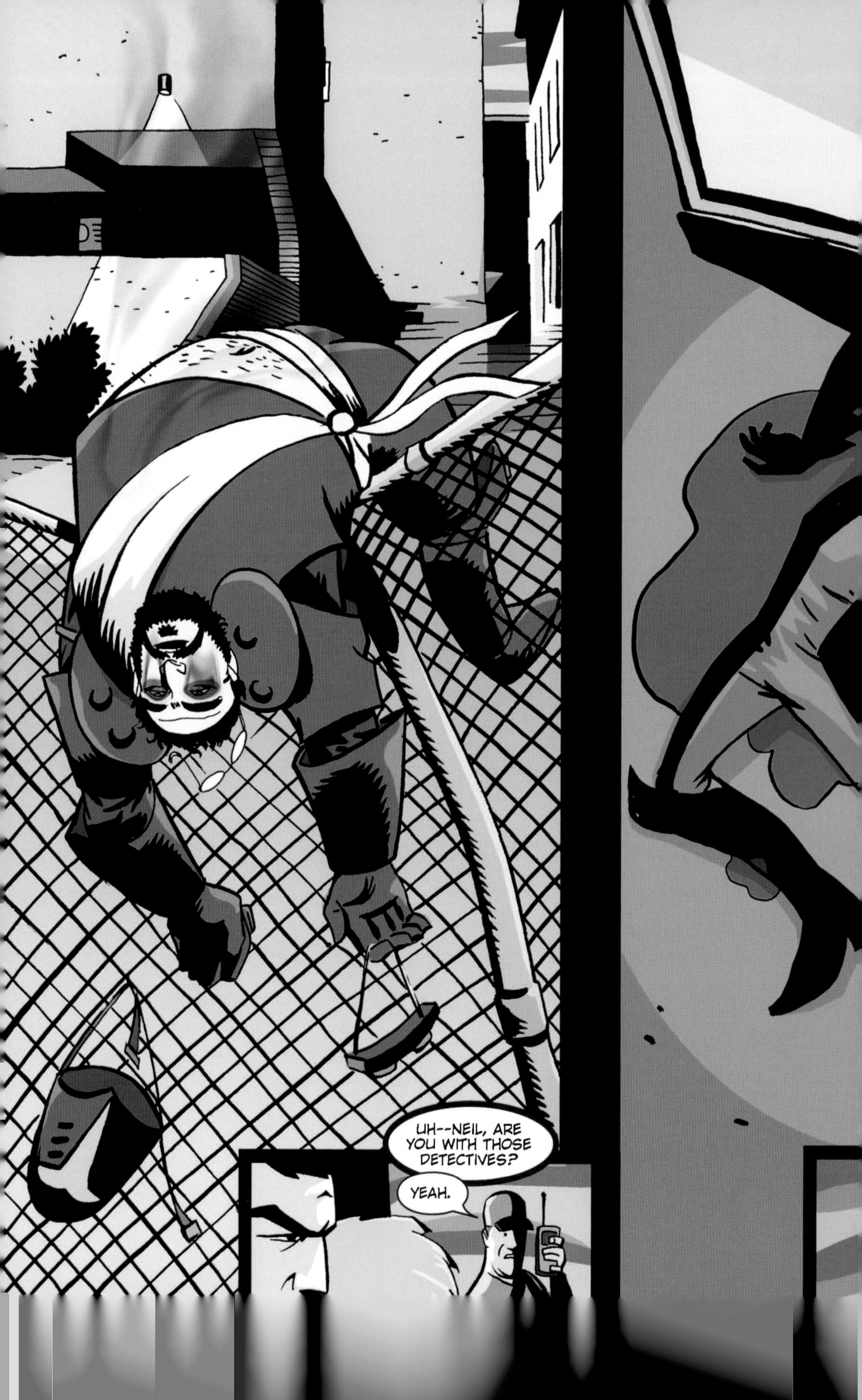
UH--NEIL, ARE YOU WITH THOSE DETECTIVES?
YEAH.

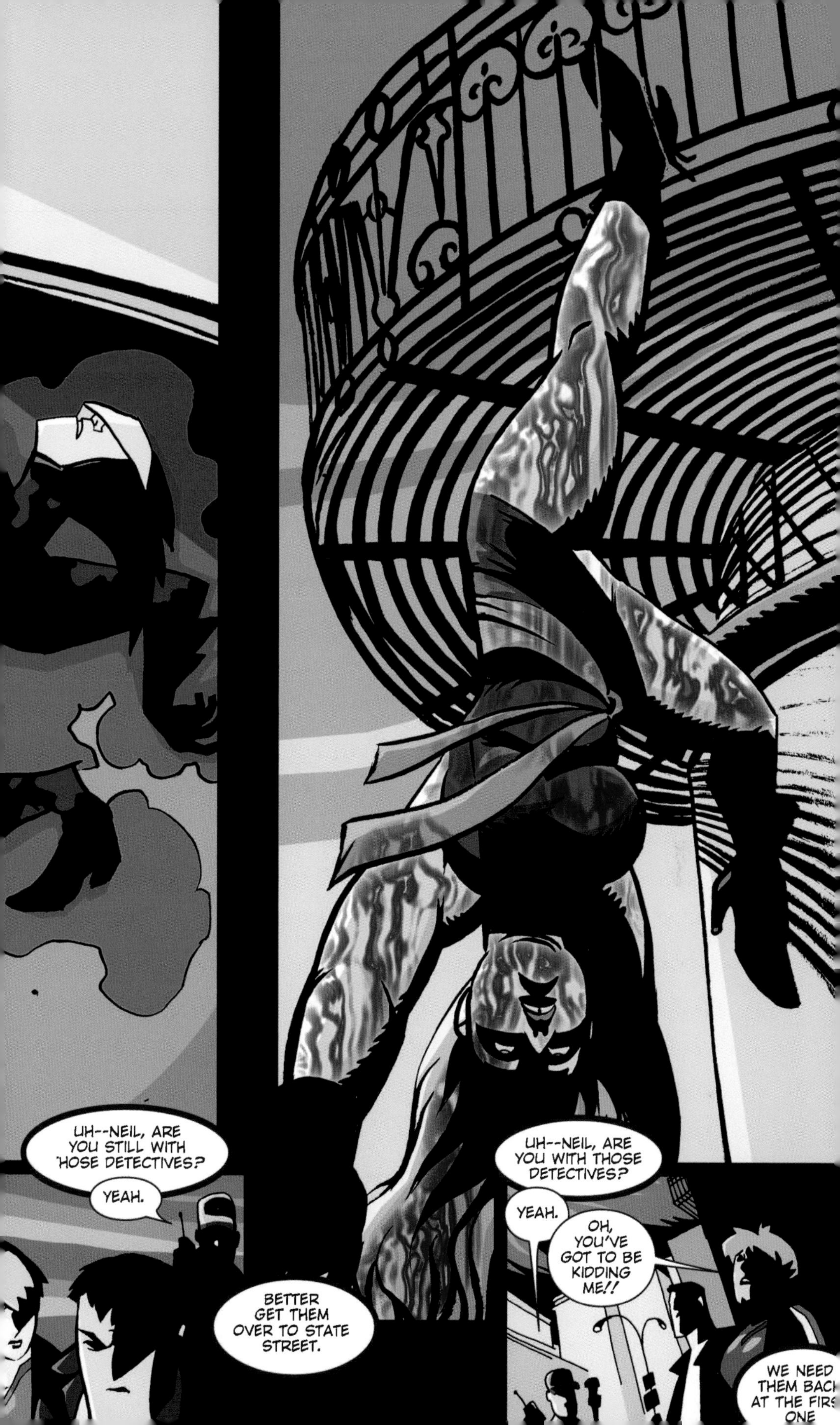
UH--NEIL, ARE YOU STILL WITH 'HOSE DETECTIVES?
YEAH.
BETTER GET THEM OVER TO STATE STREET.
UH--NEIL, ARE YOU WITH THOSE DETECTIVES?
YEAH.
OH, YOU'VE GOT TO BE KIDDING ME!!
WE NEED THEM BAC AT THE FIRS ONE

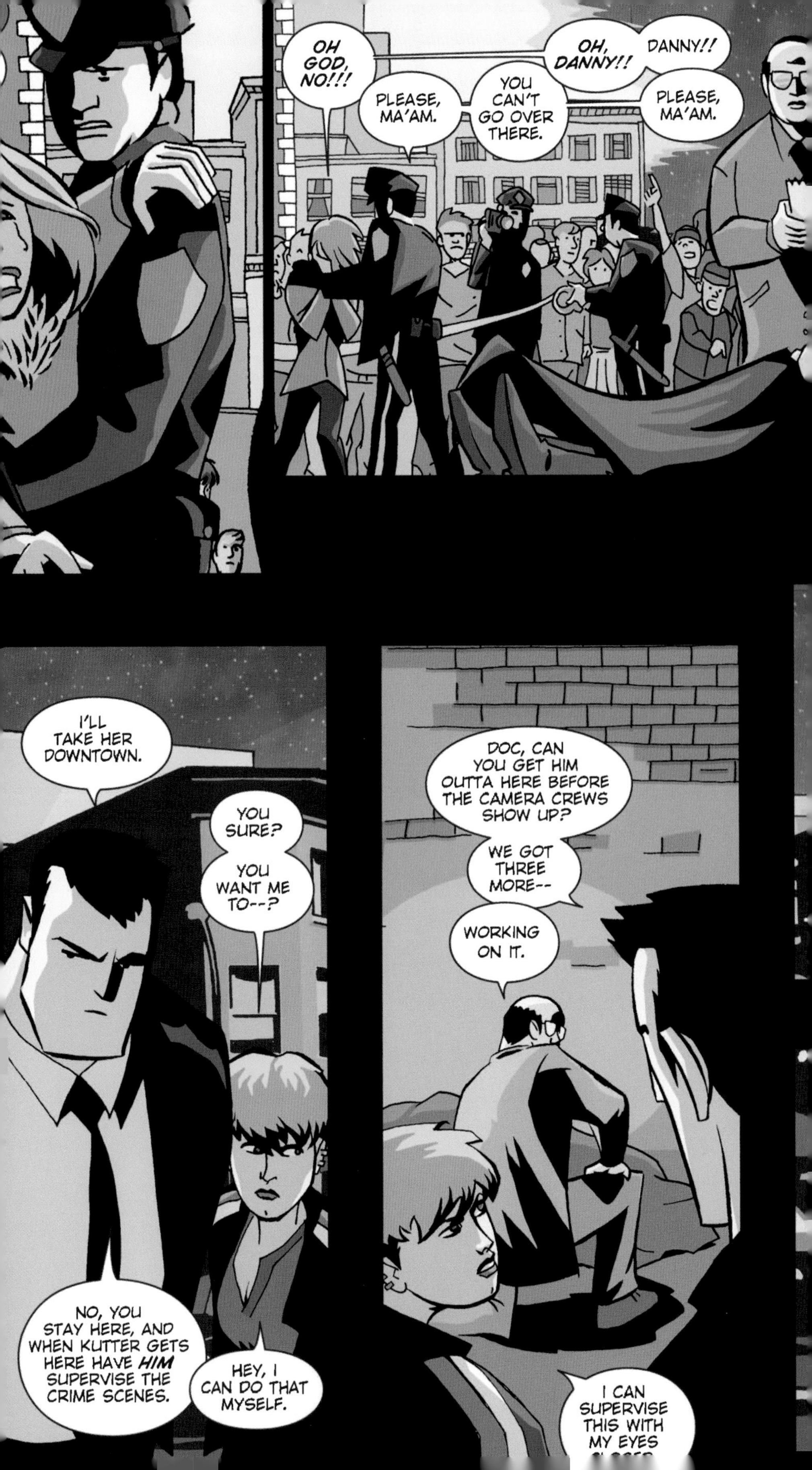
OH GOD, NO!!!
PLEASE, MA'AM.
YOU CAN'T GO OVER THERE.
OH, DANNY!!
DANNY!!
PLEASE, MA'AM.
I'LL TAKE HER DOWNTOWN.
YOU SURE?
YOU WANT ME TO--?
NO, YOU STAY HERE, AND WHEN KUTTER GETS HERE HAVE *HIM* SUPERVISE THE CRIME SCENES.
HEY, I CAN DO THAT MYSELF.
DOC, CAN YOU GET HIM OUTTA HERE BEFORE THE CAMERA CREWS SHOW UP?
WE GOT THREE MORE--
WORKING ON IT.
I CAN SUPERVISE THIS WITH MY EYES

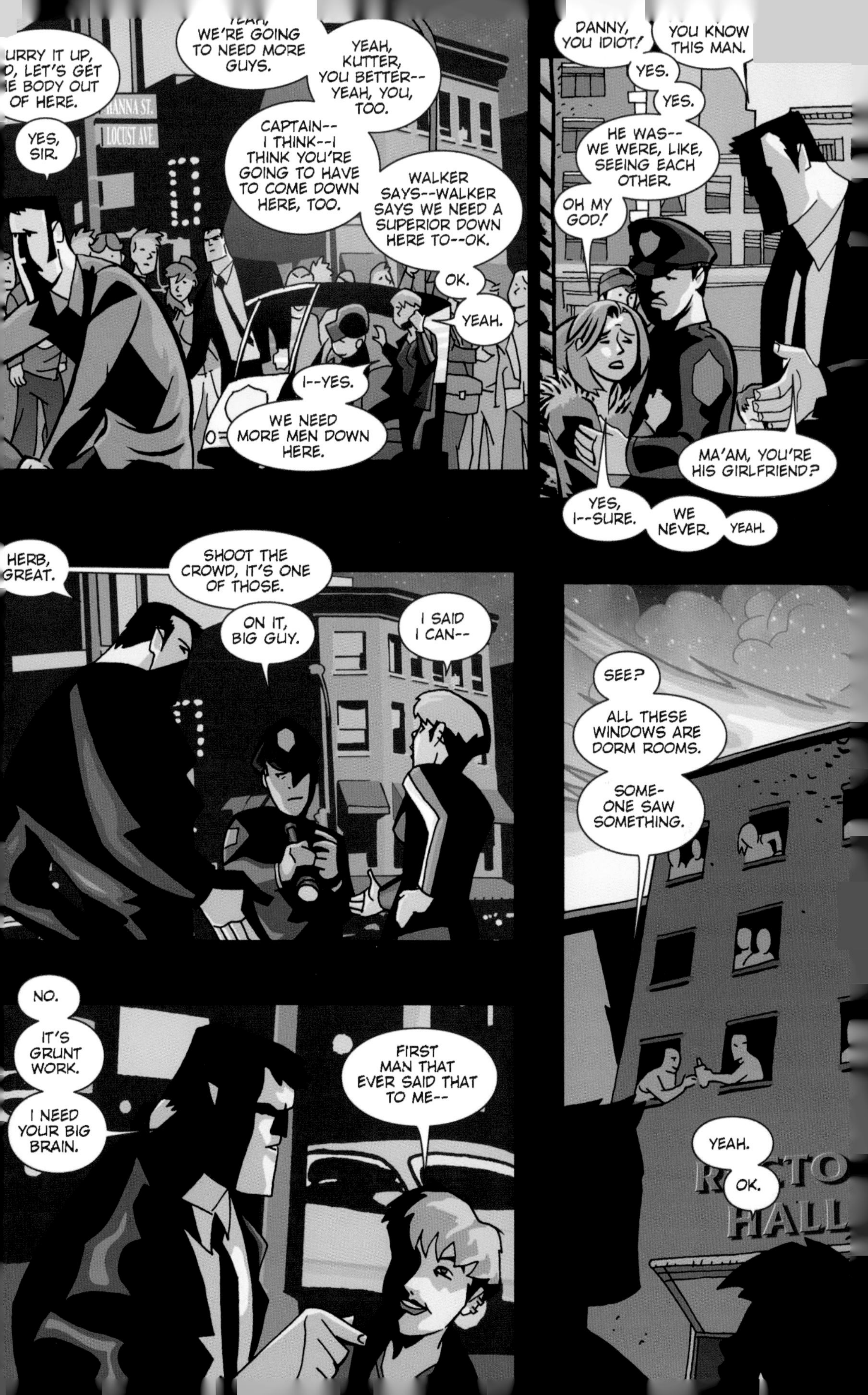
URRY IT UP, D, LET'S GET IE BODY OUT OF HERE.
HANNA ST.
LOCUST AVE.
YES, SIR.
WE'RE GOING TO NEED MORE GUYS.
YEAH, KUTTER, YOU BETTER-- YEAH, YOU, TOO.
CAPTAIN-- I THINK--I THINK YOU'RE GOING TO HAVE TO COME DOWN HERE, TOO.
WALKER SAYS--WALKER SAYS WE NEED A SUPERIOR DOWN HERE TO--OK.
OK.
YEAH.
I--YES.
WE NEED MORE MEN DOWN HERE.
DANNY, YOU IDIOT!
YOU KNOW THIS MAN.
YES.
YES.
HE WAS-- WE WERE, LIKE, SEEING EACH OTHER.
OH MY GOD!
MA'AM, YOU'RE HIS GIRLFRIEND?
YES, I--SURE.
WE NEVER.
YEAH.
HERB, GREAT.
SHOOT THE CROWD, IT'S ONE OF THOSE.
ON IT, BIG GUY.
I SAID I CAN--
NO.
IT'S GRUNT WORK.
I NEED YOUR BIG BRAIN.
FIRST MAN THAT EVER SAID THAT TO ME--
SEE?
ALL THESE WINDOWS ARE DORM ROOMS.
SOME-ONE SAW SOMETHING.
YEAH.
OK.

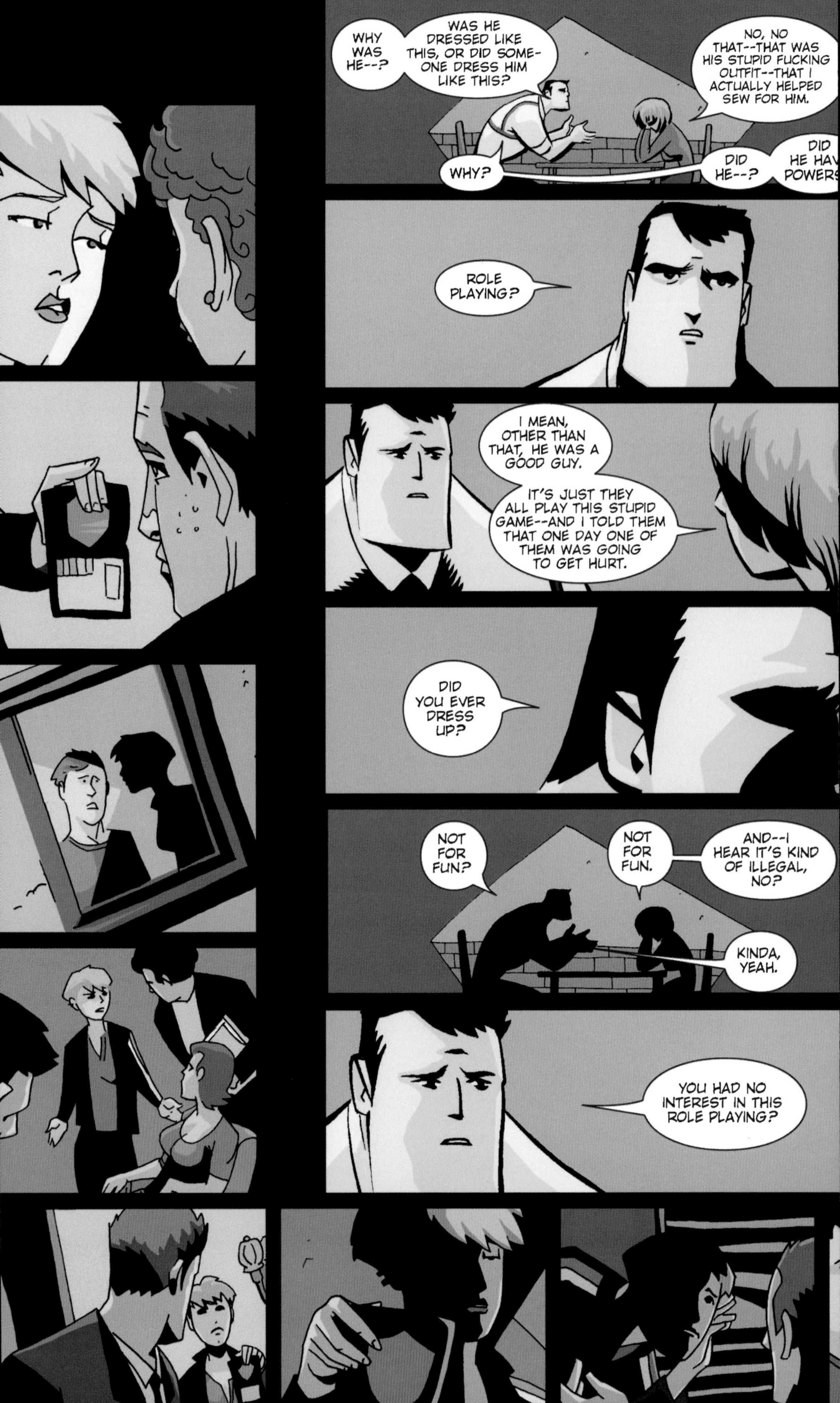
WHY WAS HE--?
WAS HE DRESSED LIKE THIS, OR DID SOME-ONE DRESS HIM LIKE THIS?
NO, NO THAT--THAT WAS HIS STUPID FUCKING OUTFIT--THAT I ACTUALLY HELPED SEW FOR HIM.
WHY?
DID HE--?
ROLE PLAYING?
I MEAN, OTHER THAN THAT, HE WAS A GOOD GUY.
IT'S JUST THEY ALL PLAY THIS STUPID GAME--AND I TOLD THEM THAT ONE DAY ONE OF THEM WAS GOING TO GET HURT.
DID YOU EVER DRESS UP?
NOT FOR FUN?
NOT FOR FUN.
AND--I HEAR IT'S KIND OF ILLEGAL, NO?
KINDA, YEAH.
YOU HAD NO INTEREST IN THIS ROLE PLAYING?

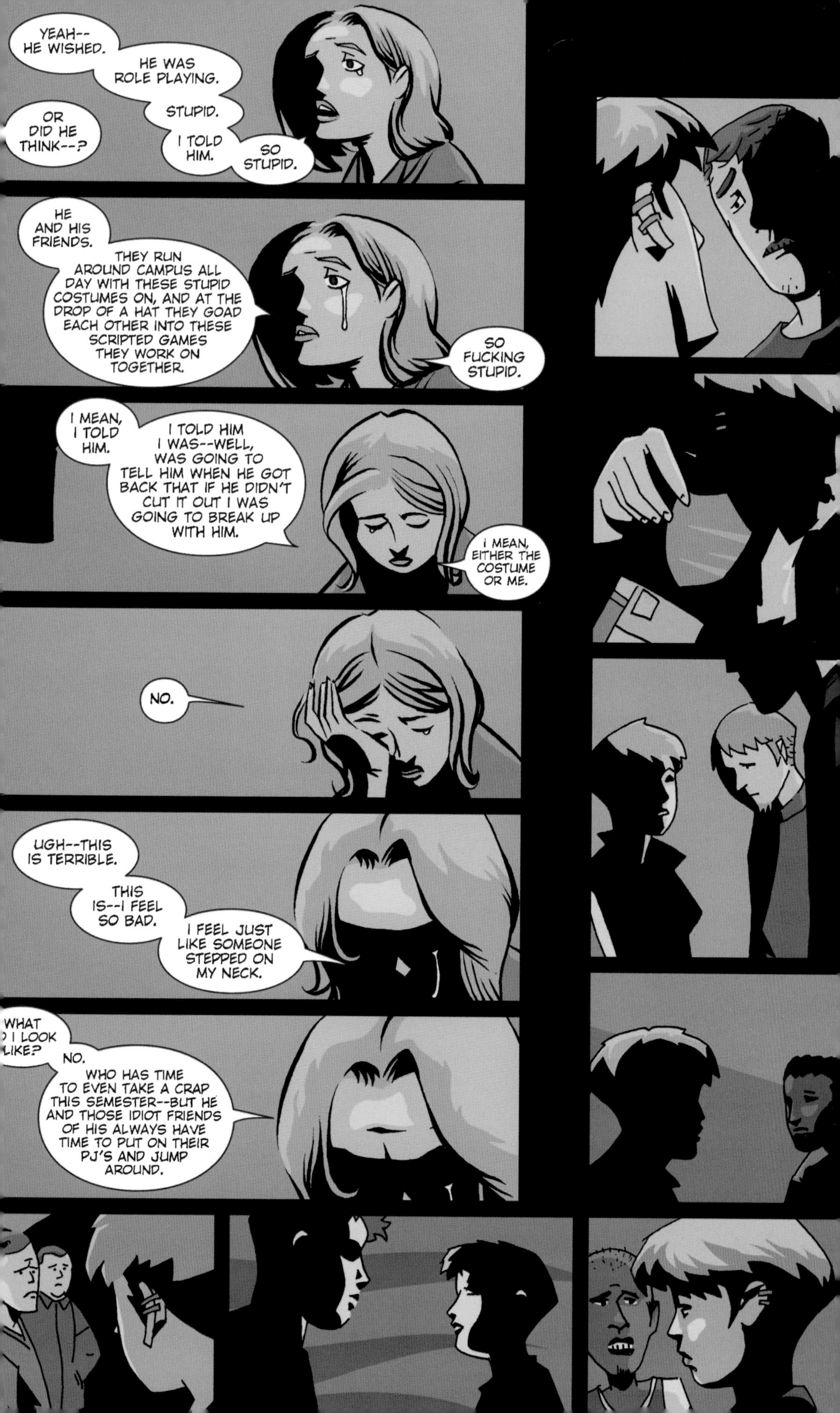
YEAH-- HE WISHED.
HE WAS ROLE PLAYING.
OR DID HE THINK--?
STUPID.
I TOLD HIM.
SO STUPID.
HE AND HIS FRIENDS.
THEY RUN AROUND CAMPUS ALL DAY WITH THESE STUPID COSTUMES ON, AND AT THE DROP OF A HAT THEY GOAD EACH OTHER INTO THESE SCRIPTED GAMES THEY WORK ON TOGETHER.
SO FUCKING STUPID.
I MEAN, I TOLD HIM.
I TOLD HIM I WAS--WELL, WAS GOING TO TELL HIM WHEN HE GOT BACK THAT IF HE DIDN'T CUT IT OUT I WAS GOING TO BREAK UP WITH HIM.
I MEAN, EITHER THE COSTUME OR ME.
NO.
UGH--THIS IS TERRIBLE.
THIS IS--I FEEL SO BAD.
I FEEL JUST LIKE SOMEONE STEPPED ON MY NECK.
NO.
WHO HAS TIME TO EVEN TAKE A CRAP THIS SEMESTER--BUT HE AND THOSE IDIOT FRIENDS OF HIS ALWAYS HAVE TIME TO PUT ON THEIR PJ'S AND JUMP AROUND.

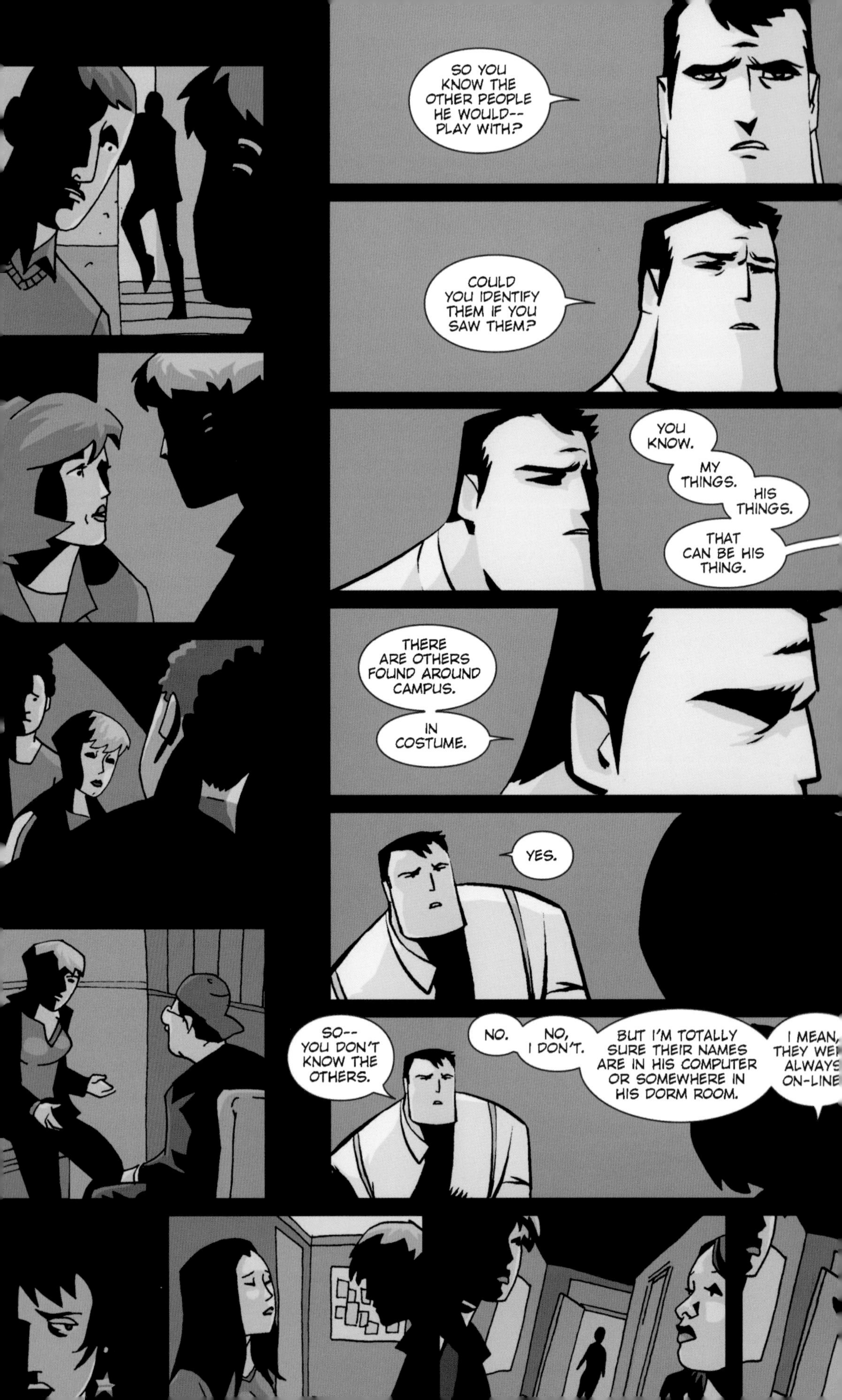
SO YOU KNOW THE OTHER PEOPLE HE WOULD-- PLAY WITH?
COULD YOU IDENTIFY THEM IF YOU SAW THEM?
YOU KNOW.
MY THINGS.
HIS THINGS.
THAT CAN BE HIS THING.
THERE ARE OTHERS FOUND AROUND CAMPUS.
IN COSTUME.
YES.
SO-- YOU DON'T KNOW THE OTHERS.
NO.
NO, I DON'T.
BUT I'M TOTALLY SURE THEIR NAMES ARE IN HIS COMPUTER OR SOMEWHERE IN HIS DORM ROOM.

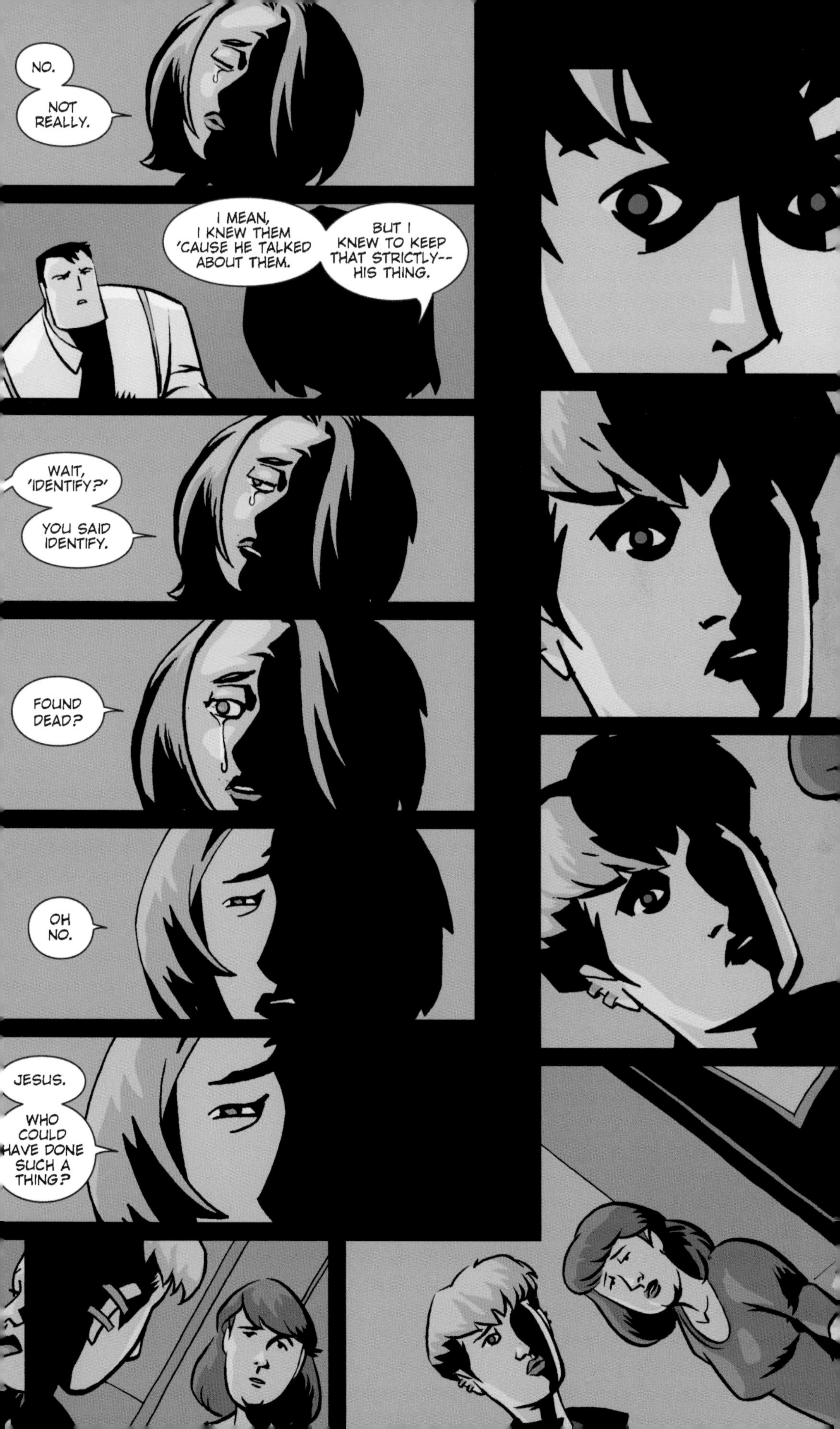
NO.
NOT REALLY.
I MEAN, I KNEW THEM 'CAUSE HE TALKED ABOUT THEM.
BUT I KNEW TO KEEP THAT STRICTLY-- HIS THING.
WAIT, 'IDENTIFY?'
YOU SAID IDENTIFY.
FOUND DEAD?
OH NO.
JESUS.
WHO COULD HAVE DONE SUCH A THING?

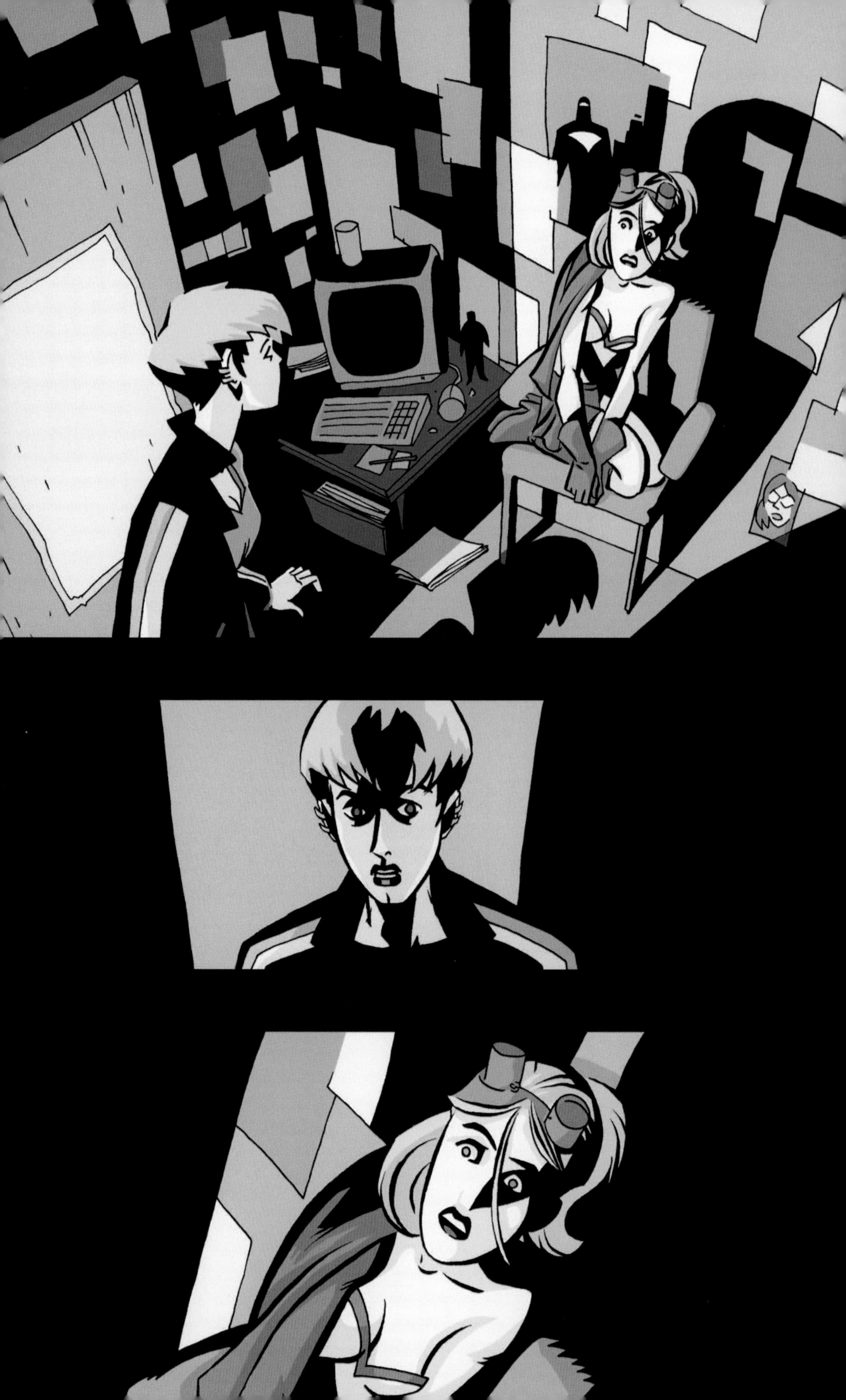

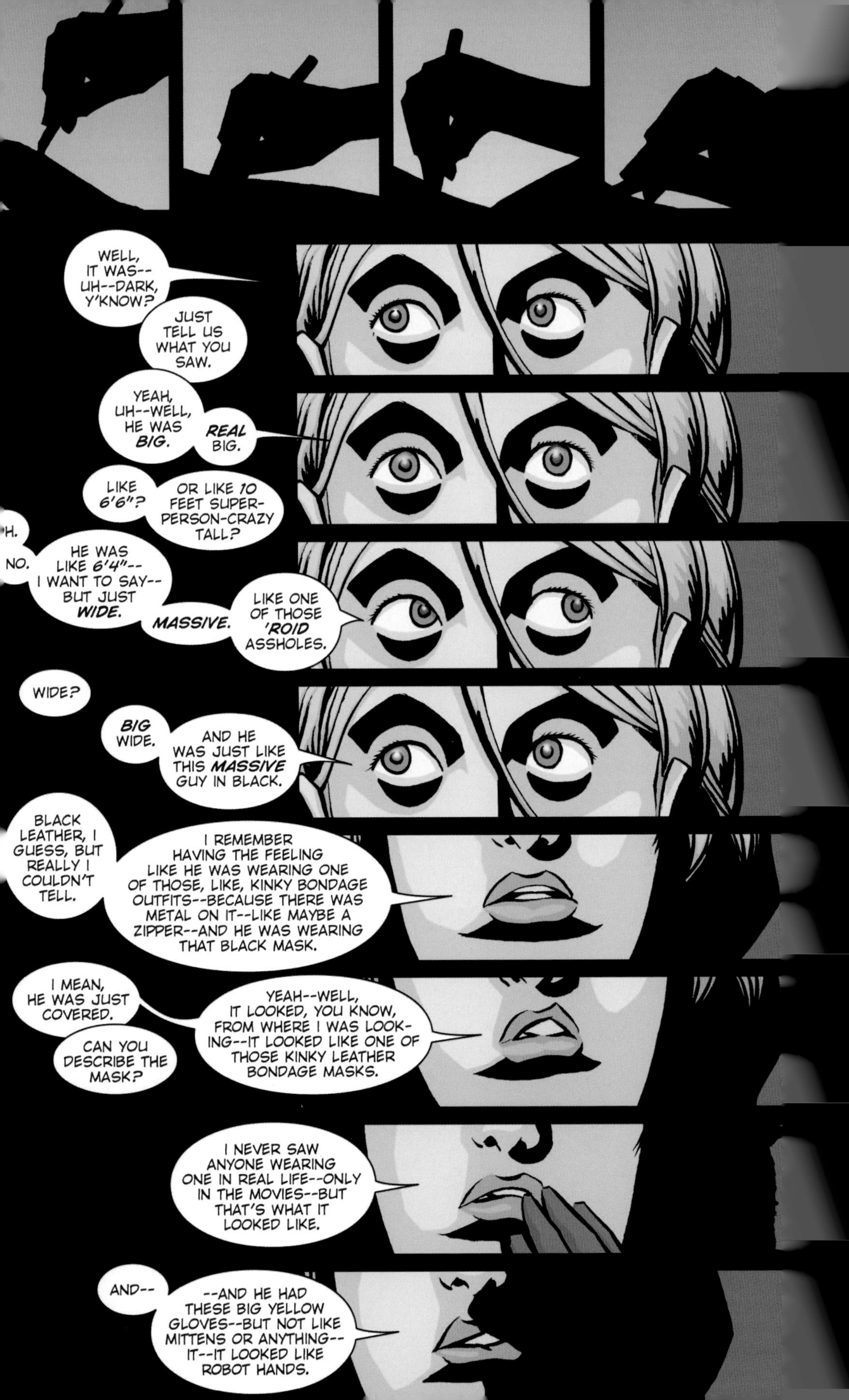

WELL, IT WAS-- UH--DARK, Y'KNOW?
JUST TELL US WHAT YOU SAW.
YEAH, UH--WELL, HE WAS BIG.
REAL BIG.
LIKE 6'6"?
OR LIKE 10 FEET SUPER-PERSON-CRAZY TALL?
NO.
HE WAS LIKE 6'4"-- I WANT TO SAY-- BUT JUST WIDE.
MASSIVE.
LIKE ONE OF THOSE 'ROID ASSHOLES.
WIDE?
BIG WIDE.
AND HE WAS JUST LIKE THIS MASSIVE GUY IN BLACK.
BLACK LEATHER, I GUESS, BUT REALLY I COULDN'T TELL.
I REMEMBER HAVING THE FEELING LIKE HE WAS WEARING ONE OF THOSE, LIKE, KINKY BONDAGE OUTFITS--BECAUSE THERE WAS METAL ON IT--LIKE MAYBE A ZIPPER--AND HE WAS WEARING THAT BLACK MASK.
I MEAN, HE WAS JUST COVERED.
CAN YOU DESCRIBE THE MASK?
YEAH--WELL, IT LOOKED, YOU KNOW, FROM WHERE I WAS LOOK-ING--IT LOOKED LIKE ONE OF THOSE KINKY LEATHER BONDAGE MASKS.
I NEVER SAW ANYONE WEARING ONE IN REAL LIFE--ONLY IN THE MOVIES--BUT THAT'S WHAT IT LOOKED LIKE.
AND--
--AND HE HAD THESE BIG YELLOW GLOVES--BUT NOT LIKE MITTENS OR ANYTHING-- IT--IT LOOKED LIKE ROBOT HANDS.

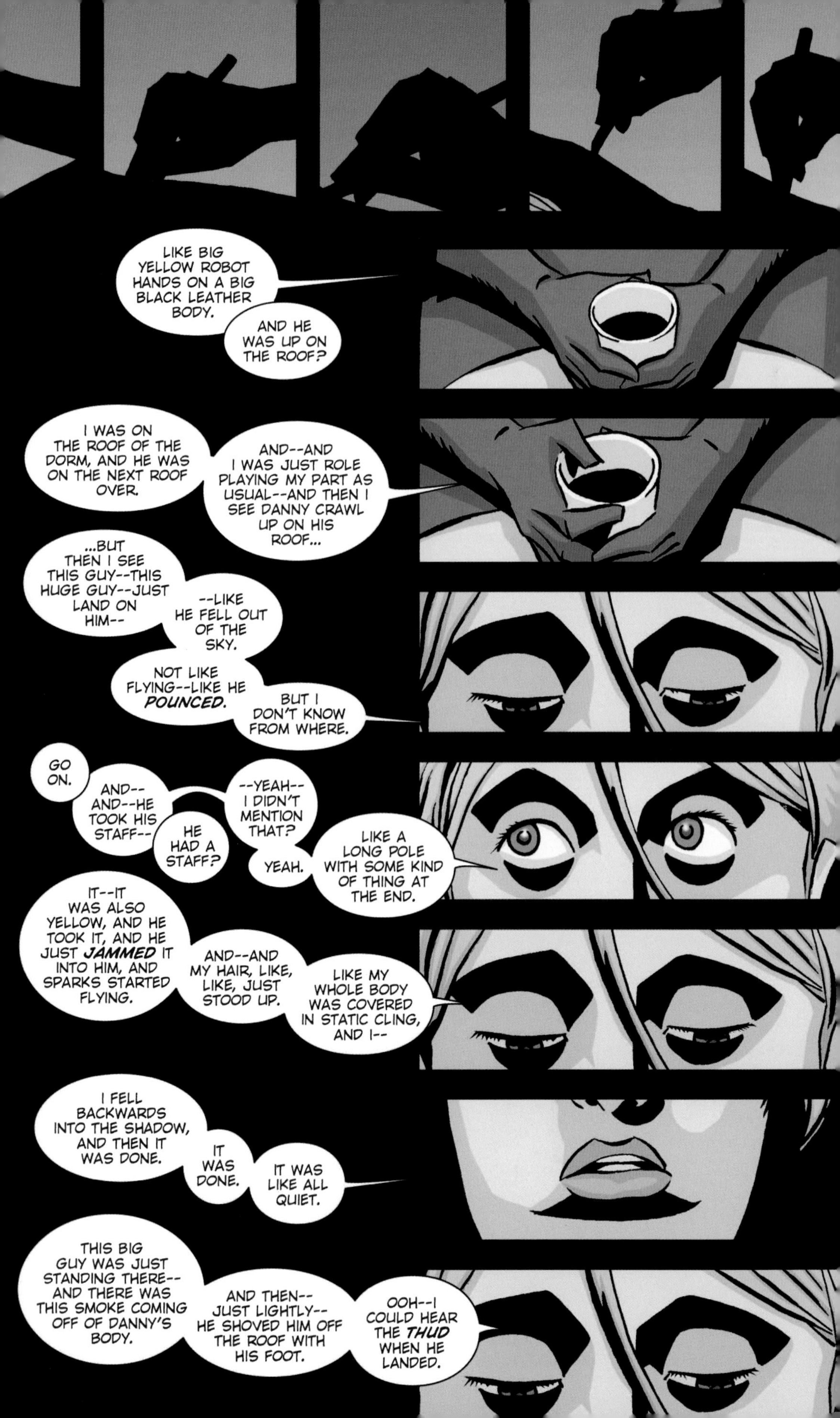
LIKE BIG YELLOW ROBOT HANDS ON A BIG BLACK LEATHER BODY.
AND HE WAS UP ON THE ROOF?
I WAS ON THE ROOF OF THE DORM, AND HE WAS ON THE NEXT ROOF OVER.
AND--AND I WAS JUST ROLE PLAYING MY PART AS USUAL--AND THEN I SEE DANNY CRAWL UP ON HIS ROOF...
...BUT THEN I SEE THIS GUY--THIS HUGE GUY--JUST LAND ON HIM--
--LIKE HE FELL OUT OF THE SKY.
NOT LIKE FLYING--LIKE HE POUNCED.
BUT I DON'T KNOW FROM WHERE.
GO ON.
AND--AND--HE TOOK HIS STAFF--
HE HAD A STAFF?
--YEAH--I DIDN'T MENTION THAT?
YEAH.
LIKE A LONG POLE WITH SOME KIND OF THING AT THE END.
IT--IT WAS ALSO YELLOW, AND HE TOOK IT, AND HE JUST JAMMED IT INTO HIM, AND SPARKS STARTED FLYING.
AND--AND MY HAIR, LIKE, LIKE, JUST STOOD UP.
LIKE MY WHOLE BODY WAS COVERED IN STATIC CLING, AND I--
I FELL BACKWARDS INTO THE SHADOW, AND THEN IT WAS DONE.
IT WAS DONE.
IT WAS LIKE ALL QUIET.
THIS BIG GUY WAS JUST STANDING THERE--AND THERE WAS THIS SMOKE COMING OFF OF DANNY'S BODY.
AND THEN--JUST LIGHTLY--HE SHOVED HIM OFF THE ROOF WITH HIS FOOT.
OOH--I COULD HEAR THE THUD WHEN HE LANDED.

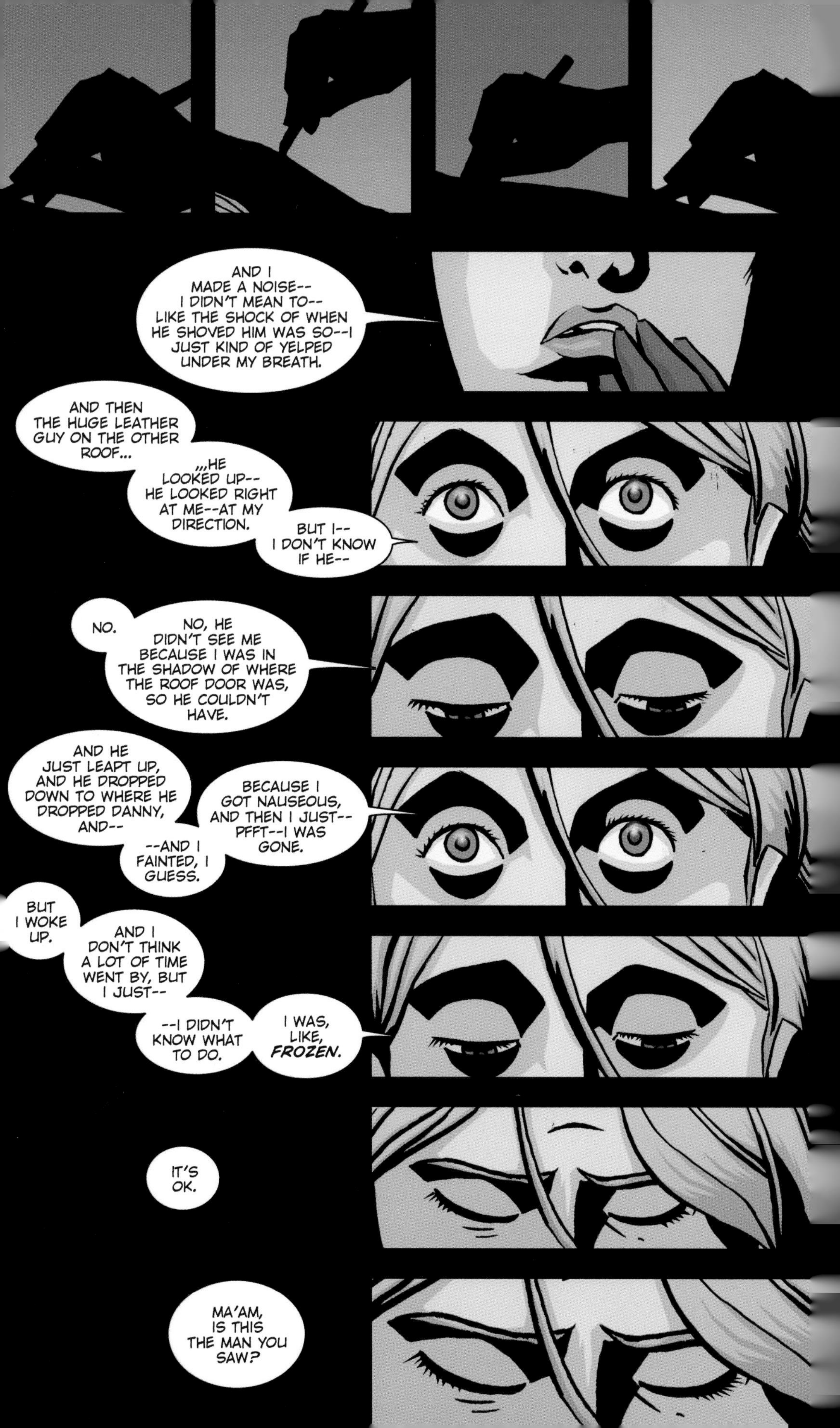
AND I MADE A NOISE-- I DIDN'T MEAN TO-- LIKE THE SHOCK OF WHEN HE SHOVED HIM WAS SO--I JUST KIND OF YELPED UNDER MY BREATH.
AND THEN THE HUGE LEATHER GUY ON THE OTHER ROOF...
...HE LOOKED UP-- HE LOOKED RIGHT AT ME--AT MY DIRECTION.
BUT I-- I DON'T KNOW IF HE--
NO.
NO, HE DIDN'T SEE ME BECAUSE I WAS IN THE SHADOW OF WHERE THE ROOF DOOR WAS, SO HE COULDN'T HAVE.
AND HE JUST LEAPT UP, AND HE DROPPED DOWN TO WHERE HE DROPPED DANNY, AND--
--AND I FAINTED, I GUESS.
BECAUSE I GOT NAUSEOUS, AND THEN I JUST-- PFFT--I WAS GONE.
BUT I WOKE UP.
AND I DON'T THINK A LOT OF TIME WENT BY, BUT I JUST--
--I DIDN'T KNOW WHAT TO DO.
I WAS, LIKE, ***FROZEN***.
IT'S OK.
MA'AM, IS THIS THE MAN YOU SAW?

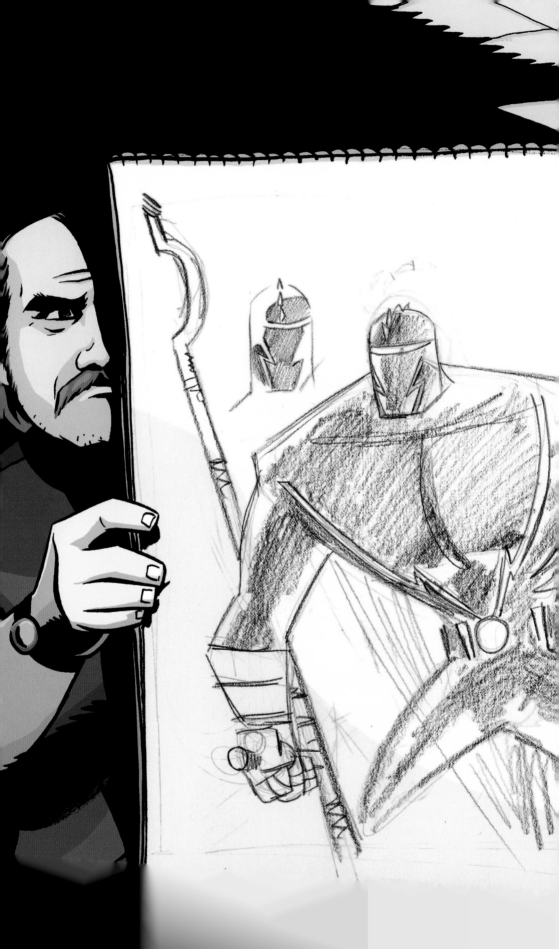

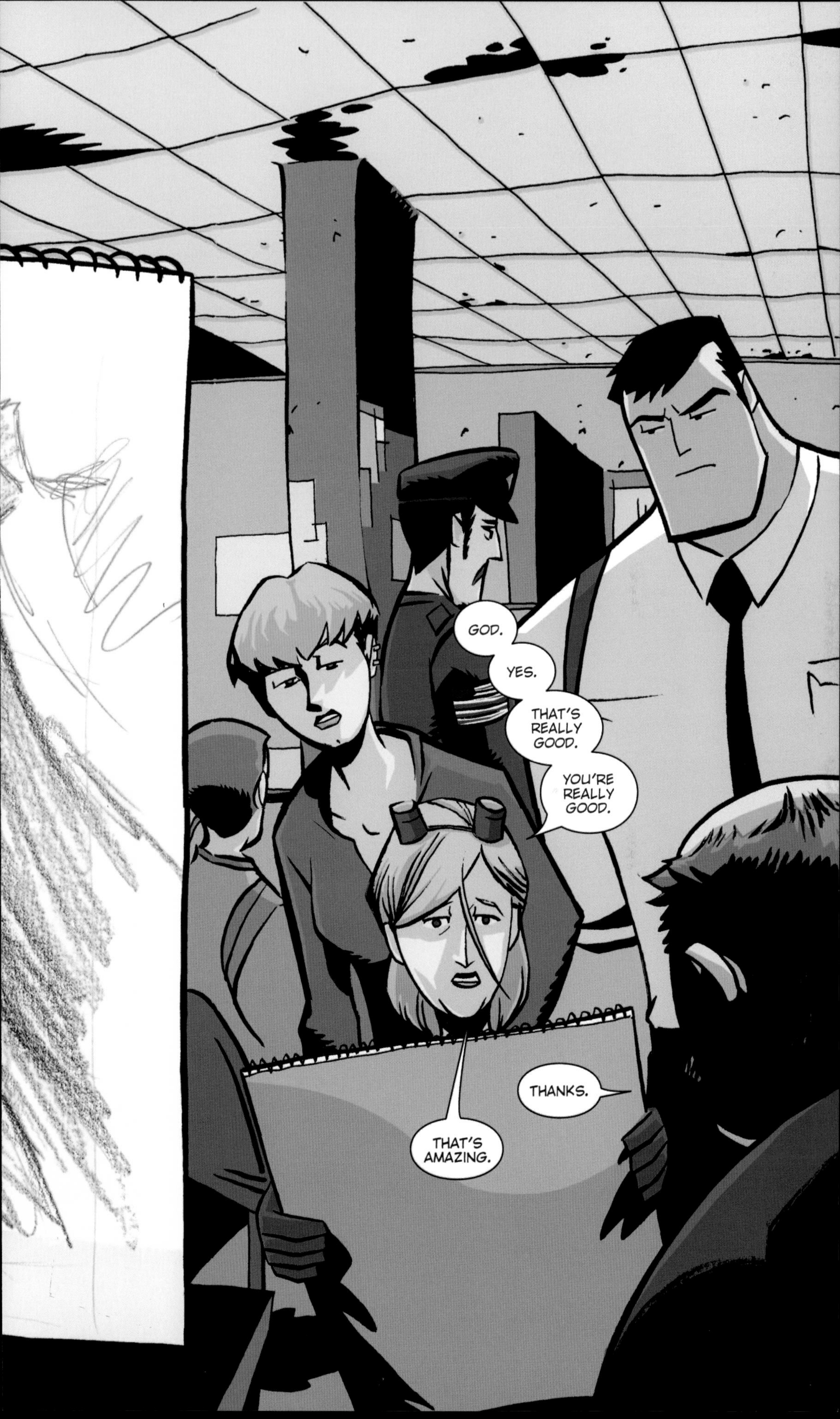
GOD.
YES.
THAT'S REALLY GOOD.
YOU'RE REALLY GOOD.
THAT'S AMAZING.
THANKS.

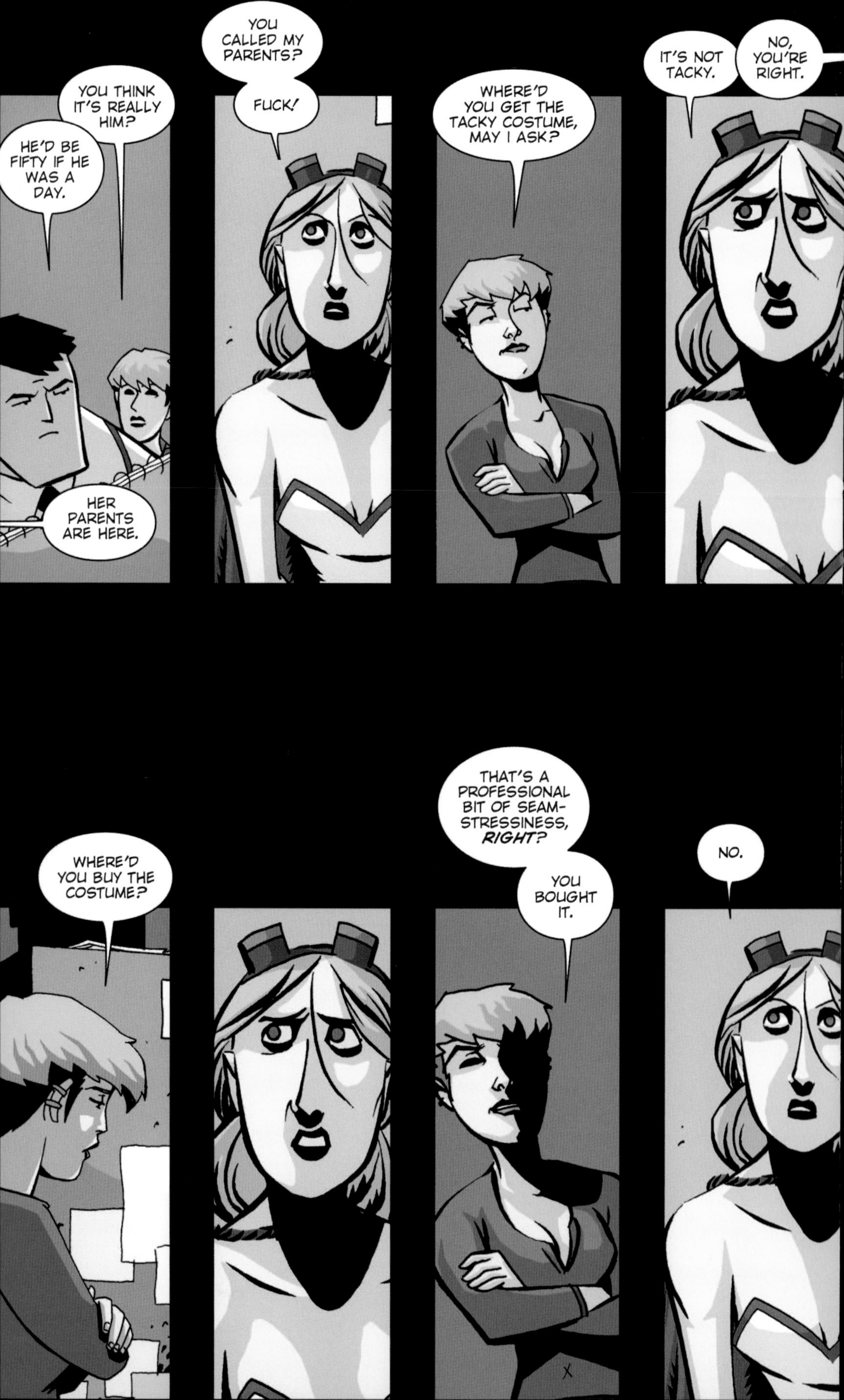
HE'D BE FIFTY IF HE WAS A DAY.
YOU THINK IT'S REALLY HIM?
HER PARENTS ARE HERE.
YOU CALLED MY PARENTS?
FUCK!
WHERE'D YOU GET THE TACKY COSTUME, MAY I ASK?
IT'S NOT TACKY.
NO, YOU'RE RIGHT.
WHERE'D YOU BUY THE COSTUME?
THAT'S A PROFESSIONAL BIT OF SEAM-STRESSINESS, ***RIGHT?***
YOU BOUGHT IT.
NO.

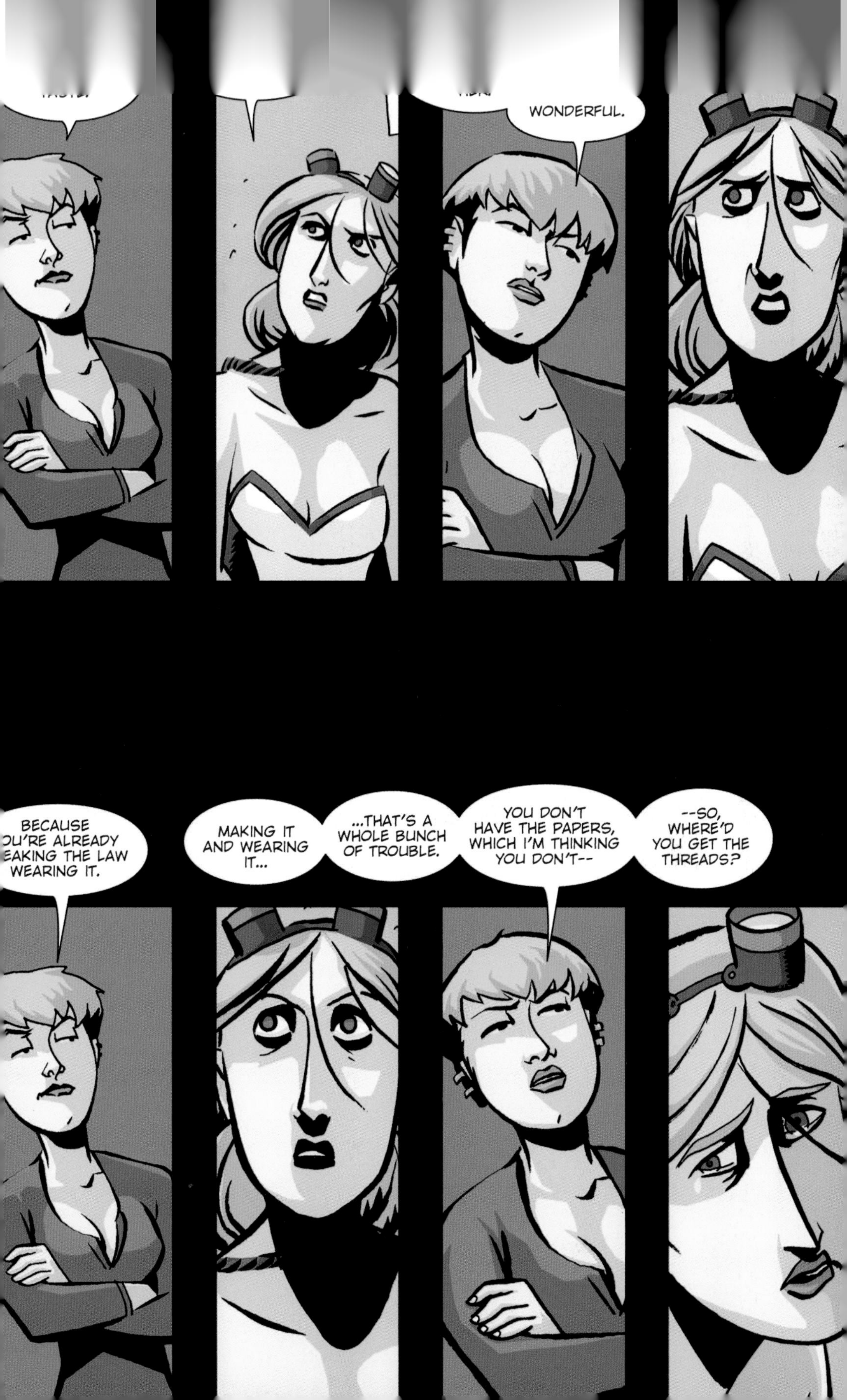
WONDERFUL.
BECAUSE
OU'RE ALREADY
EAKING THE LAW
WEARING IT.
MAKING IT AND WEARING IT...
...THAT'S A WHOLE BUNCH OF TROUBLE.
YOU DON'T HAVE THE PAPERS, WHICH I'M THINKING YOU DON'T--
--SO, WHERE'D YOU GET THE THREADS?

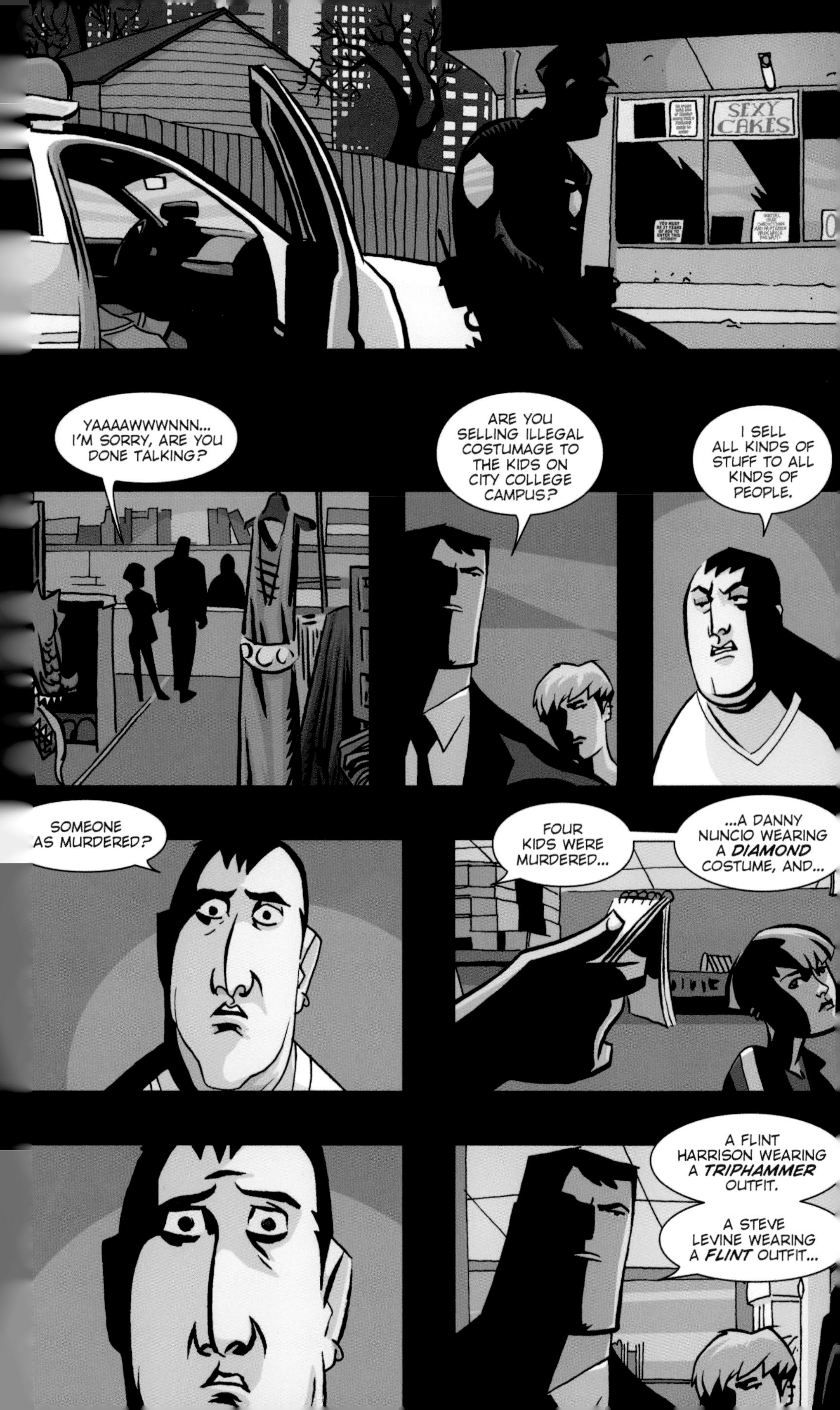
SEXY CAKES
YOU MUST BE 21 YEARS OF AGE TO ENTER THIS STORE!!
YAAAAWWWNNN... I'M SORRY, ARE YOU DONE TALKING?
ARE YOU SELLING ILLEGAL COSTUMAGE TO THE KIDS ON CITY COLLEGE CAMPUS?
I SELL ALL KINDS OF STUFF TO ALL KINDS OF PEOPLE.
SOMEONE AS MURDERED?
FOUR KIDS WERE MURDERED...
...A DANNY NUNCIO WEARING A DIAMOND COSTUME, AND...
A FLINT HARRISON WEARING A TRIPHAMMER OUTFIT.
A STEVE LEVINE WEARING A FLINT OUTFIT...

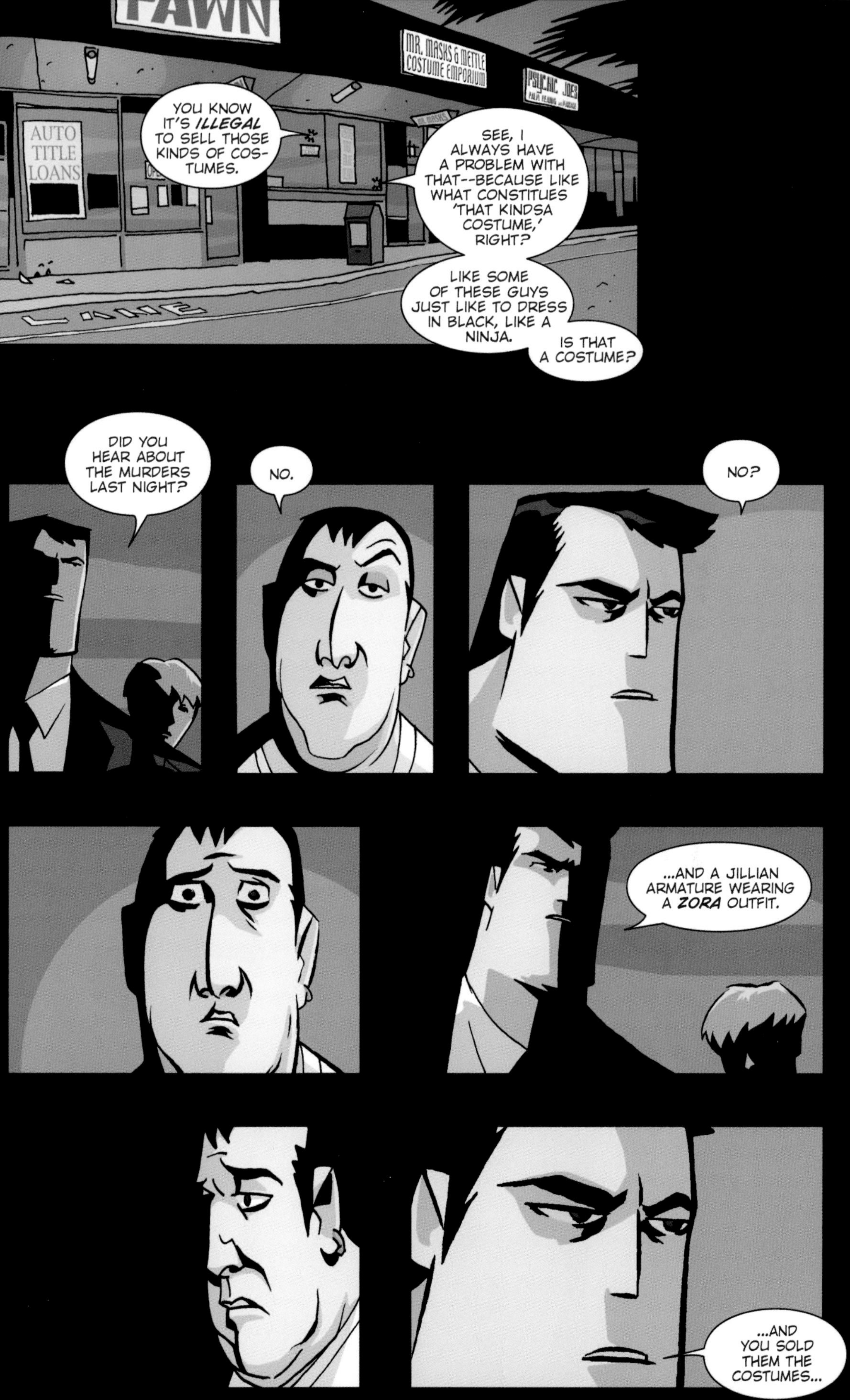
PAWN
MR. MASKS & METTLE COSTUME EMPORIUM
PSYCHIC JOES
AUTO TITLE LOANS
LANE
YOU KNOW IT'S ILLEGAL TO SELL THOSE KINDS OF COS-TUMES.
SEE, I ALWAYS HAVE A PROBLEM WITH THAT--BECAUSE LIKE WHAT CONSTITUES 'THAT KINDSA COSTUME,' RIGHT?
LIKE SOME OF THESE GUYS JUST LIKE TO DRESS IN BLACK, LIKE A NINJA.
IS THAT A COSTUME?
DID YOU HEAR ABOUT THE MURDERS LAST NIGHT?
NO.
NO?
...AND A JILLIAN ARMATURE WEARING A ZORA OUTFIT.
...AND YOU SOLD THEM THE COSTUMES...

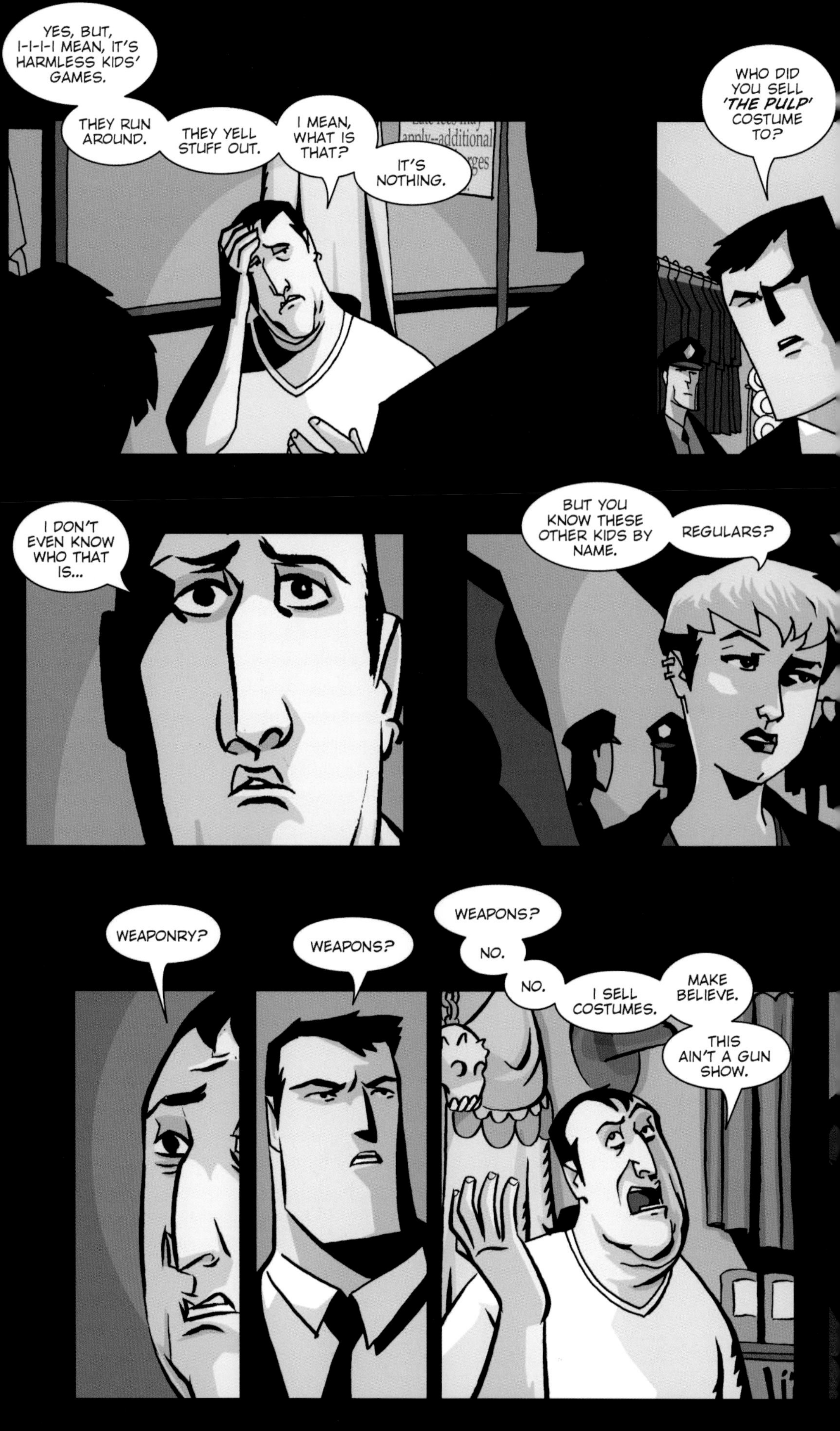

YES, BUT, I-I-I-I MEAN, IT'S HARMLESS KIDS' GAMES.
THEY RUN AROUND.
THEY YELL STUFF OUT.
I MEAN, WHAT IS THAT?
IT'S NOTHING.
WHO DID YOU SELL *'THE PULP'* COSTUME TO?
I DON'T EVEN KNOW WHO THAT IS...
BUT YOU KNOW THESE OTHER KIDS BY NAME.
REGULARS?
WEAPONRY?
WEAPONS?
WEAPONS?
NO.
NO.
I SELL COSTUMES.
MAKE BELIEVE.
THIS AIN'T A GUN SHOW.

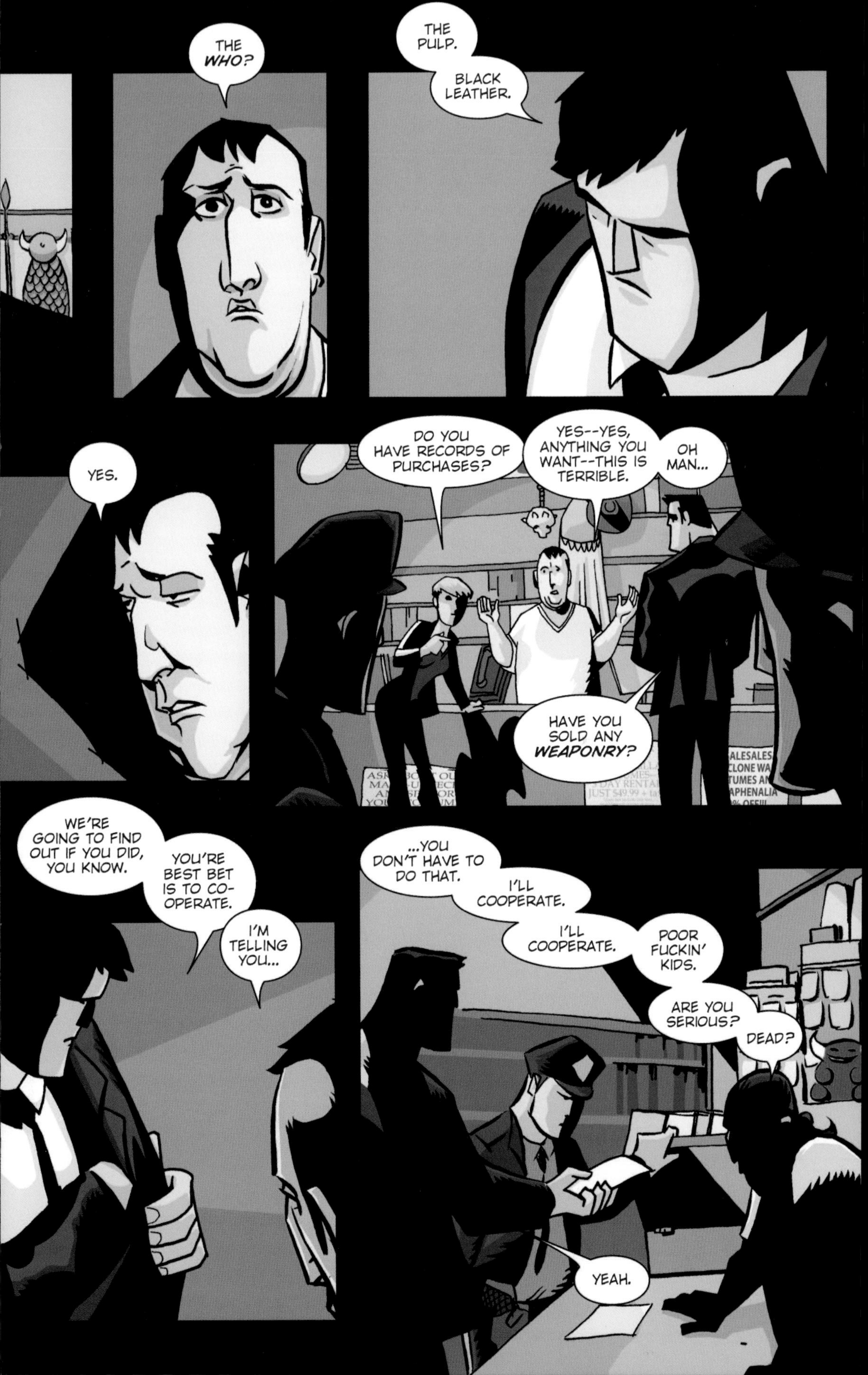
THE *WHO?*
THE PULP.
BLACK LEATHER.
YES.
DO YOU HAVE RECORDS OF PURCHASES?
YES--YES, ANYTHING YOU WANT--THIS IS TERRIBLE.
OH MAN...
HAVE YOU SOLD ANY *WEAPONRY?*
WE'RE GOING TO FIND OUT IF YOU DID, YOU KNOW.
YOU'RE BEST BET IS TO CO-OPERATE.
I'M TELLING YOU...
...YOU DON'T HAVE TO DO THAT.
I'LL COOPERATE.
I'LL COOPERATE.
POOR FUCKIN' KIDS.
ARE YOU SERIOUS?
DEAD?
YEAH.

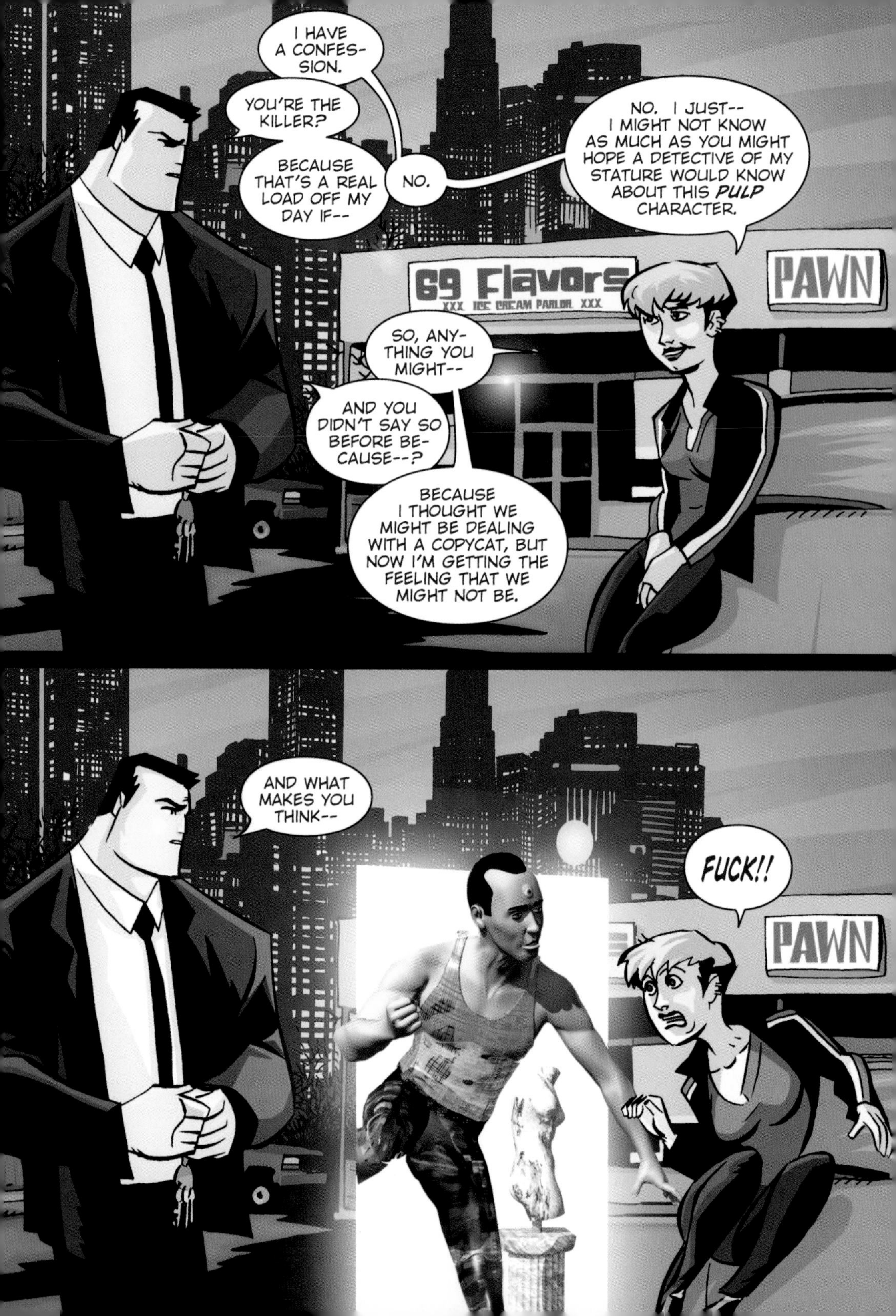
I HAVE A CONFESSION.
YOU'RE THE KILLER?
BECAUSE THAT'S A REAL LOAD OFF MY DAY IF--
NO.
NO. I JUST-- I MIGHT NOT KNOW AS MUCH AS YOU MIGHT HOPE A DETECTIVE OF MY STATURE WOULD KNOW ABOUT THIS *PULP* CHARACTER.
69 Flavors
XXX ICE CREAM PARLOR XXX
PAWN
SO, ANYTHING YOU MIGHT--
AND YOU DIDN'T SAY SO BEFORE BECAUSE--?
BECAUSE I THOUGHT WE MIGHT BE DEALING WITH A COPYCAT, BUT NOW I'M GETTING THE FEELING THAT WE MIGHT NOT BE.
AND WHAT MAKES YOU THINK--
FUCK!!
PAWN

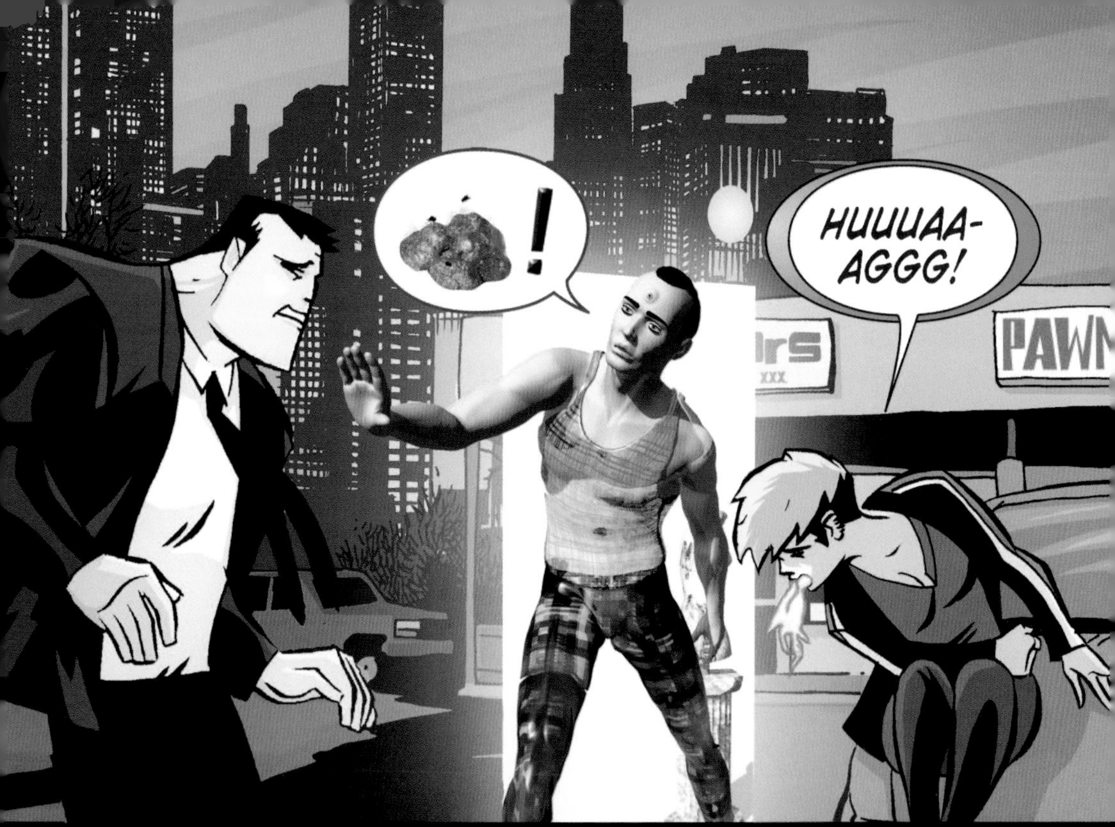
!
HUUUAA-AGGG!
PAWN
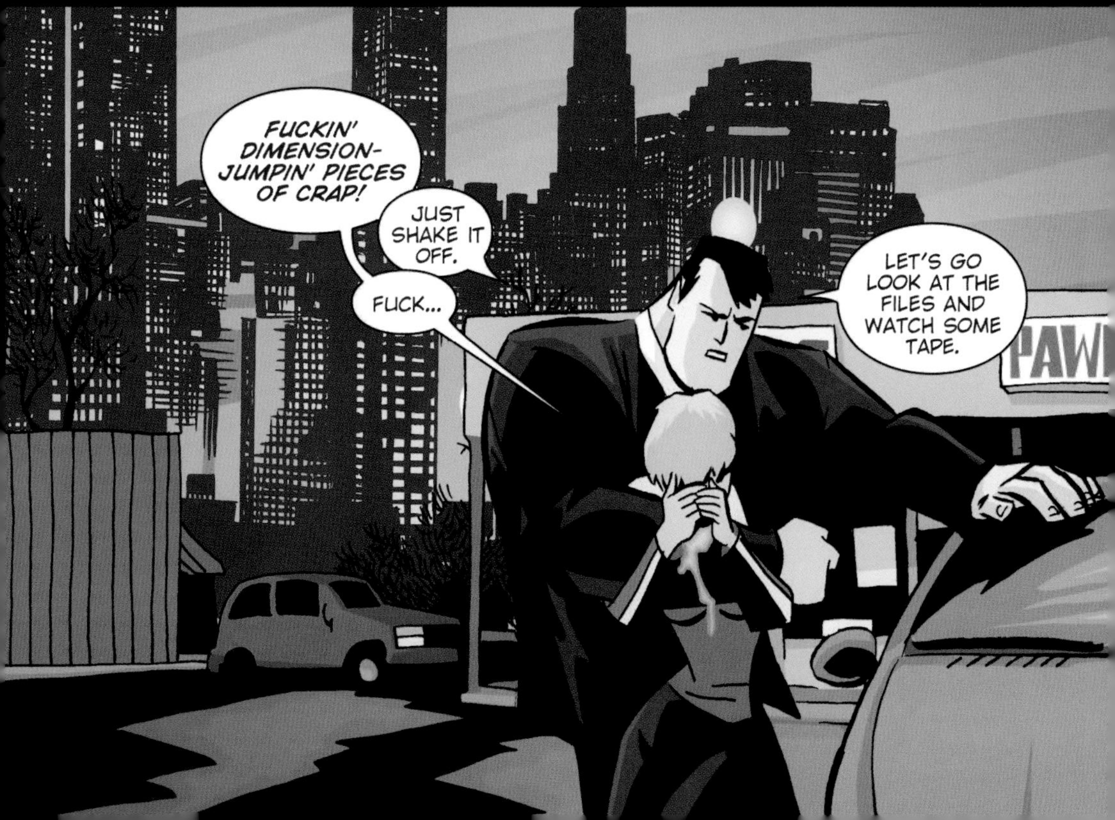
FUCKIN' DIMENSION-JUMPIN' PIECES OF CRAP!
JUST SHAKE IT OFF.
FUCK...
LET'S GO LOOK AT THE FILES AND WATCH SOME TAPE.
PAWN

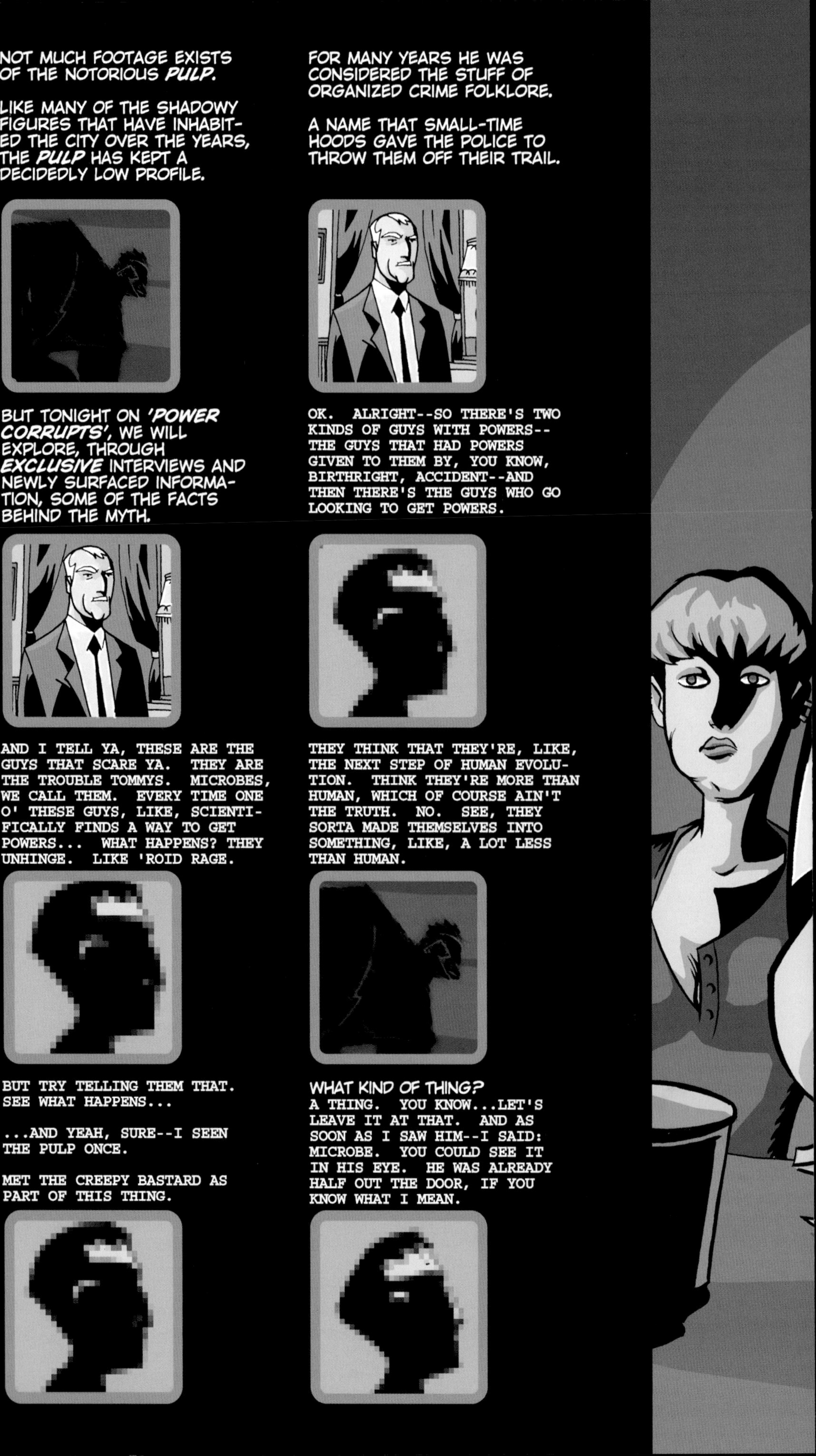

NOT MUCH FOOTAGE EXISTS OF THE NOTORIOUS *PULP*.
LIKE MANY OF THE SHADOWY FIGURES THAT HAVE INHABITED THE CITY OVER THE YEARS, THE *PULP* HAS KEPT A DECIDEDLY LOW PROFILE.
FOR MANY YEARS HE WAS CONSIDERED THE STUFF OF ORGANIZED CRIME FOLKLORE.
A NAME THAT SMALL-TIME HOODS GAVE THE POLICE TO THROW THEM OFF THEIR TRAIL.
BUT TONIGHT ON *'POWER CORRUPTS'*, WE WILL EXPLORE, THROUGH *EXCLUSIVE* INTERVIEWS AND NEWLY SURFACED INFORMATION, SOME OF THE FACTS BEHIND THE MYTH.
OK. ALRIGHT--SO THERE'S TWO KINDS OF GUYS WITH POWERS--THE GUYS THAT HAD POWERS GIVEN TO THEM BY, YOU KNOW, BIRTHRIGHT, ACCIDENT--AND THEN THERE'S THE GUYS WHO GO LOOKING TO GET POWERS.
AND I TELL YA, THESE ARE THE GUYS THAT SCARE YA. THEY ARE THE TROUBLE TOMMYS. MICROBES, WE CALL THEM. EVERY TIME ONE O' THESE GUYS, LIKE, SCIENTIFICALLY FINDS A WAY TO GET POWERS... WHAT HAPPENS? THEY UNHINGE. LIKE 'ROID RAGE.
THEY THINK THAT THEY'RE, LIKE, THE NEXT STEP OF HUMAN EVOLUTION. THINK THEY'RE MORE THAN HUMAN, WHICH OF COURSE AIN'T THE TRUTH. NO. SEE, THEY SORTA MADE THEMSELVES INTO SOMETHING, LIKE, A LOT LESS THAN HUMAN.
BUT TRY TELLING THEM THAT. SEE WHAT HAPPENS...
...AND YEAH, SURE--I SEEN THE PULP ONCE.
MET THE CREEPY BASTARD AS PART OF THIS THING.
WHAT KIND OF THING?
A THING. YOU KNOW...LET'S LEAVE IT AT THAT. AND AS SOON AS I SAW HIM--I SAID: MICROBE. YOU COULD SEE IT IN HIS EYE. HE WAS ALREADY HALF OUT THE DOOR, IF YOU KNOW WHAT I MEAN.

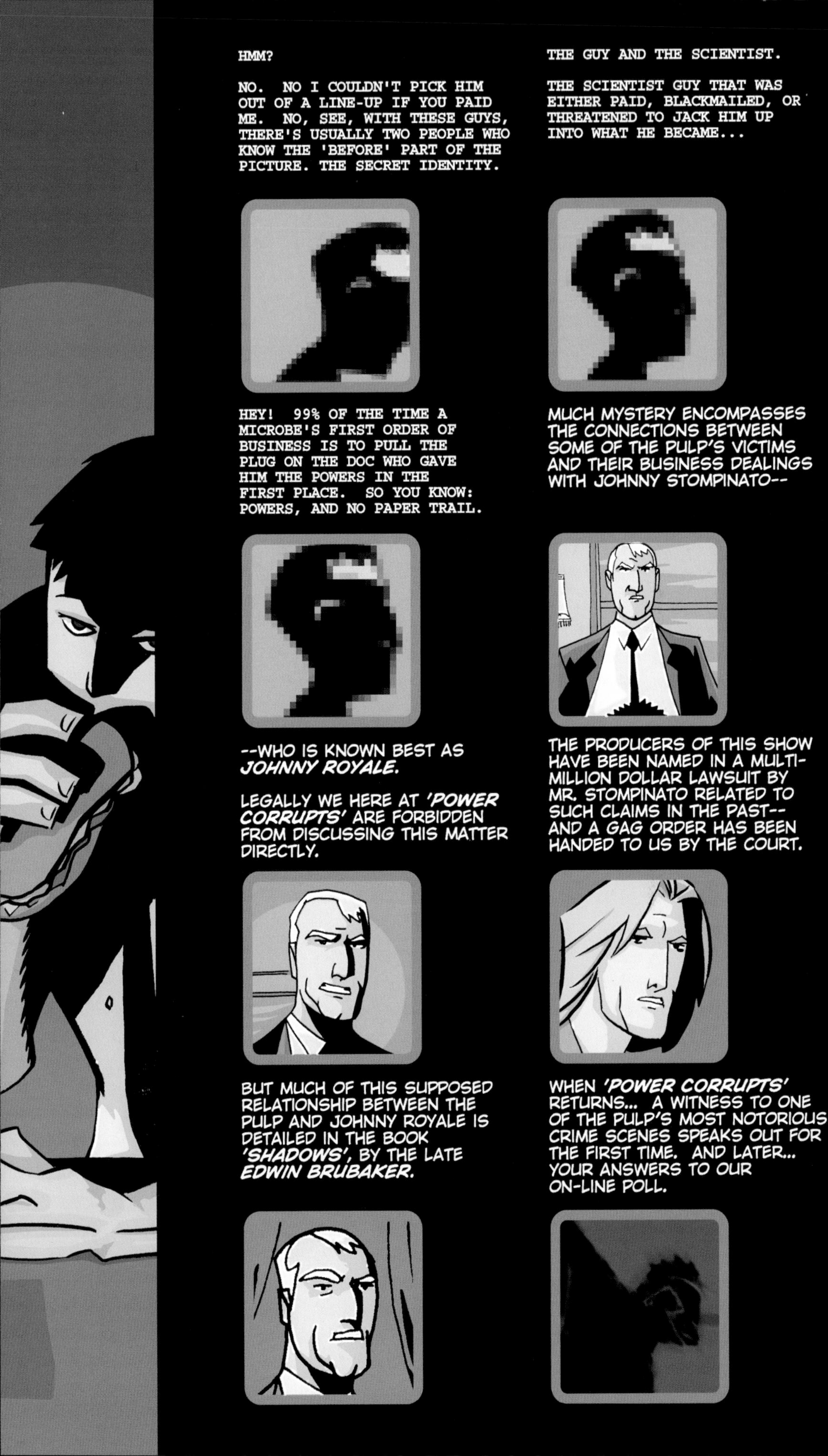
HMM?
NO. NO I COULDN'T PICK HIM OUT OF A LINE-UP IF YOU PAID ME. NO, SEE, WITH THESE GUYS, THERE'S USUALLY TWO PEOPLE WHO KNOW THE 'BEFORE' PART OF THE PICTURE. THE SECRET IDENTITY.
THE GUY AND THE SCIENTIST.
THE SCIENTIST GUY THAT WAS EITHER PAID, BLACKMAILED, OR THREATENED TO JACK HIM UP INTO WHAT HE BECAME...
HEY! 99% OF THE TIME A MICROBE'S FIRST ORDER OF BUSINESS IS TO PULL THE PLUG ON THE DOC WHO GAVE HIM THE POWERS IN THE FIRST PLACE. SO YOU KNOW: POWERS, AND NO PAPER TRAIL.
MUCH MYSTERY ENCOMPASSES THE CONNECTIONS BETWEEN SOME OF THE PULP'S VICTIMS AND THEIR BUSINESS DEALINGS WITH JOHNNY STOMPINATO--
--WHO IS KNOWN BEST AS JOHNNY ROYALE.
LEGALLY WE HERE AT 'POWER CORRUPTS' ARE FORBIDDEN FROM DISCUSSING THIS MATTER DIRECTLY.
THE PRODUCERS OF THIS SHOW HAVE BEEN NAMED IN A MULTI-MILLION DOLLAR LAWSUIT BY MR. STOMPINATO RELATED TO SUCH CLAIMS IN THE PAST--AND A GAG ORDER HAS BEEN HANDED TO US BY THE COURT.
BUT MUCH OF THIS SUPPOSED RELATIONSHIP BETWEEN THE PULP AND JOHNNY ROYALE IS DETAILED IN THE BOOK 'SHADOWS', BY THE LATE EDWIN BRUBAKER.
WHEN 'POWER CORRUPTS' RETURNS... A WITNESS TO ONE OF THE PULP'S MOST NOTORIOUS CRIME SCENES SPEAKS OUT FOR THE FIRST TIME. AND LATER... YOUR ANSWERS TO OUR ON-LINE POLL.

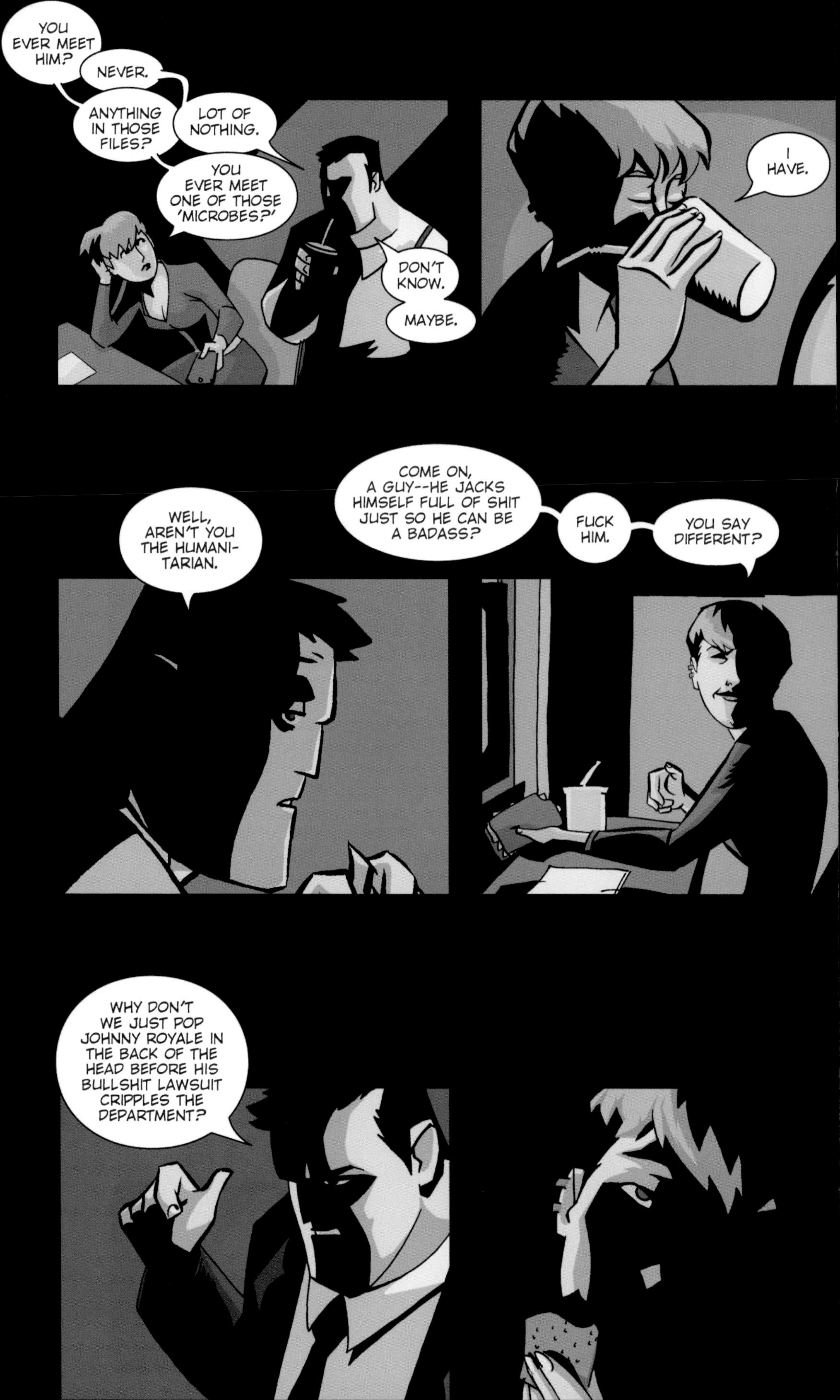
YOU EVER MEET HIM?
NEVER.
ANYTHING IN THOSE FILES?
LOT OF NOTHING.
YOU EVER MEET ONE OF THOSE 'MICROBES?'
DON'T KNOW.
MAYBE.
I HAVE.
WELL, AREN'T YOU THE HUMANI-TARIAN.
COME ON, A GUY--HE JACKS HIMSELF FULL OF SHIT JUST SO HE CAN BE A BADASS?
FUCK HIM.
YOU SAY DIFFERENT?
WHY DON'T WE JUST POP JOHNNY ROYALE IN THE BACK OF THE HEAD BEFORE HIS BULLSHIT LAWSUIT CRIPPLES THE DEPARTMENT?

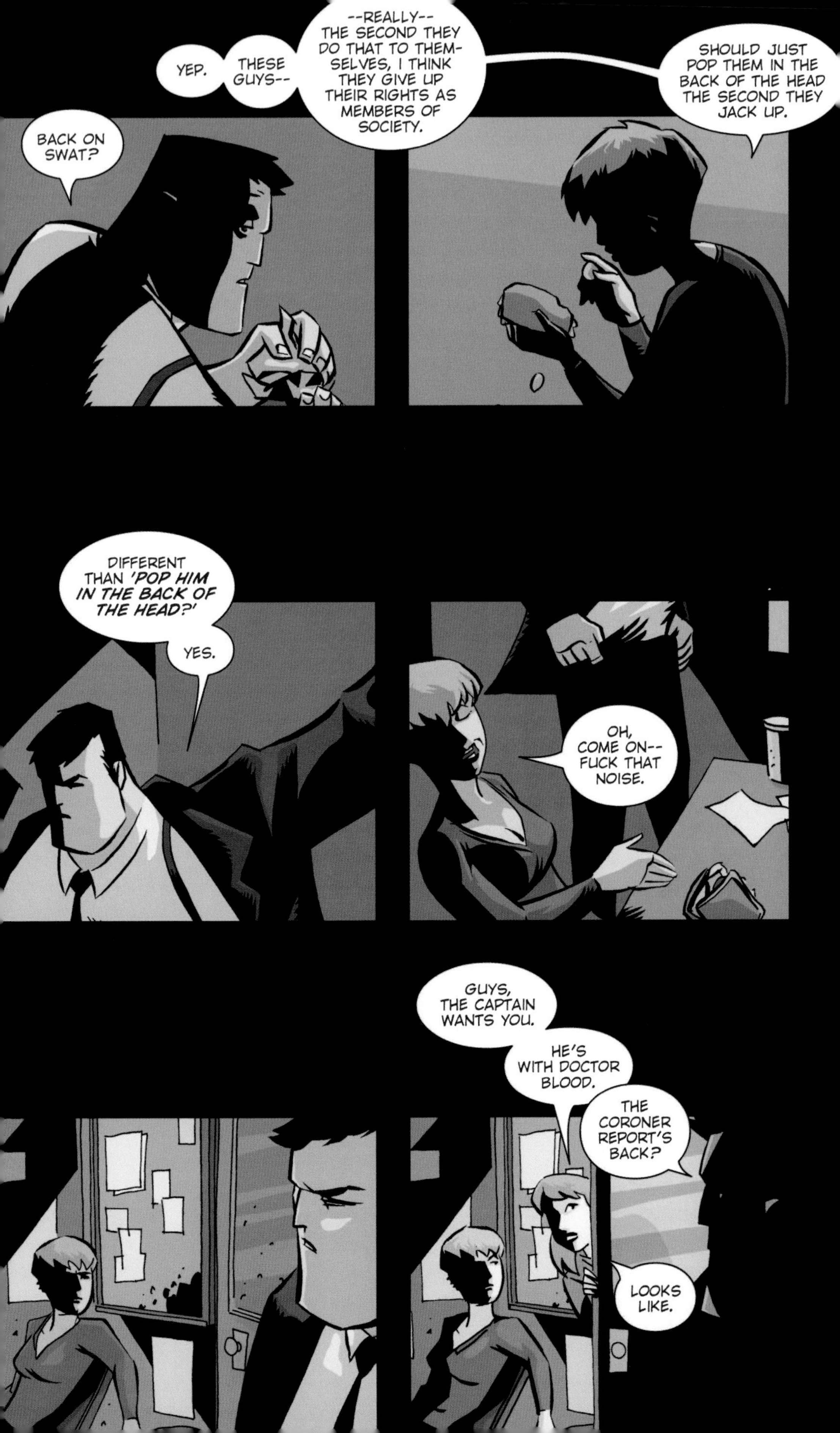
BACK ON SWAT?
YEP.
THESE GUYS--
--REALLY-- THE SECOND THEY DO THAT TO THEM-SELVES, I THINK THEY GIVE UP THEIR RIGHTS AS MEMBERS OF SOCIETY.
SHOULD JUST POP THEM IN THE BACK OF THE HEAD THE SECOND THEY JACK UP.
DIFFERENT THAN *'POP HIM IN THE BACK OF THE HEAD?'*
YES.
OH, COME ON-- FUCK THAT NOISE.
GUYS, THE CAPTAIN WANTS YOU.
HE'S WITH DOCTOR BLOOD.
THE CORONER REPORT'S BACK?
LOOKS LIKE.

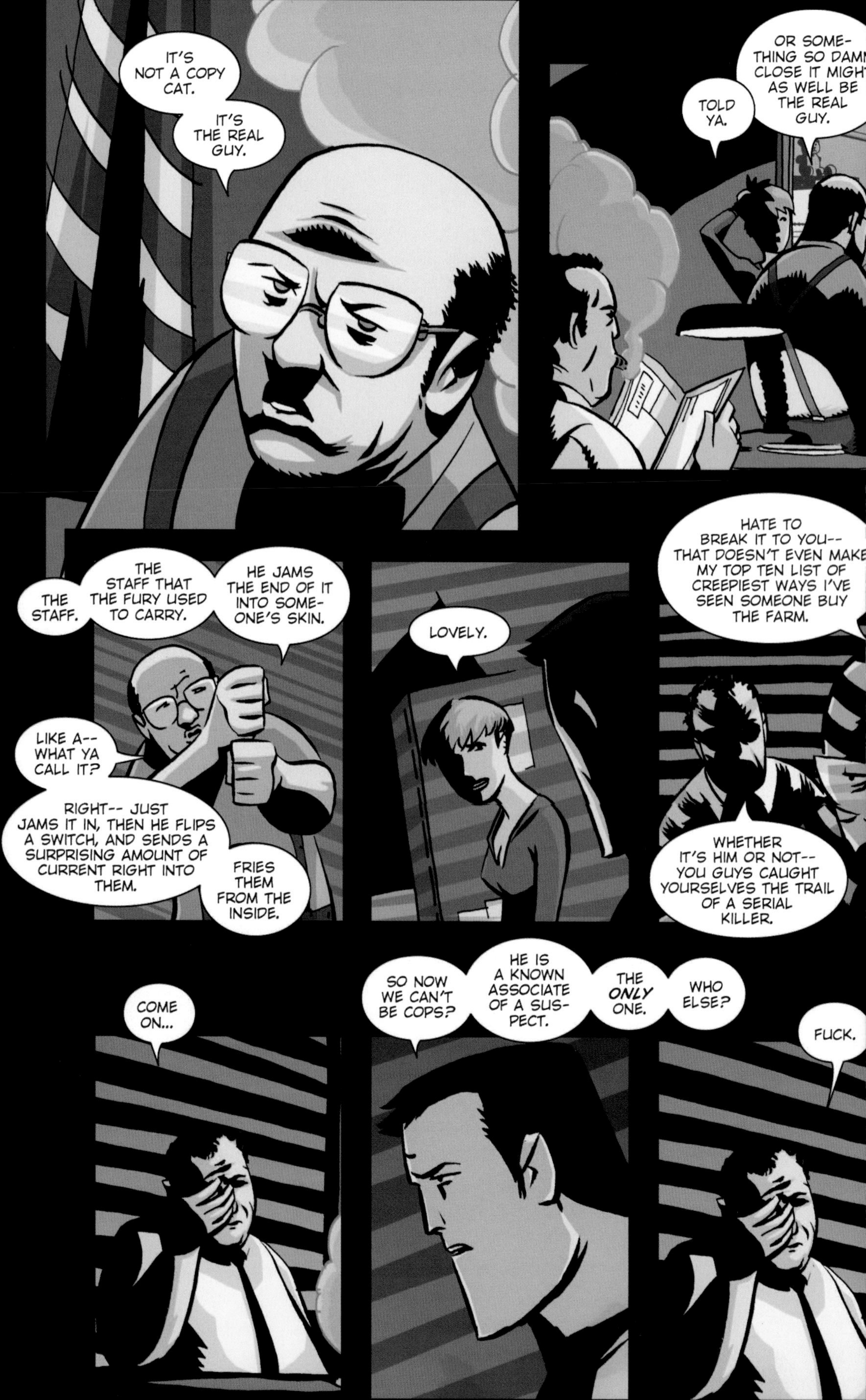
IT'S NOT A COPY CAT.
IT'S THE REAL GUY.
TOLD YA.
OR SOME-THING SO DAMN CLOSE IT MIGHT AS WELL BE THE REAL GUY.
THE STAFF.
THE STAFF THAT THE FURY USED TO CARRY.
HE JAMS THE END OF IT INTO SOME-ONE'S SKIN.
LIKE A-- WHAT YA CALL IT?
RIGHT-- JUST JAMS IT IN, THEN HE FLIPS A SWITCH, AND SENDS A SURPRISING AMOUNT OF CURRENT RIGHT INTO THEM.
FRIES THEM FROM THE INSIDE.
LOVELY.
HATE TO BREAK IT TO YOU-- THAT DOESN'T EVEN MAKE MY TOP TEN LIST OF CREEPIEST WAYS I'VE SEEN SOMEONE BUY THE FARM.
WHETHER IT'S HIM OR NOT-- YOU GUYS CAUGHT YOURSELVES THE TRAIL OF A SERIAL KILLER.
COME ON...
SO NOW WE CAN'T BE COPS?
HE IS A KNOWN ASSOCIATE OF A SUS-PECT.
THE *ONLY* ONE.
WHO ELSE?
FUCK.

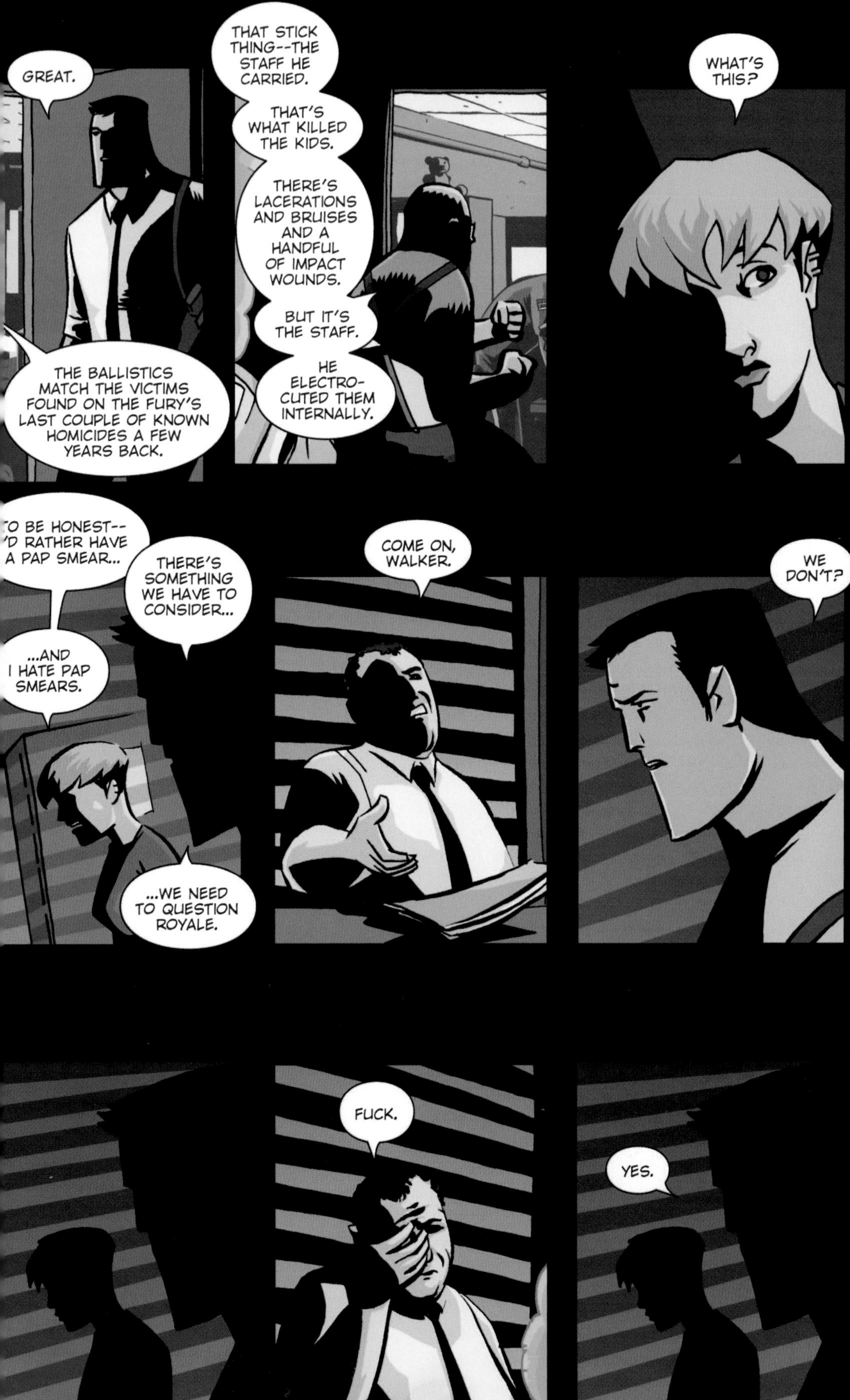

GREAT.
THE BALLISTICS MATCH THE VICTIMS FOUND ON THE FURY'S LAST COUPLE OF KNOWN HOMICIDES A FEW YEARS BACK.
THAT STICK THING--THE STAFF HE CARRIED.
THAT'S WHAT KILLED THE KIDS.
THERE'S LACERATIONS AND BRUISES AND A HANDFUL OF IMPACT WOUNDS.
BUT IT'S THE STAFF.
HE ELECTRO-CUTED THEM INTERNALLY.
WHAT'S THIS?
TO BE HONEST--I'D RATHER HAVE A PAP SMEAR...
...AND I HATE PAP SMEARS.
THERE'S SOMETHING WE HAVE TO CONSIDER...
...WE NEED TO QUESTION ROYALE.
COME ON, WALKER.
WE DON'T?
FUCK.
YES.

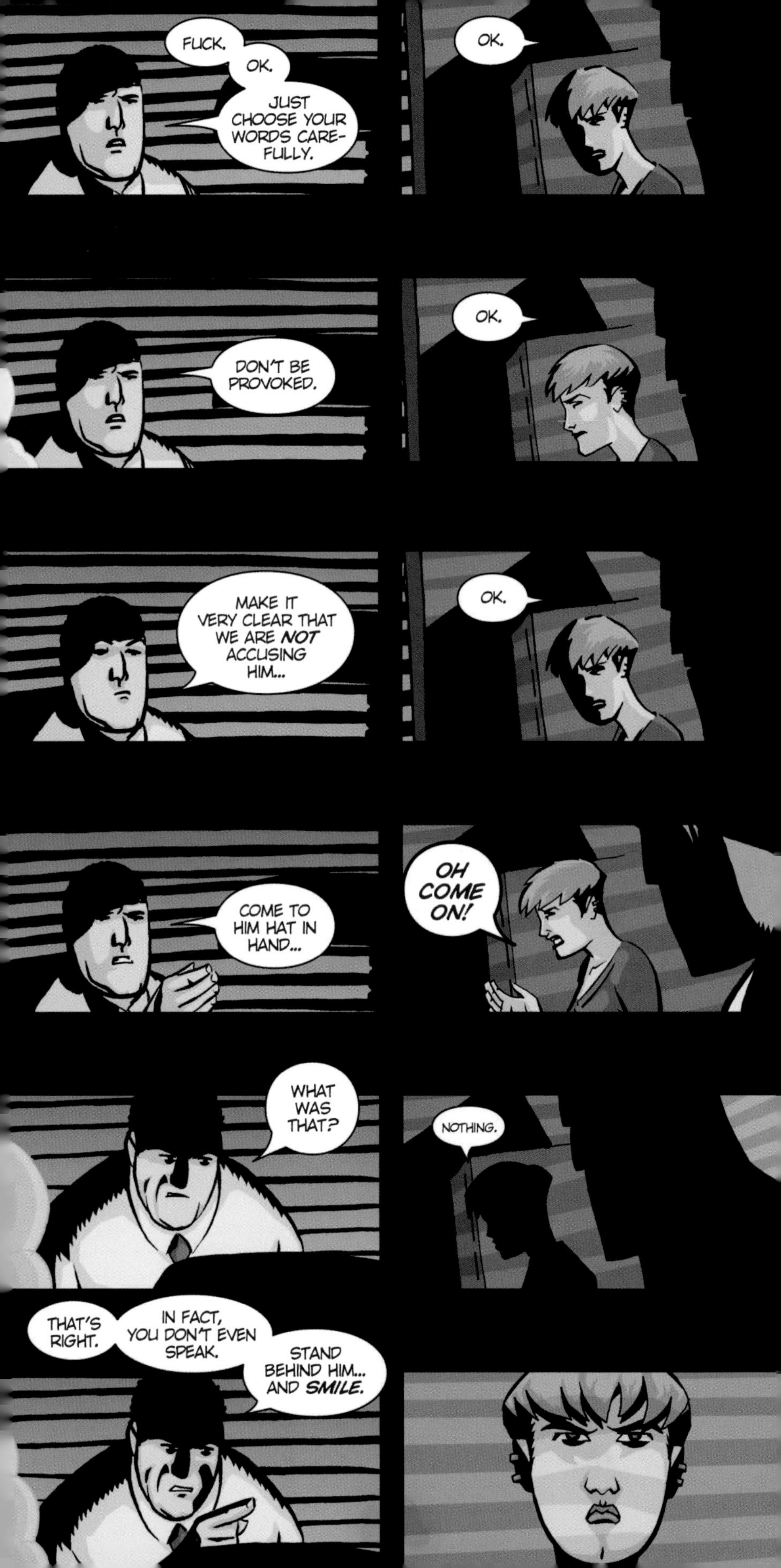
FUCK.
OK.
JUST CHOOSE YOUR WORDS CARE-FULLY.
OK.
DON'T BE PROVOKED.
OK.
MAKE IT VERY CLEAR THAT WE ARE NOT ACCUSING HIM...
OK.
COME TO HIM HAT IN HAND...
OH COME ON!
WHAT WAS THAT?
NOTHING.
THAT'S RIGHT.
IN FACT, YOU DON'T EVEN SPEAK.
STAND BEHIND HIM... AND SMILE.

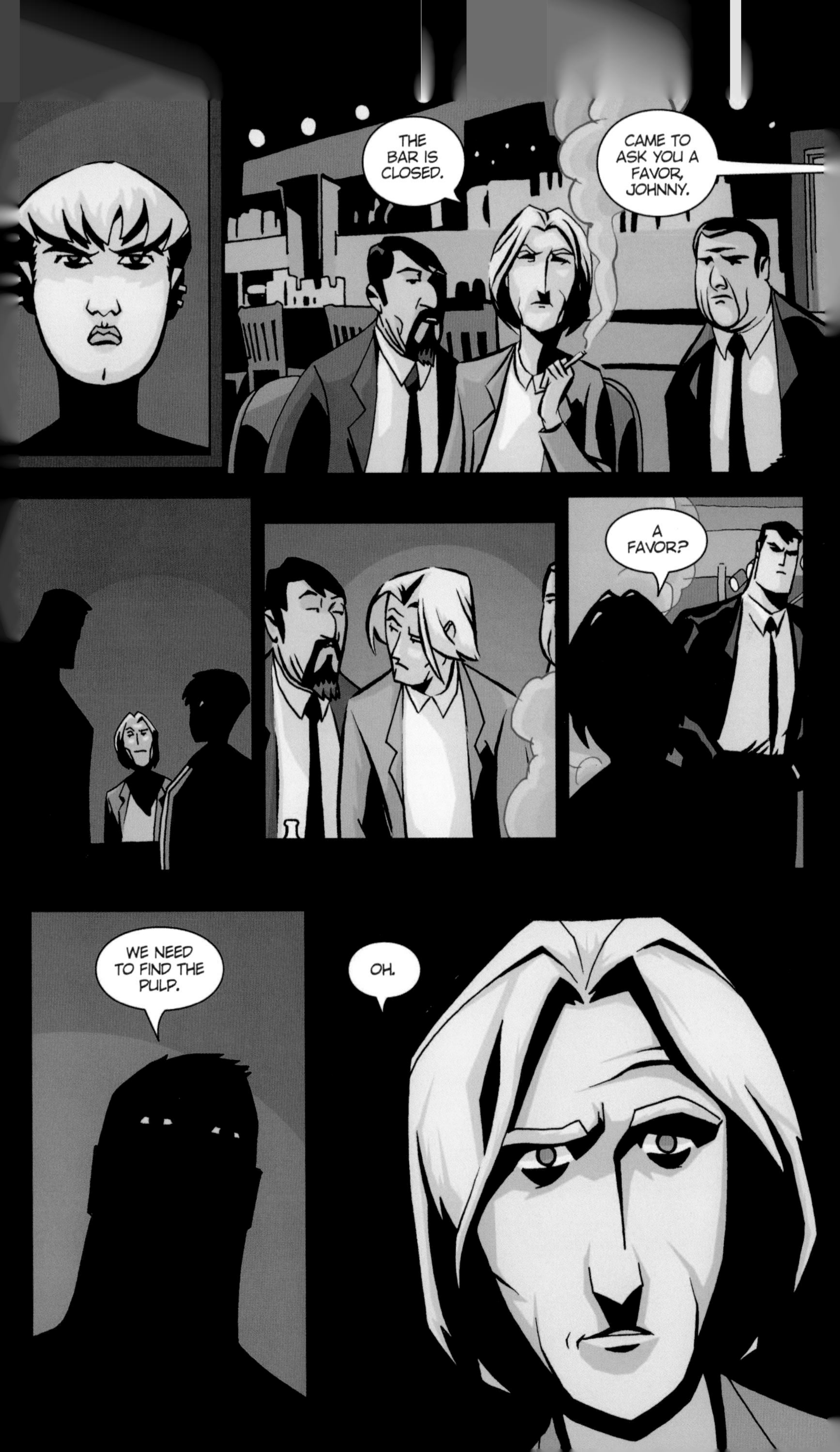
THE BAR IS CLOSED.
CAME TO ASK YOU A FAVOR, JOHNNY.
A FAVOR?
WE NEED TO FIND THE PULP.
OH.

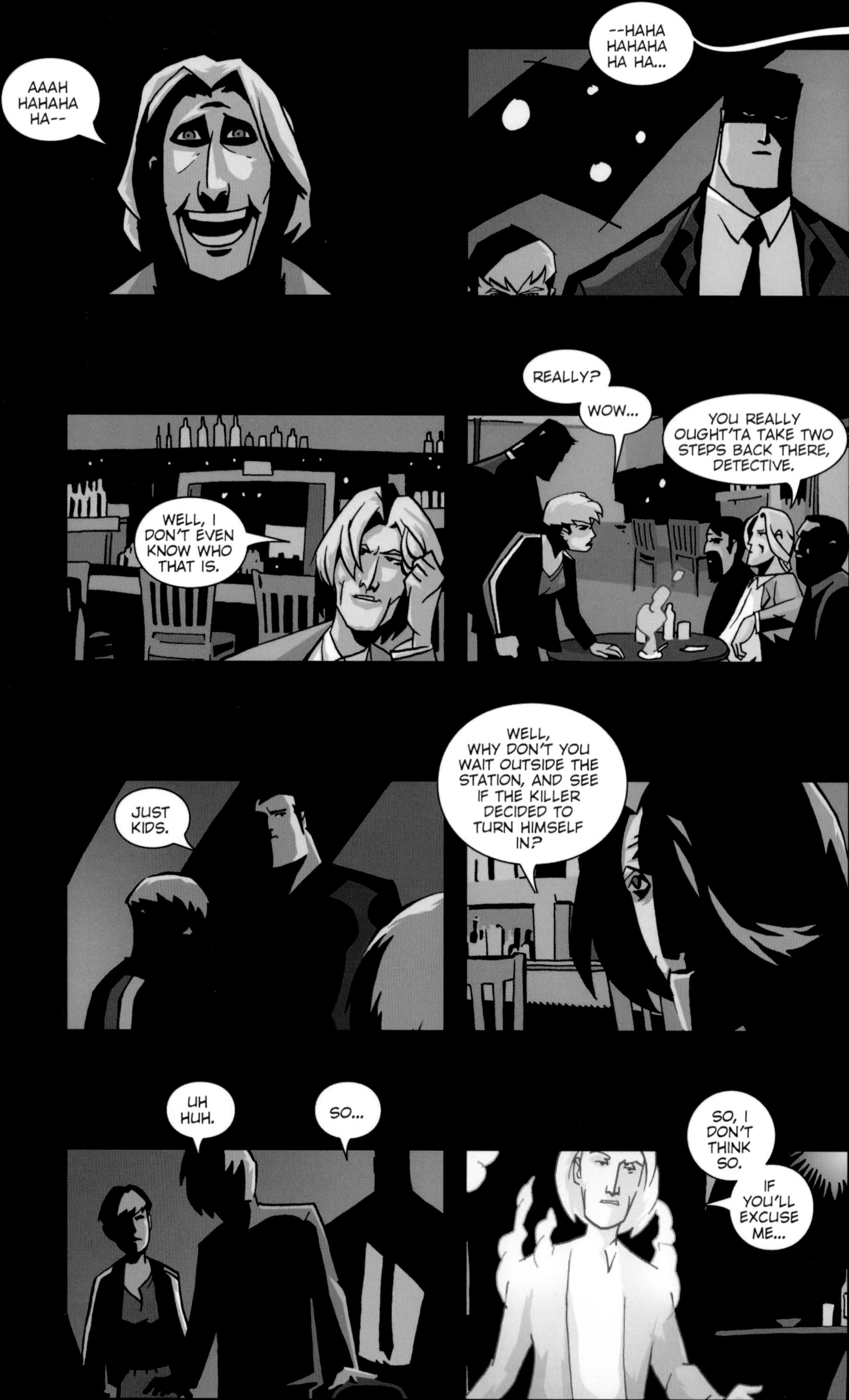
AAAH HAHAHA HA--
--HAHA HAHAHA HA HA...
WELL, I DON'T EVEN KNOW WHO THAT IS.
REALLY?
WOW...
YOU REALLY OUGHT'TA TAKE TWO STEPS BACK THERE, DETECTIVE.
JUST KIDS.
WELL, WHY DON'T YOU WAIT OUTSIDE THE STATION, AND SEE IF THE KILLER DECIDED TO TURN HIMSELF IN?
UH HUH.
SO...
SO, I DON'T THINK SO.
IF YOU'LL EXCUSE ME...

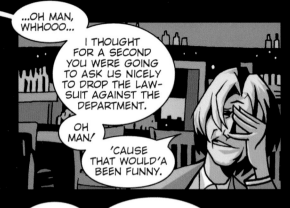

...OH MAN, WHHOOO...

I THOUGHT FOR A SECOND YOU WERE GOING TO ASK US NICELY TO DROP THE LAWSUIT AGAINST THE DEPARTMENT.

OH MAN!

'CAUSE THAT WOULD'A BEEN FUNNY.

NO, JOHNNY, WE JUST NEED TO FIND THE PULP.

THERE HAVE BEEN SOME MURDERS.

KIDS PLAYING DRESS UP--NOTHING TO DO WITH YOU, ME OR ANYTHING...

...WE JUST NEED TO FIND THE PULP

KIDS?

SOMEONE KILLED SOME KIDS?

HA HA HA LIKE THAT GUY WHO OFFED THE RETRO CUNT.

YOU GONNA HELP US OR NOT?

I WOULD CONSIDER IT A PERSONAL FAVOR.

HEY!-- NO TELE-PORTING!

WE'RE NOT DONE TALKING TO YOU.

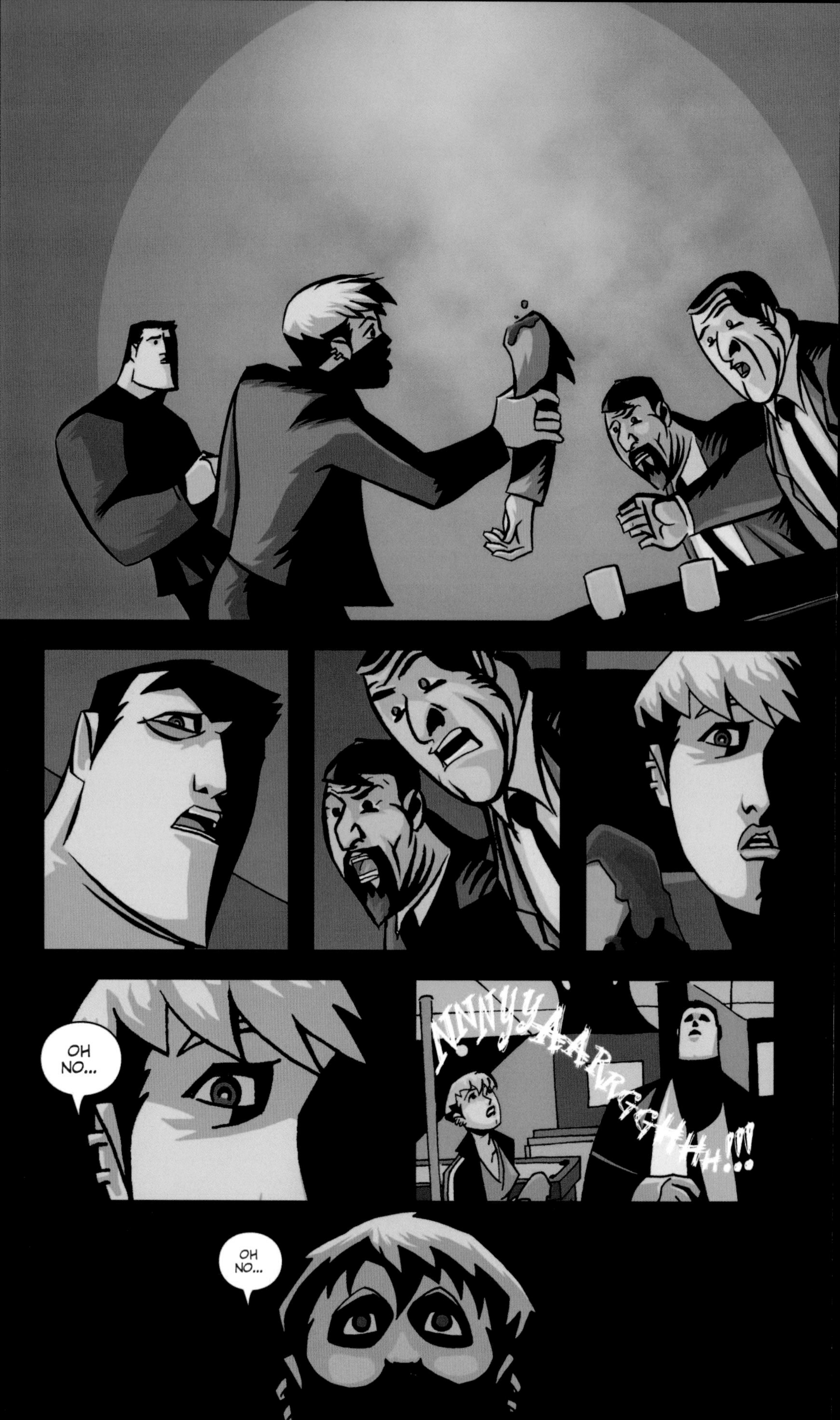
OH NO...
NNNYAARRGHHH!!!
OH NO...

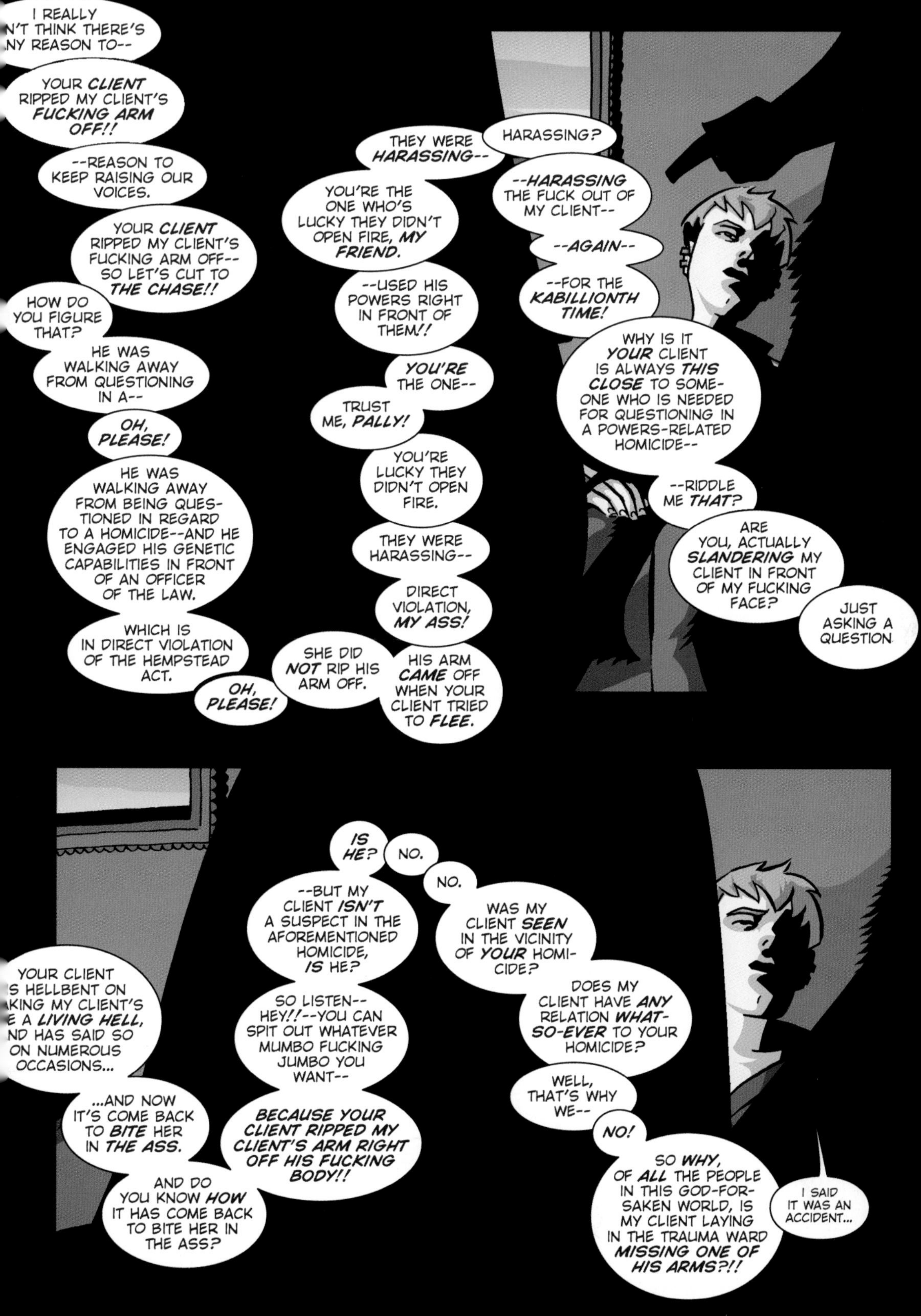

I REALLY N'T THINK THERE'S NY REASON TO--
YOUR CLIENT RIPPED MY CLIENT'S FUCKING ARM OFF!!
--REASON TO KEEP RAISING OUR VOICES.
YOUR CLIENT RIPPED MY CLIENT'S FUCKING ARM OFF-- SO LET'S CUT TO THE CHASE!!
HOW DO YOU FIGURE THAT?
HE WAS WALKING AWAY FROM QUESTIONING IN A--
OH, PLEASE!
HE WAS WALKING AWAY FROM BEING QUESTIONED IN REGARD TO A HOMICIDE--AND HE ENGAGED HIS GENETIC CAPABILITIES IN FRONT OF AN OFFICER OF THE LAW.
WHICH IS IN DIRECT VIOLATION OF THE HEMPSTEAD ACT.
OH, PLEASE!
SHE DID NOT RIP HIS ARM OFF.
HIS ARM CAME OFF WHEN YOUR CLIENT TRIED TO FLEE.
THEY WERE HARASSING--
HARASSING?
YOU'RE THE ONE WHO'S LUCKY THEY DIDN'T OPEN FIRE, MY FRIEND.
--HARASSING THE FUCK OUT OF MY CLIENT--
--AGAIN--
--USED HIS POWERS RIGHT IN FRONT OF THEM!!
--FOR THE KABILLIONTH TIME!
YOU'RE THE ONE--
TRUST ME, PALLY!
YOU'RE LUCKY THEY DIDN'T OPEN FIRE.
THEY WERE HARASSING--
DIRECT VIOLATION, MY ASS!
WHY IS IT YOUR CLIENT IS ALWAYS THIS CLOSE TO SOMEONE WHO IS NEEDED FOR QUESTIONING IN A POWERS-RELATED HOMICIDE--
--RIDDLE ME THAT?
ARE YOU, ACTUALLY SLANDERING MY CLIENT IN FRONT OF MY FUCKING FACE?
JUST ASKING A QUESTION.
IS HE?
NO.
NO.
--BUT MY CLIENT ISN'T A SUSPECT IN THE AFOREMENTIONED HOMICIDE, IS HE?
WAS MY CLIENT SEEN IN THE VICINITY OF YOUR HOMICIDE?
YOUR CLIENT S HELLBENT ON KING MY CLIENT'S E A LIVING HELL, ND HAS SAID SO ON NUMEROUS OCCASIONS...
...AND NOW IT'S COME BACK TO BITE HER IN THE ASS.
AND DO YOU KNOW HOW IT HAS COME BACK TO BITE HER IN THE ASS?
SO LISTEN-- HEY!!--YOU CAN SPIT OUT WHATEVER MUMBO FUCKING JUMBO YOU WANT--
BECAUSE YOUR CLIENT RIPPED MY CLIENT'S ARM RIGHT OFF HIS FUCKING BODY!!
DOES MY CLIENT HAVE ANY RELATION WHATSO-EVER TO YOUR HOMICIDE?
WELL, THAT'S WHY WE--
NO!
SO WHY, OF ALL THE PEOPLE IN THIS GOD-FORSAKEN WORLD, IS MY CLIENT LAYING IN THE TRAUMA WARD MISSING ONE OF HIS ARMS?!!
I SAID IT WAS AN ACCIDENT...

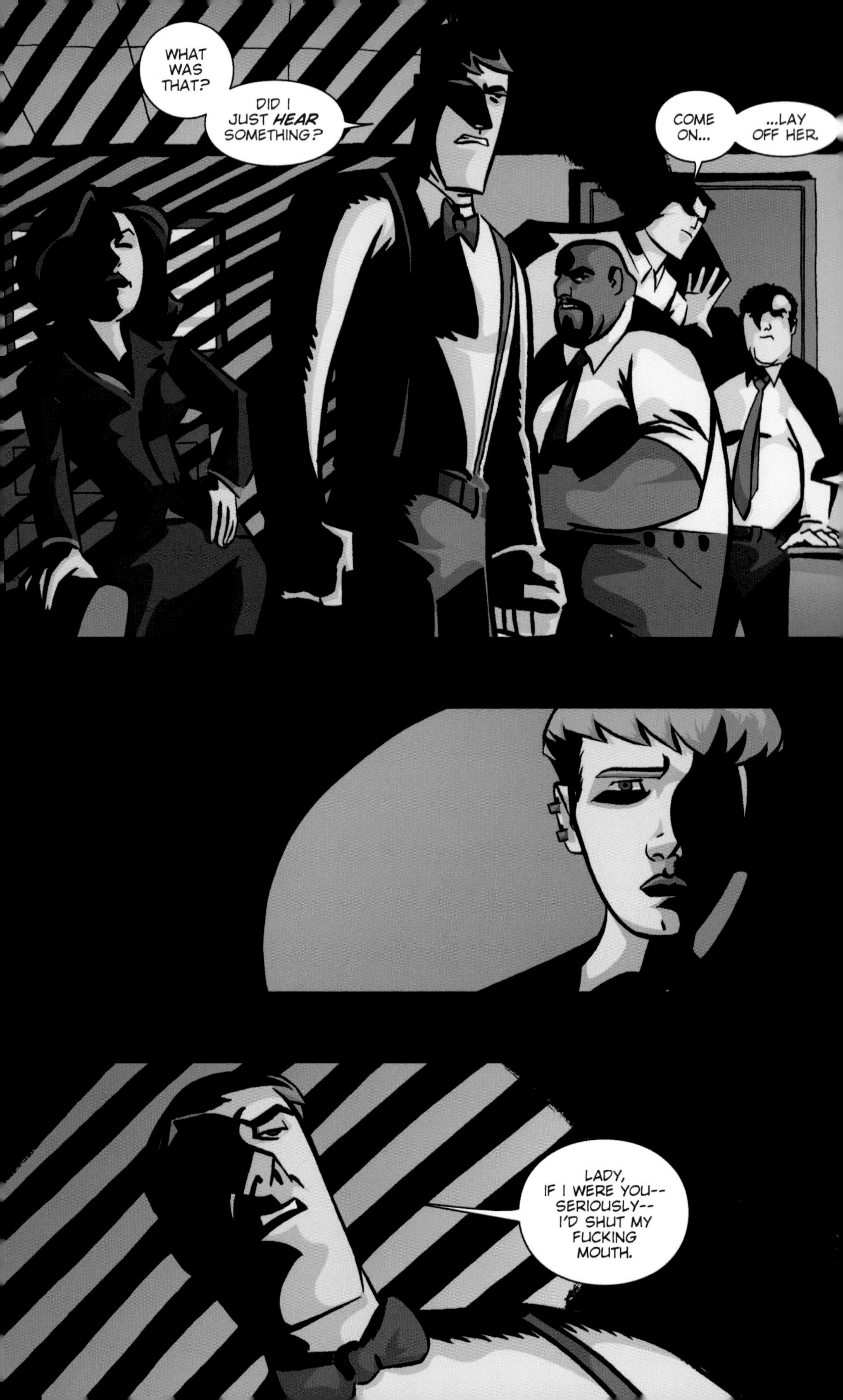
WHAT WAS THAT?
DID I JUST HEAR SOMETHING?
COME ON...
...LAY OFF HER.
LADY, IF I WERE YOU-- SERIOUSLY-- I'D SHUT MY FUCKING MOUTH.

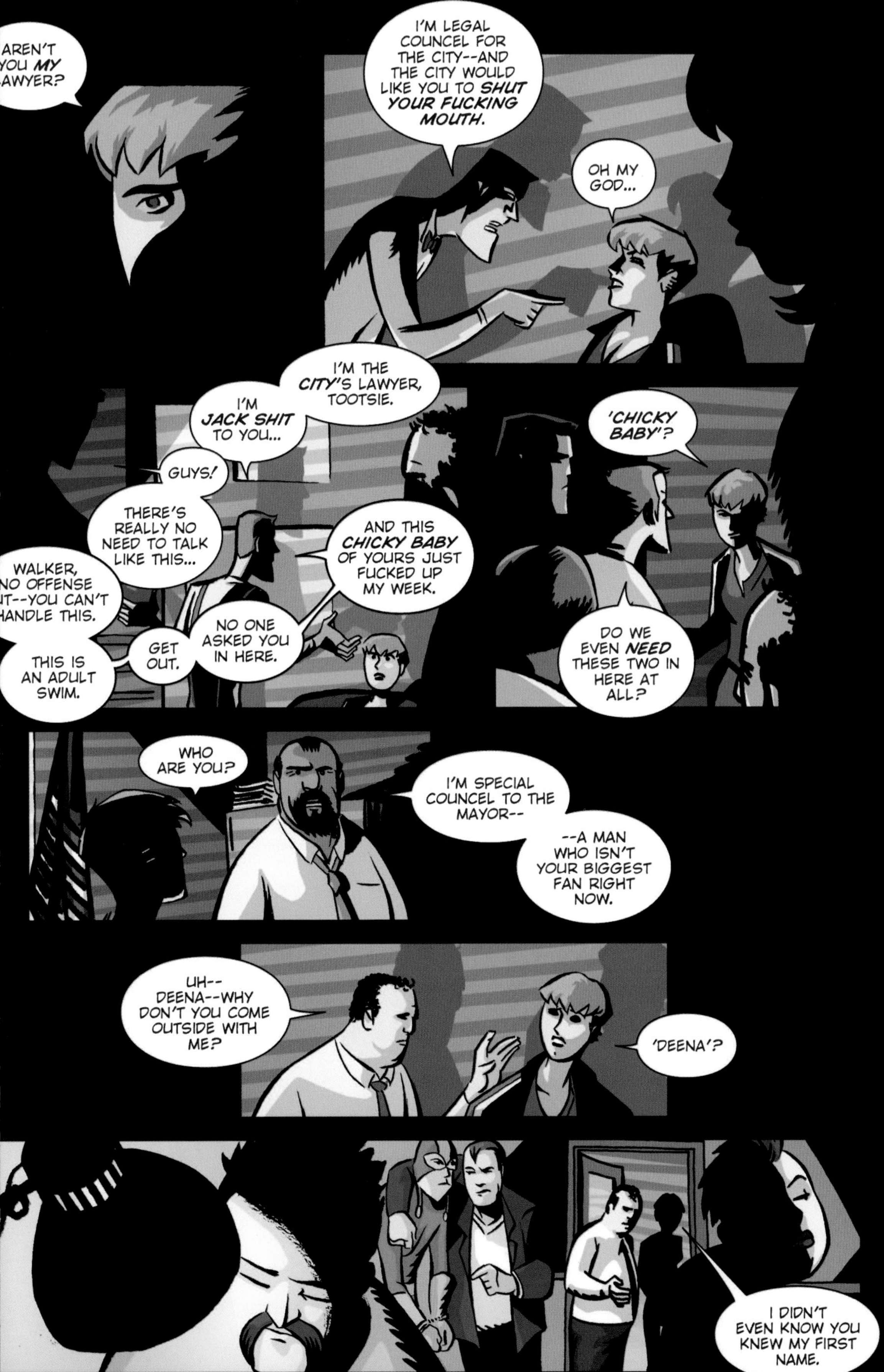
AREN'T YOU MY LAWYER?
I'M LEGAL COUNCEL FOR THE CITY--AND THE CITY WOULD LIKE YOU TO SHUT YOUR FUCKING MOUTH.
OH MY GOD...
I'M JACK SHIT TO YOU...
I'M THE CITY'S LAWYER, TOOTSIE.
GUYS!
THERE'S REALLY NO NEED TO TALK LIKE THIS...
AND THIS CHICKY BABY OF YOURS JUST FUCKED UP MY WEEK.
WALKER, NO OFFENSE BUT--YOU CAN'T HANDLE THIS.
NO ONE ASKED YOU IN HERE.
GET OUT.
THIS IS AN ADULT SWIM.
'CHICKY BABY'?
DO WE EVEN NEED THESE TWO IN HERE AT ALL?
WHO ARE YOU?
I'M SPECIAL COUNCEL TO THE MAYOR--
--A MAN WHO ISN'T YOUR BIGGEST FAN RIGHT NOW.
UH--DEENA--WHY DON'T YOU COME OUTSIDE WITH ME?
'DEENA'?
I DIDN'T EVEN KNOW YOU KNEW MY FIRST NAME.

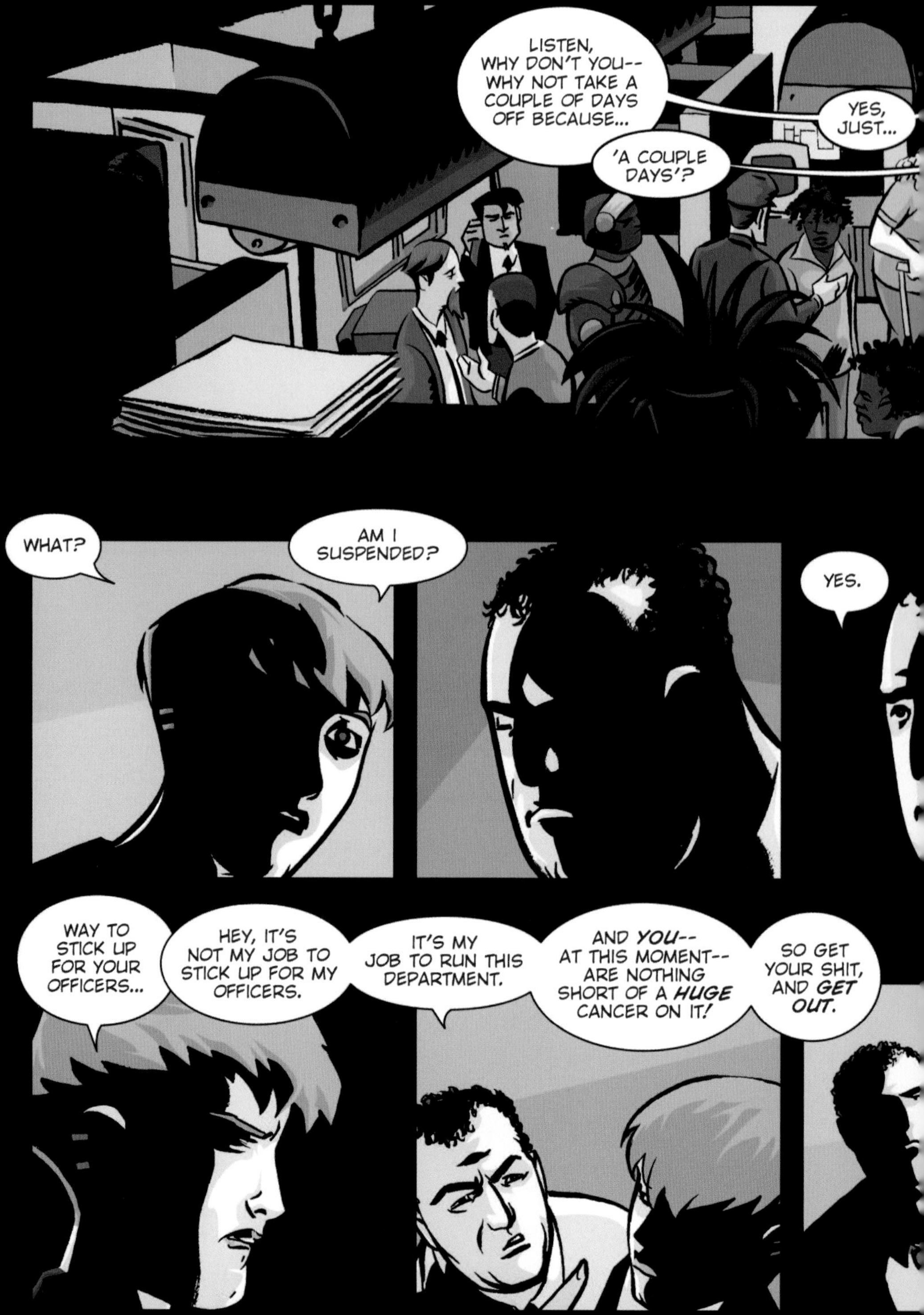
LISTEN, WHY DON'T YOU-- WHY NOT TAKE A COUPLE OF DAYS OFF BECAUSE...
'A COUPLE DAYS'?
YES, JUST...
WHAT?
AM I SUSPENDED?
YES.
WAY TO STICK UP FOR YOUR OFFICERS...
HEY, IT'S NOT MY JOB TO STICK UP FOR MY OFFICERS.
IT'S MY JOB TO RUN THIS DEPARTMENT.
AND YOU-- AT THIS MOMENT-- ARE NOTHING SHORT OF A HUGE CANCER ON IT!
SO GET YOUR SHIT, AND GET OUT.

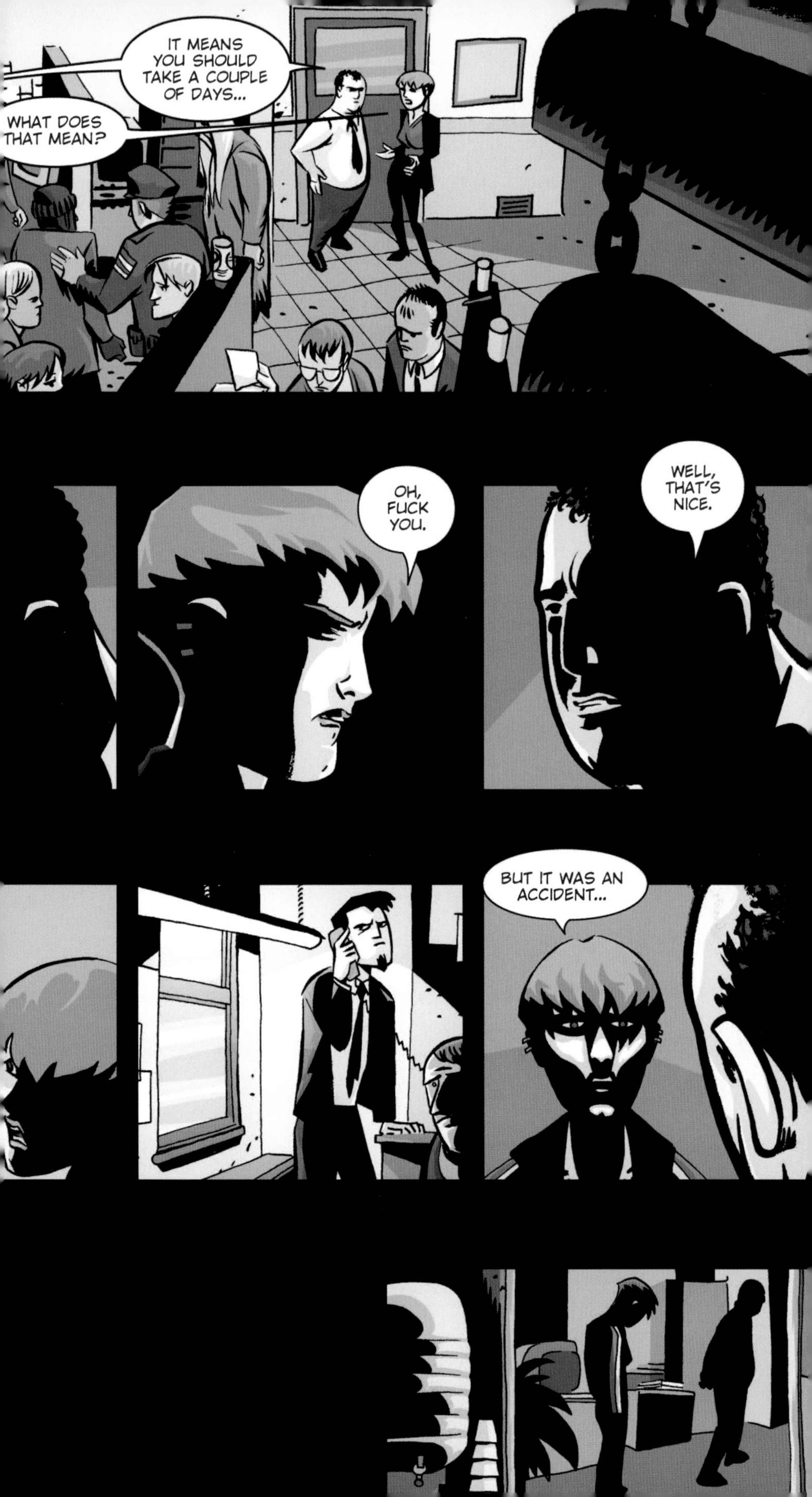
WHAT DOES THAT MEAN?
IT MEANS YOU SHOULD TAKE A COUPLE OF DAYS...
OH, FUCK YOU.
WELL, THAT'S NICE.
BUT IT WAS AN ACCIDENT...

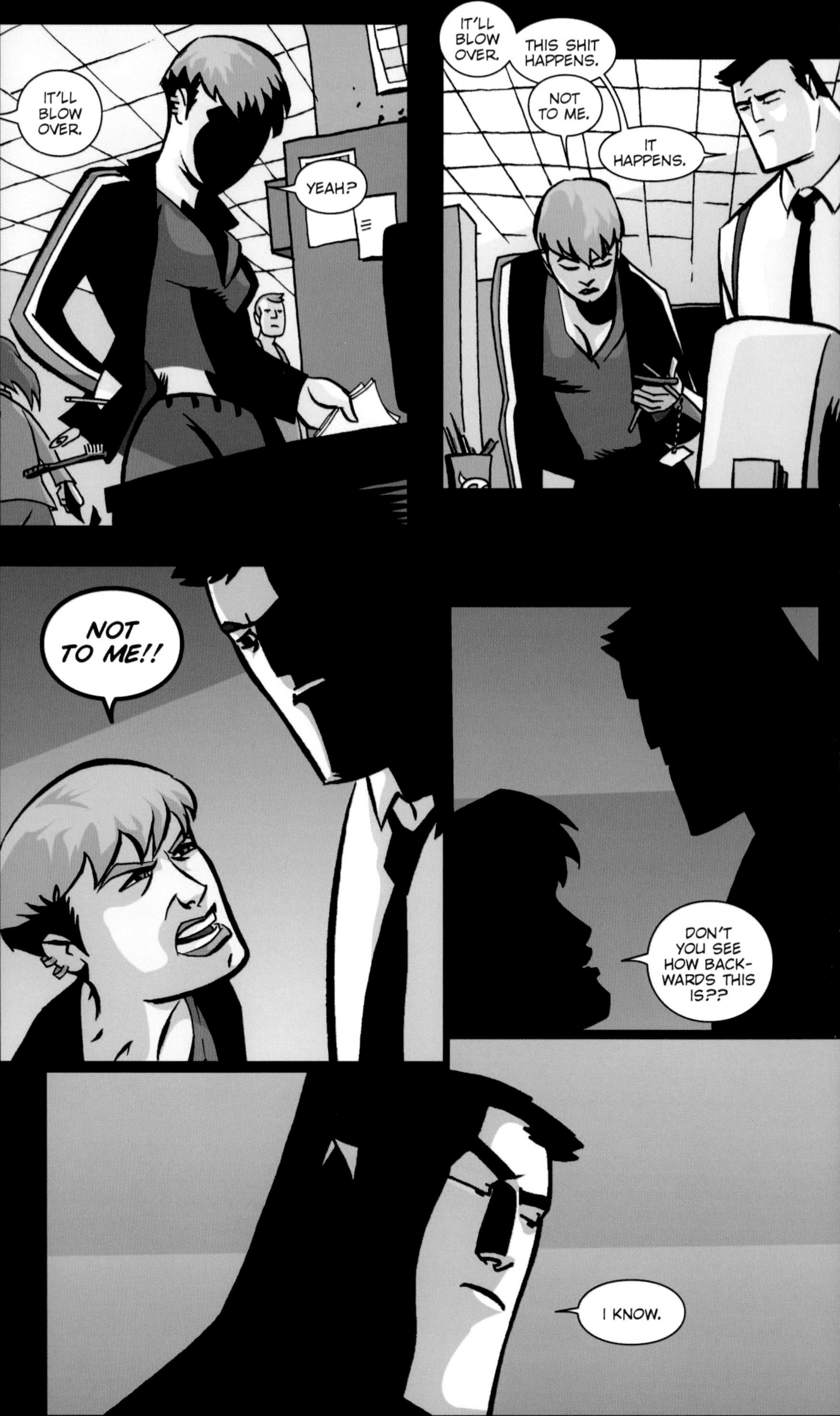
IT'LL BLOW OVER.
YEAH?
IT'LL BLOW OVER.
THIS SHIT HAPPENS.
NOT TO ME.
IT HAPPENS.
NOT TO ME!!
DON'T YOU SEE HOW BACK-WARDS THIS IS??
I KNOW.

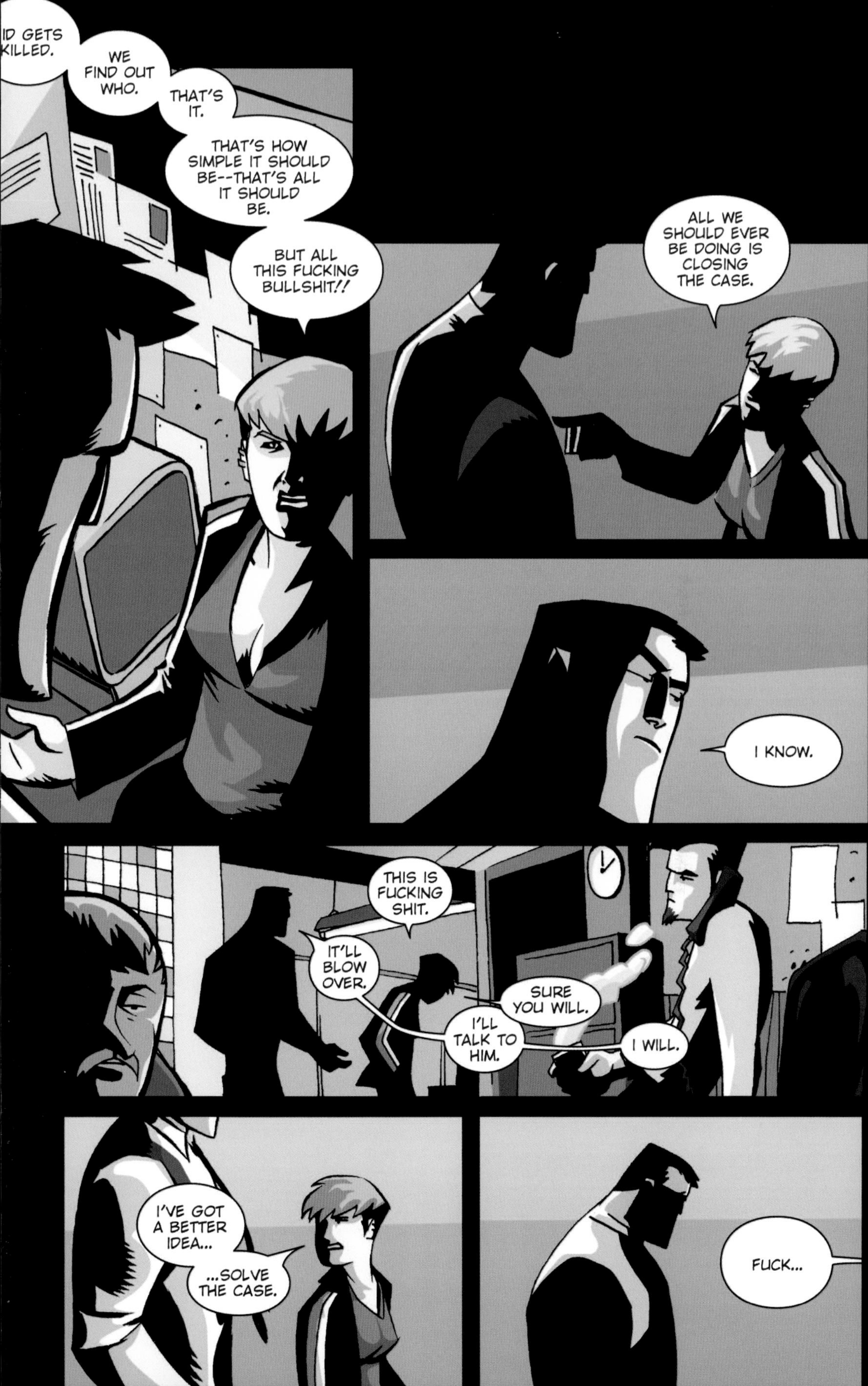
ID GETS KILLED.
WE FIND OUT WHO.
THAT'S IT.
THAT'S HOW SIMPLE IT SHOULD BE--THAT'S ALL IT SHOULD BE.
BUT ALL THIS FUCKING BULLSHIT!!
ALL WE SHOULD EVER BE DOING IS CLOSING THE CASE.
I KNOW.
THIS IS FUCKING SHIT.
IT'LL BLOW OVER.
SURE YOU WILL.
I'LL TALK TO HIM.
I WILL.
I'VE GOT A BETTER IDEA...
...SOLVE THE CASE.
FUCK...

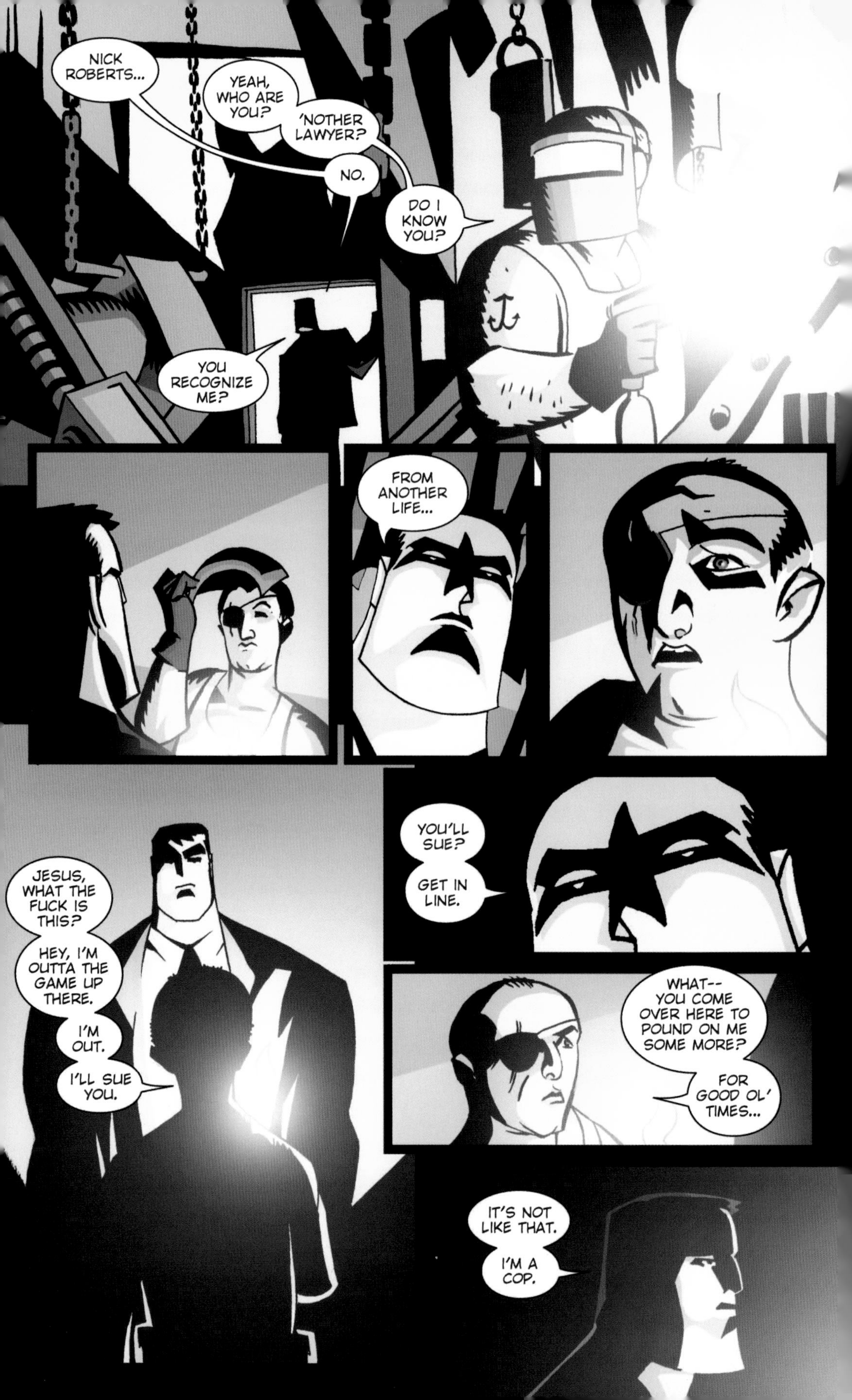
NICK ROBERTS...
YEAH, WHO ARE YOU?
'NOTHER LAWYER?
NO.
DO I KNOW YOU?
YOU RECOGNIZE ME?
FROM ANOTHER LIFE...
JESUS, WHAT THE FUCK IS THIS?
HEY, I'M OUTTA THE GAME UP THERE.
I'M OUT.
I'LL SUE YOU.
YOU'LL SUE?
GET IN LINE.
WHAT-- YOU COME OVER HERE TO POUND ON ME SOME MORE?
FOR GOOD OL' TIMES...
IT'S NOT LIKE THAT.
I'M A COP.

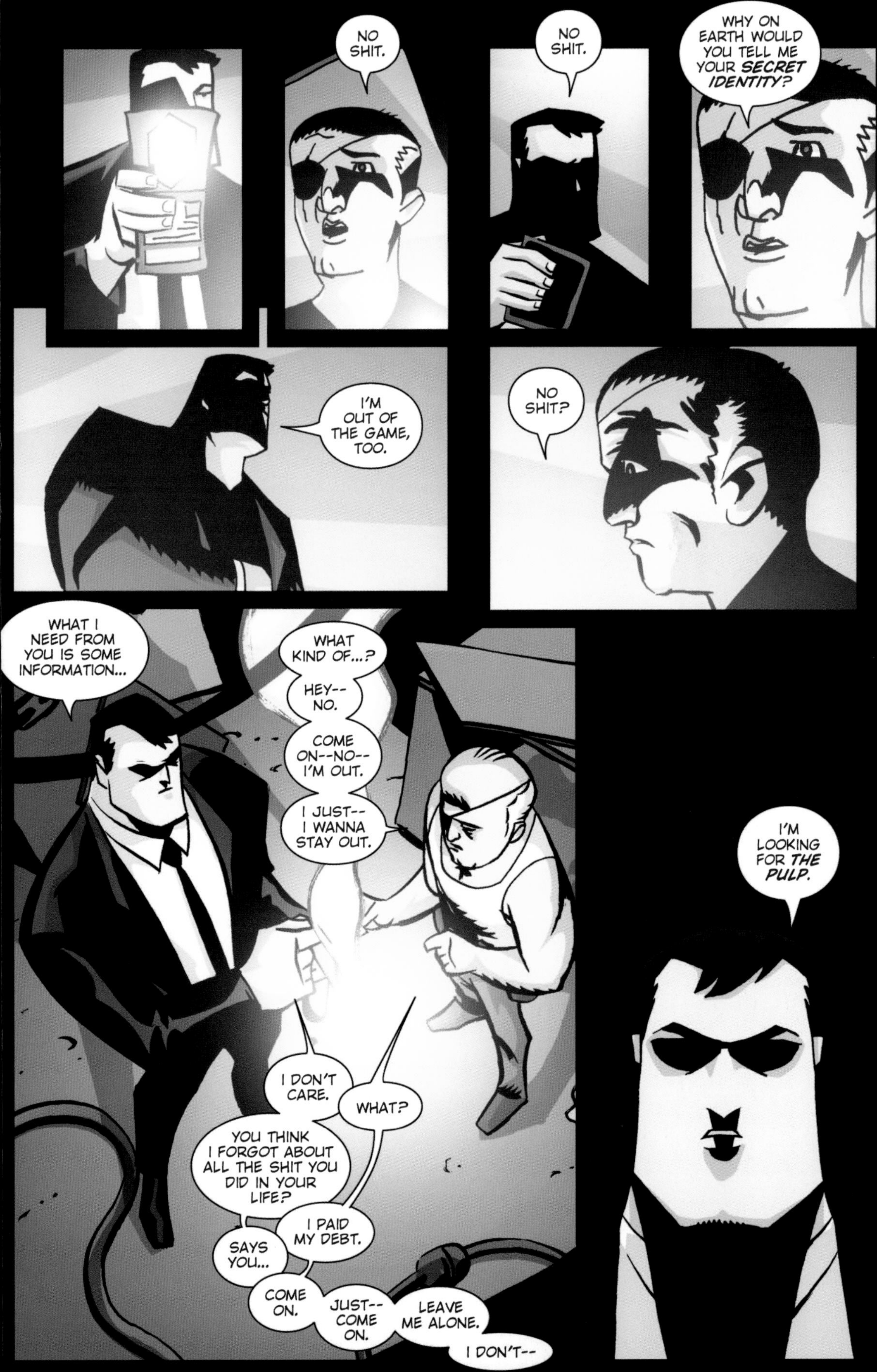
NO SHIT.
NO SHIT.
WHY ON EARTH WOULD YOU TELL ME YOUR SECRET IDENTITY?
I'M OUT OF THE GAME, TOO.
NO SHIT?
WHAT I NEED FROM YOU IS SOME INFORMATION...
WHAT KIND OF...?
HEY-- NO.
COME ON--NO-- I'M OUT.
I JUST-- I WANNA STAY OUT.
I DON'T CARE.
WHAT?
YOU THINK I FORGOT ABOUT ALL THE SHIT YOU DID IN YOUR LIFE?
I PAID MY DEBT.
SAYS YOU...
COME ON.
JUST-- COME ON.
LEAVE ME ALONE.
I DON'T--
I'M LOOKING FOR THE PULP.

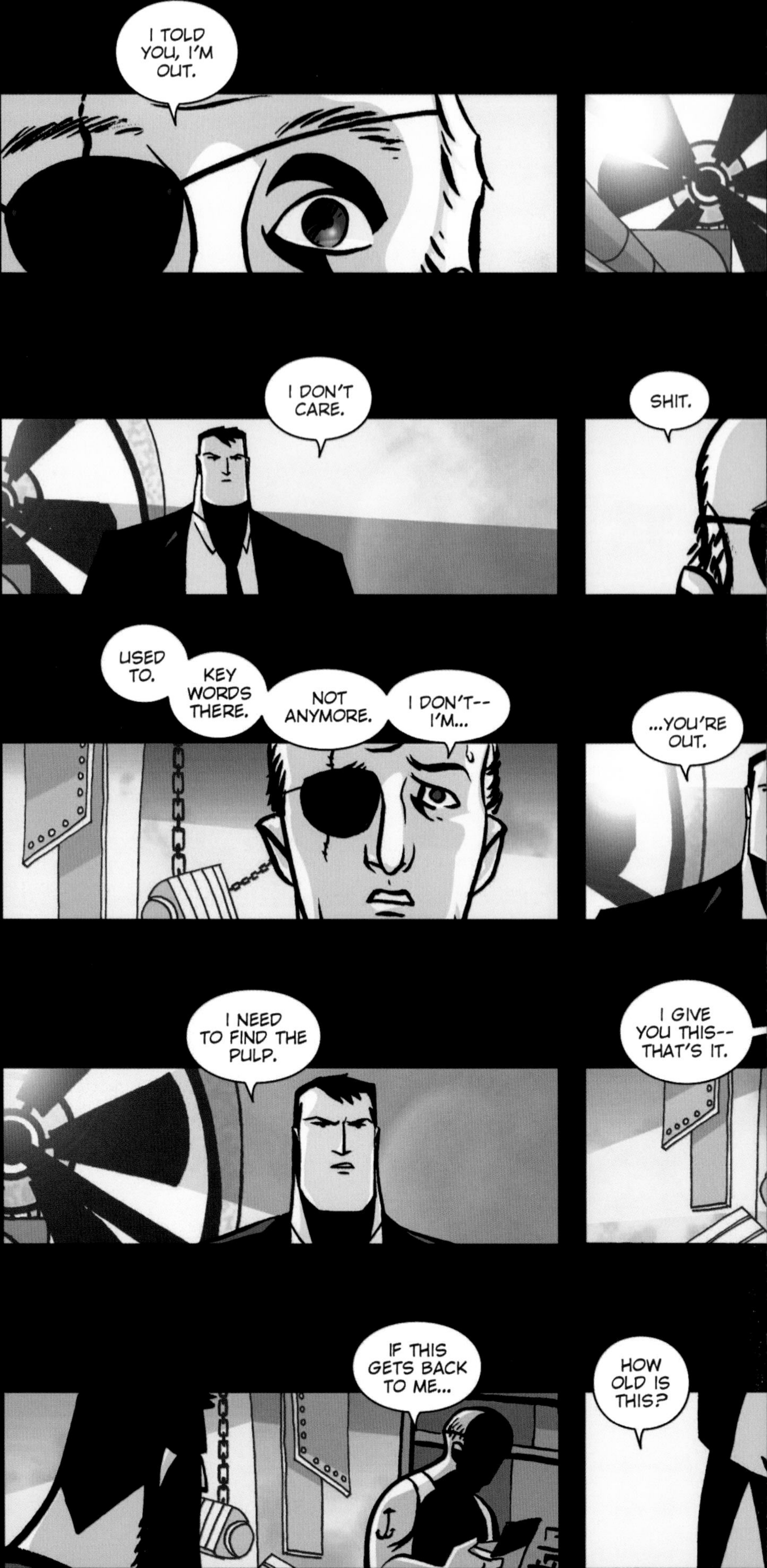
I TOLD YOU, I'M OUT.
I DON'T CARE.
SHIT.
USED TO.
KEY WORDS THERE.
NOT ANYMORE.
I DON'T-- I'M...
...YOU'RE OUT.
I NEED TO FIND THE PULP.
I GIVE YOU THIS-- THAT'S IT.
IF THIS GETS BACK TO ME...
HOW OLD IS THIS?

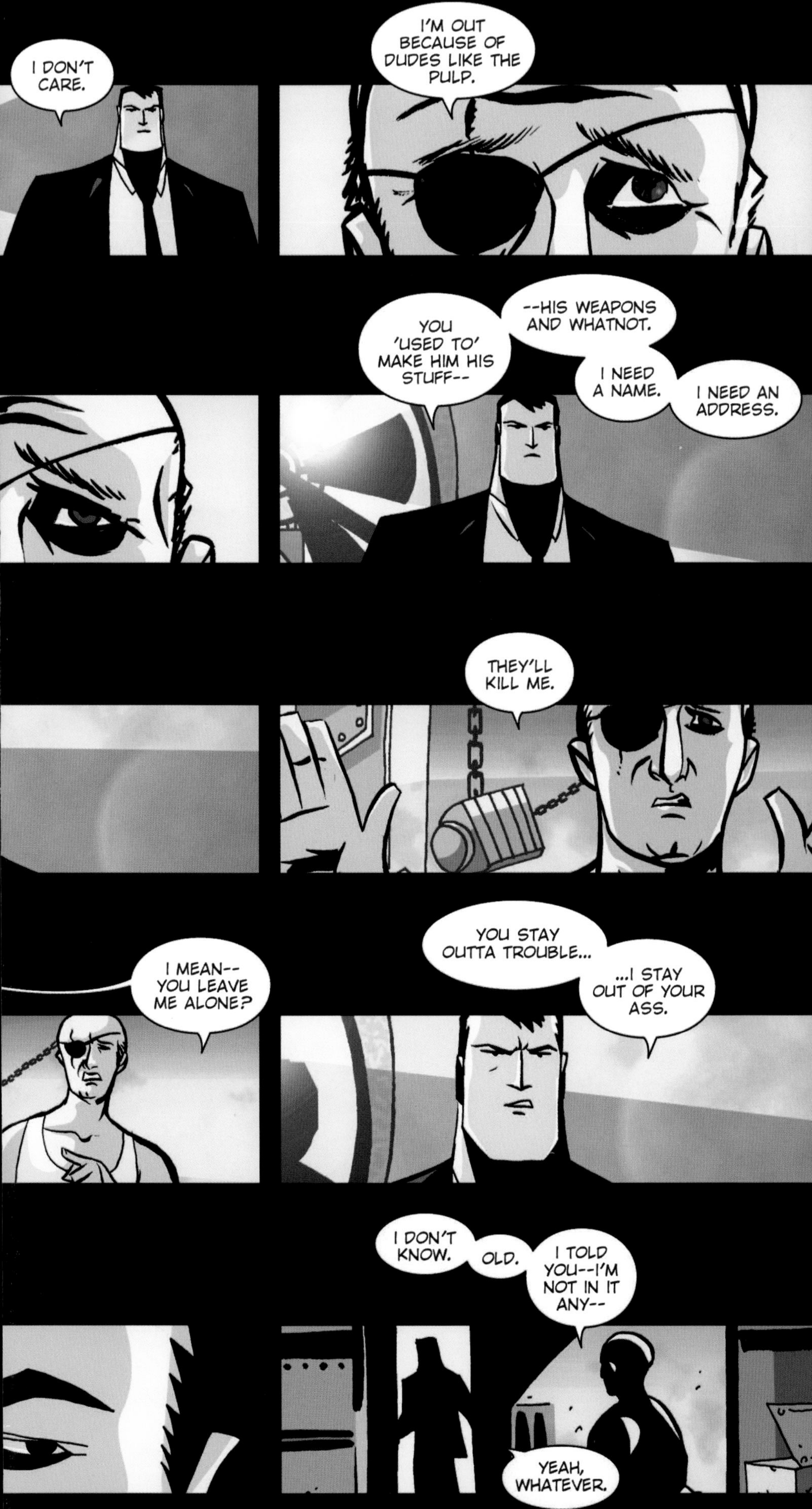
I DON'T CARE.
I'M OUT BECAUSE OF DUDES LIKE THE PULP.
YOU 'USED TO' MAKE HIM HIS STUFF--
--HIS WEAPONS AND WHATNOT.
I NEED A NAME.
I NEED AN ADDRESS.
THEY'LL KILL ME.
I MEAN-- YOU LEAVE ME ALONE?
YOU STAY OUTTA TROUBLE...
...I STAY OUT OF YOUR ASS.
I DON'T KNOW.
OLD.
I TOLD YOU--I'M NOT IN IT ANY--
YEAH, WHATEVER.

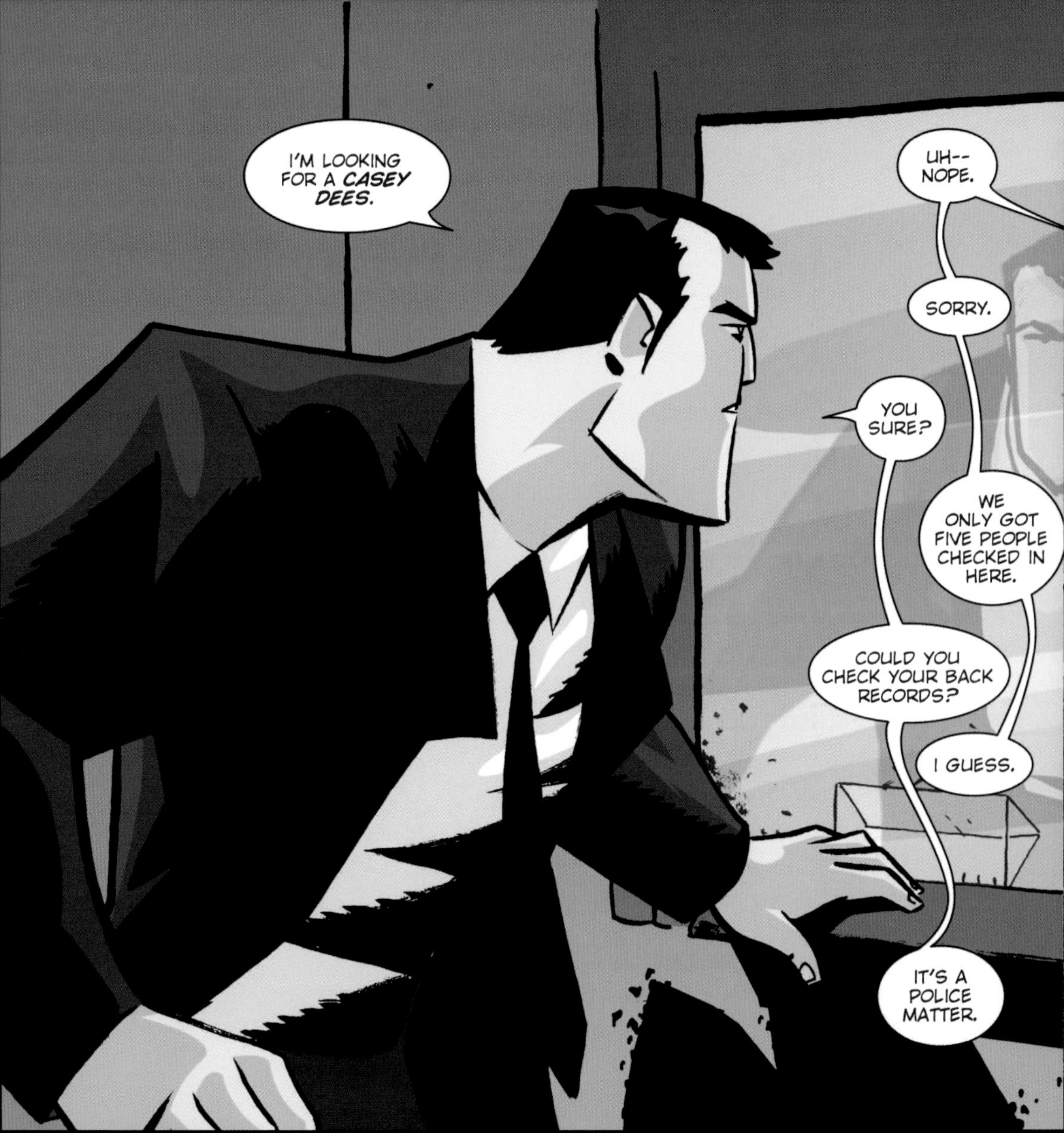
I'M LOOKING FOR A CASEY DEES.
UH--NOPE.
SORRY.
YOU SURE?
WE ONLY GOT FIVE PEOPLE CHECKED IN HERE.
COULD YOU CHECK YOUR BACK RECORDS?
I GUESS.
IT'S A POLICE MATTER.

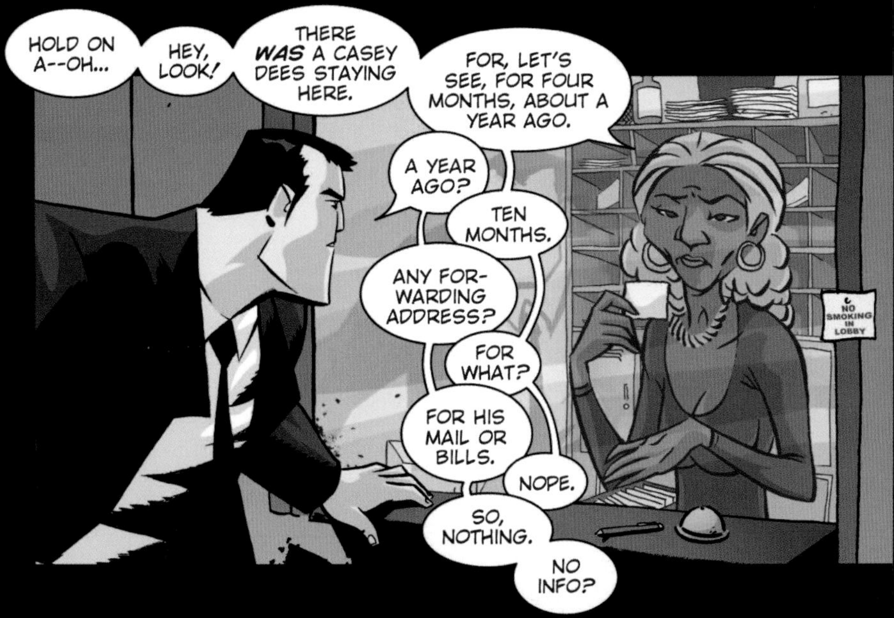
HOLD ON A--OH...
HEY, LOOK!
THERE WAS A CASEY DEES STAYING HERE.
FOR, LET'S SEE, FOR FOUR MONTHS, ABOUT A YEAR AGO.
A YEAR AGO?
TEN MONTHS.
ANY FOR-WARDING ADDRESS?
FOR WHAT?
FOR HIS MAIL OR BILLS.
NOPE.
SO, NOTHING.
NO INFO?
NO SMOKING IN LOBBY

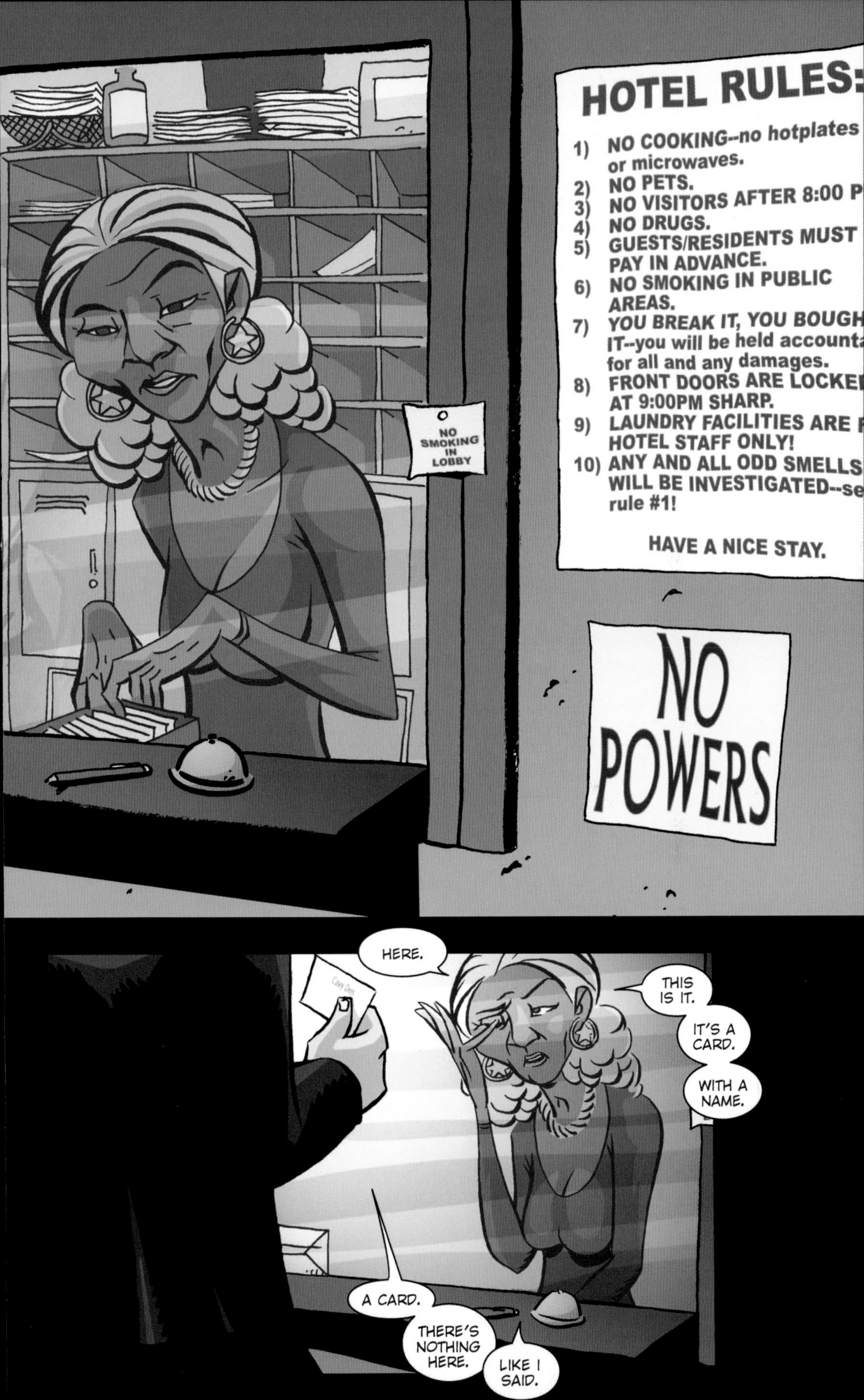
NO SMOKING IN LOBBY
HOTEL RULES:
1) NO COOKING--no hotplates or microwaves.
2) NO PETS.
3) NO VISITORS AFTER 8:00 P
4) NO DRUGS.
5) GUESTS/RESIDENTS MUST PAY IN ADVANCE.
6) NO SMOKING IN PUBLIC AREAS.
7) YOU BREAK IT, YOU BOUGH IT--you will be held accounta for all and any damages.
8) FRONT DOORS ARE LOCKE AT 9:00PM SHARP.
9) LAUNDRY FACILITIES ARE HOTEL STAFF ONLY!
10) ANY AND ALL ODD SMELLS WILL BE INVESTIGATED--se rule #1!
HAVE A NICE STAY.
NO POWERS
HERE.
THIS IS IT.
IT'S A CARD.
WITH A NAME.
A CARD.
THERE'S NOTHING HERE.
LIKE I SAID.

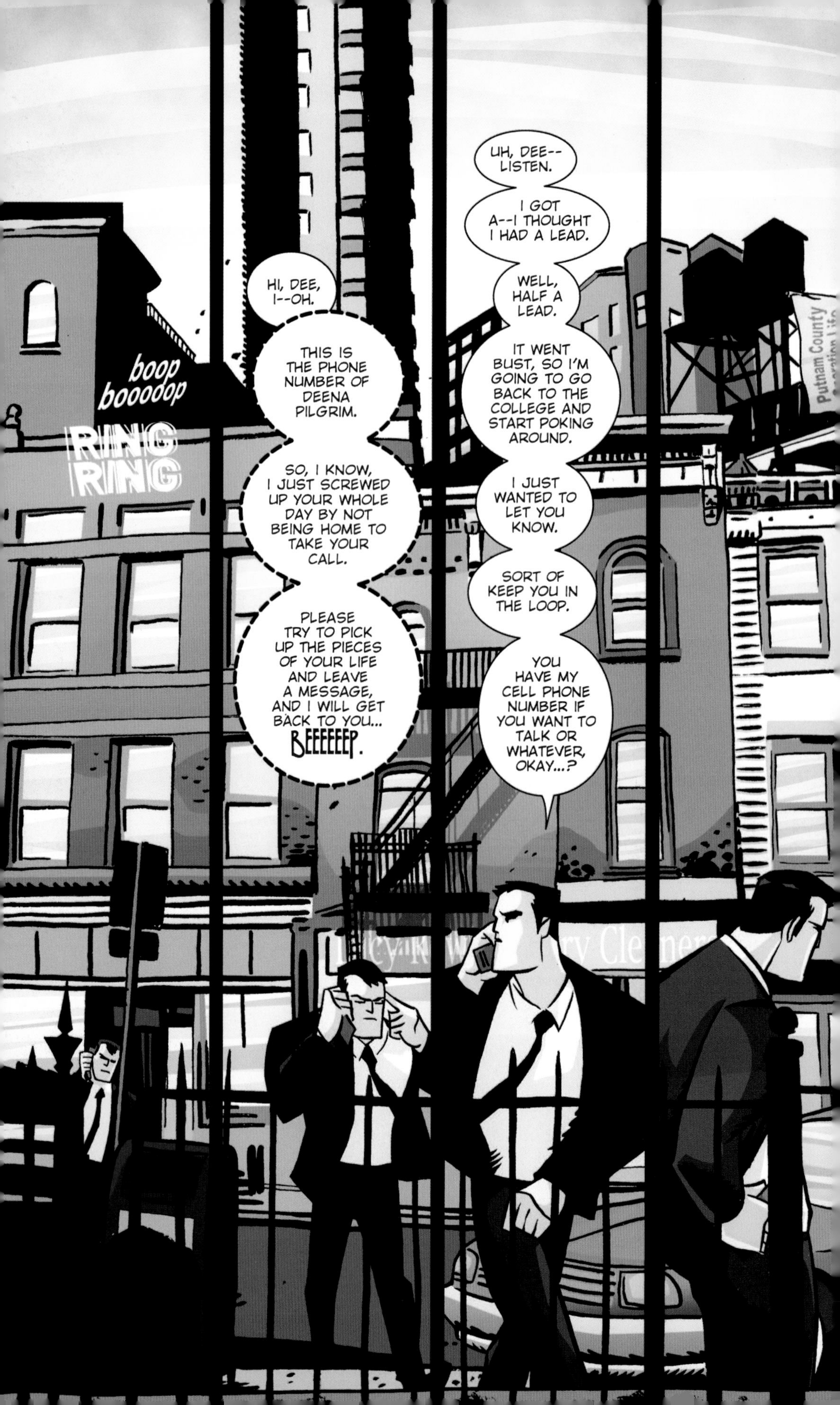
boop boooop
RING RING
HI, DEE, I--OH.
THIS IS THE PHONE NUMBER OF DEENA PILGRIM.
SO, I KNOW, I JUST SCREWED UP YOUR WHOLE DAY BY NOT BEING HOME TO TAKE YOUR CALL.
PLEASE TRY TO PICK UP THE PIECES OF YOUR LIFE AND LEAVE A MESSAGE, AND I WILL GET BACK TO YOU... BEEEEEEP.
UH, DEE-- LISTEN.
I GOT A--I THOUGHT I HAD A LEAD.
WELL, HALF A LEAD.
IT WENT BUST, SO I'M GOING TO GO BACK TO THE COLLEGE AND START POKING AROUND.
I JUST WANTED TO LET YOU KNOW.
SORT OF KEEP YOU IN THE LOOP.
YOU HAVE MY CELL PHONE NUMBER IF YOU WANT TO TALK OR WHATEVER, OKAY...?
Putnam County

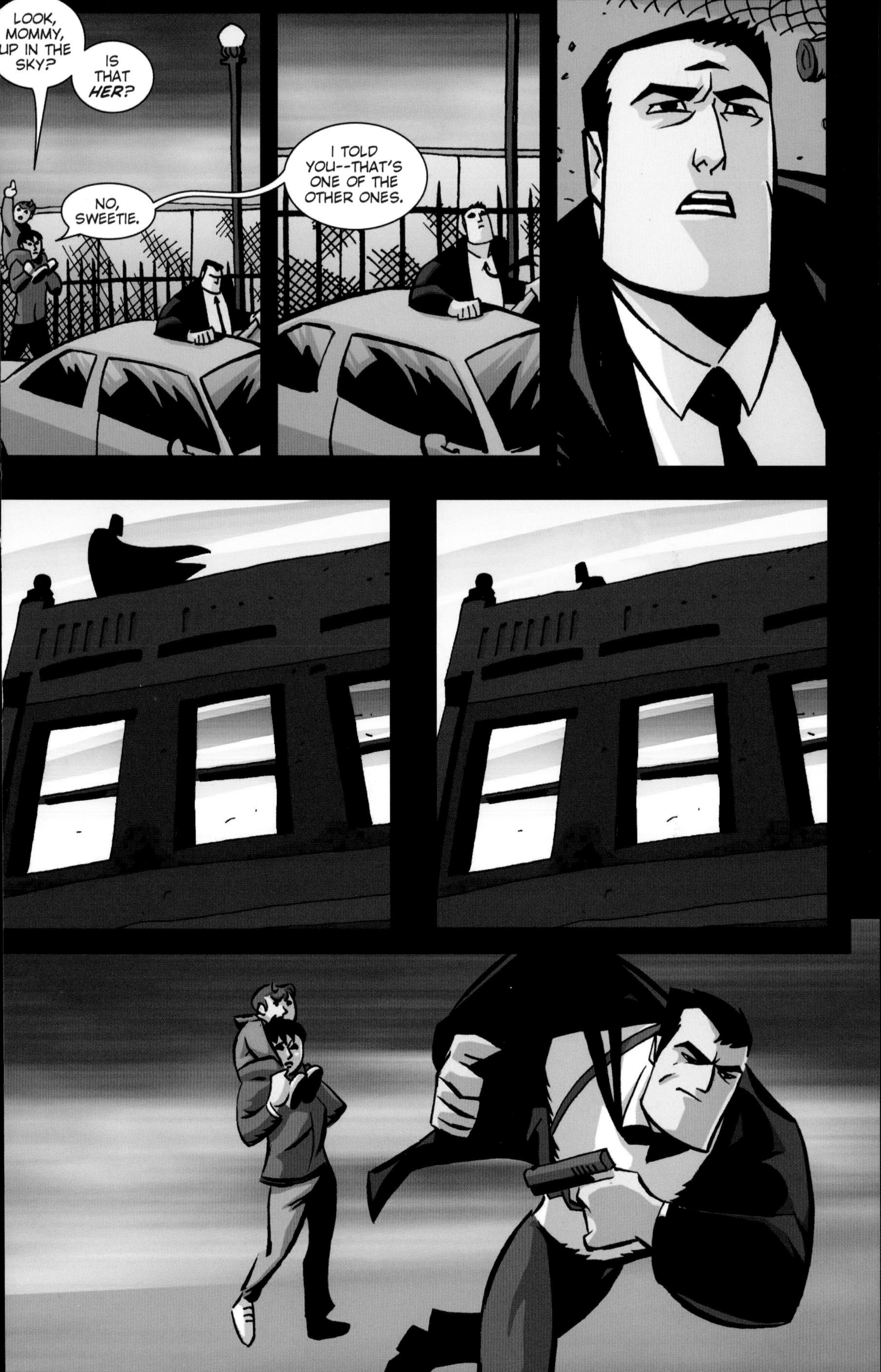
LOOK, MOMMY, UP IN THE SKY?
IS THAT *HER?*
NO, SWEETIE.
I TOLD YOU--THAT'S ONE OF THE OTHER ONES.

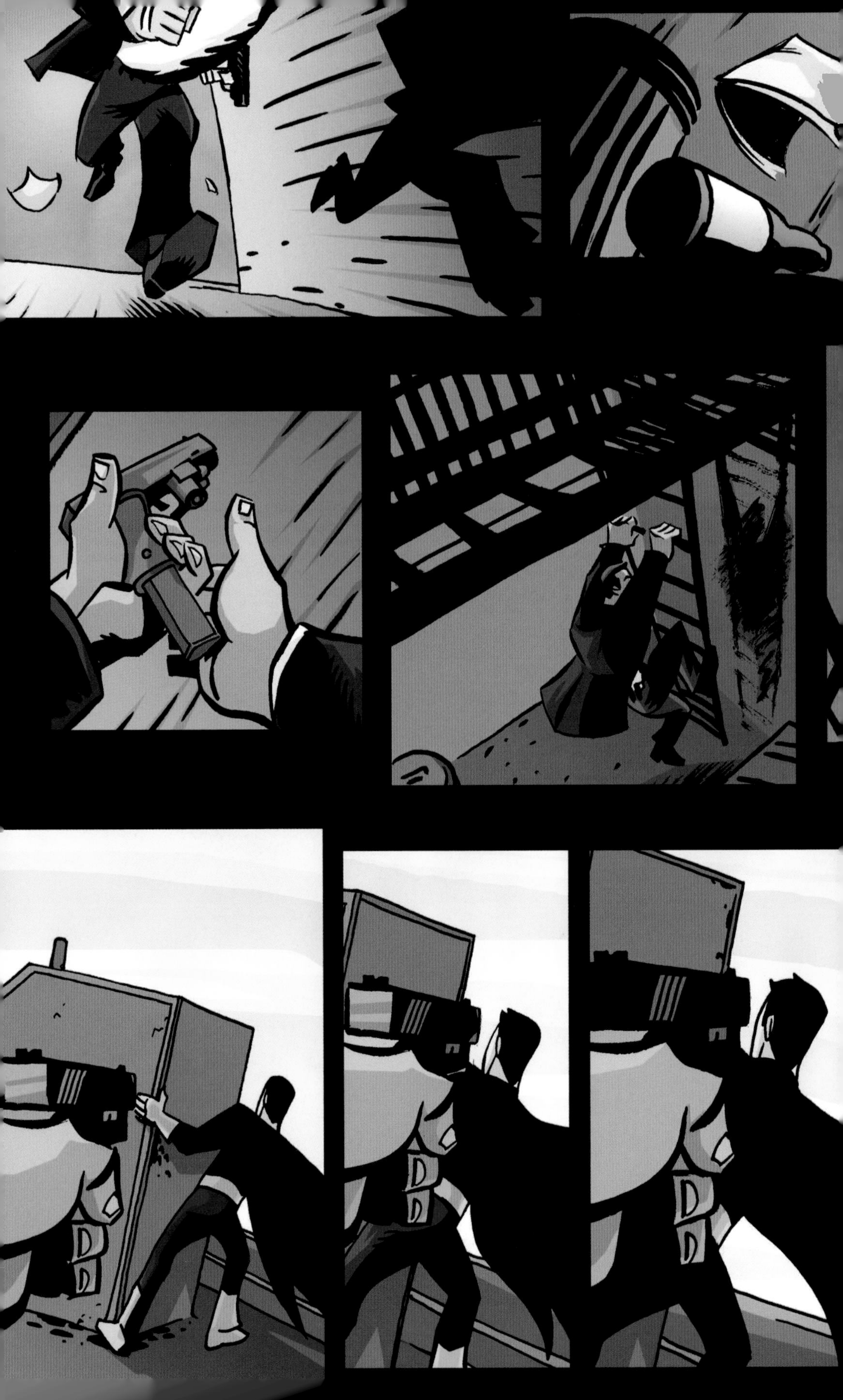

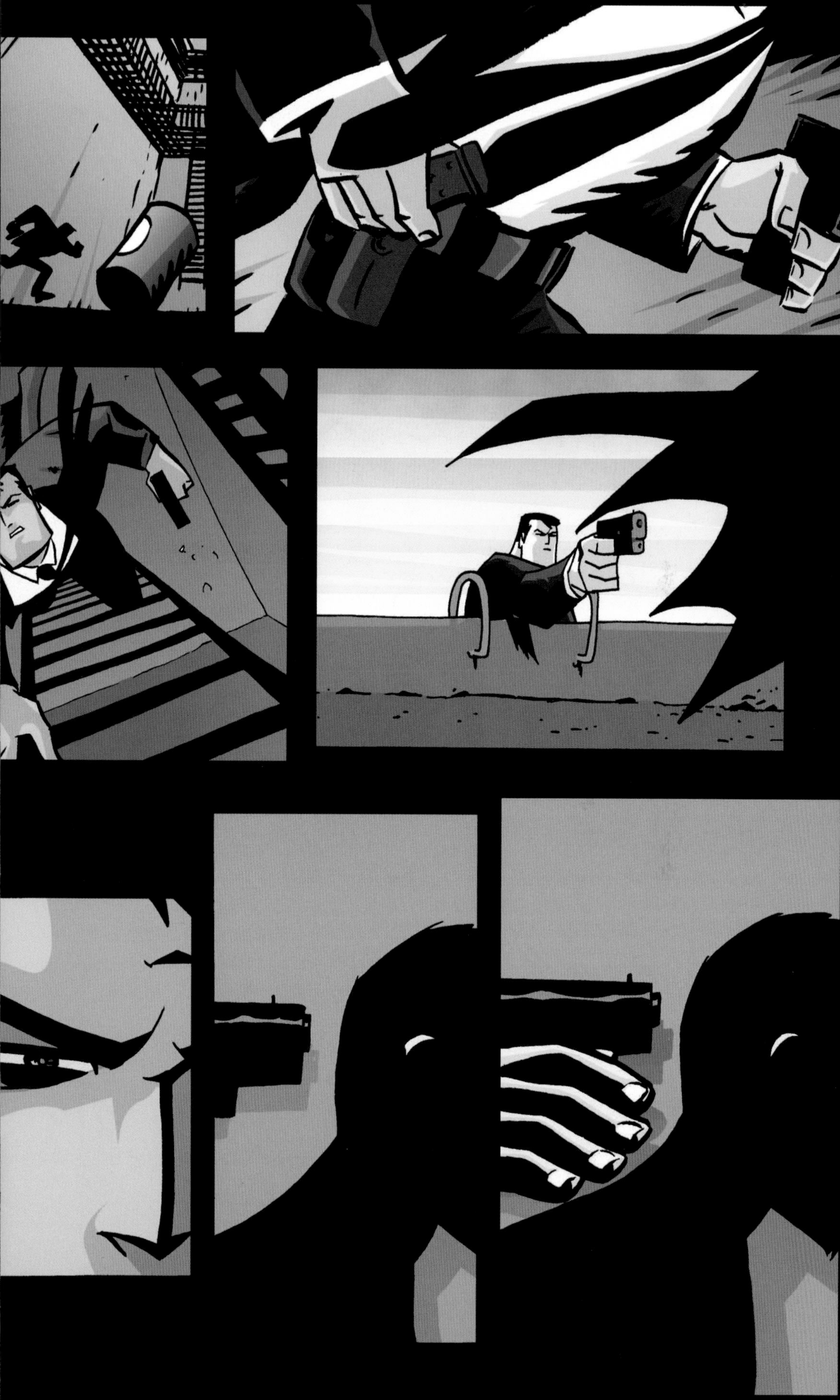

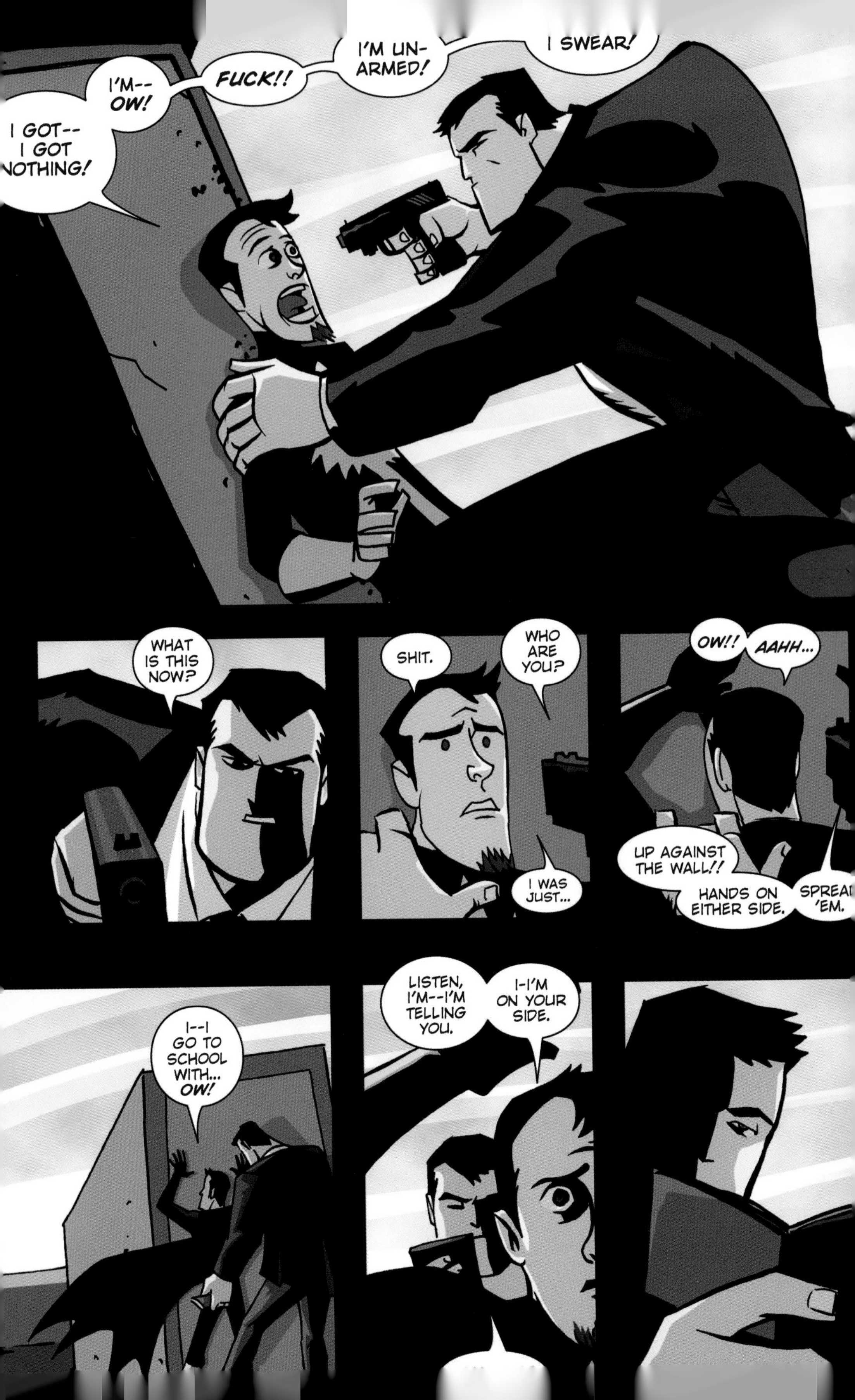
I GOT--
I GOT
NOTHING!
I'M--
OW!
FUCK!!
I'M UN-
ARMED!
I SWEAR!
WHAT
IS THIS
NOW?
SHIT.
WHO
ARE
YOU?
I WAS
JUST...
OW!!
AAHH...
UP AGAINST
THE WALL!!
HANDS ON
EITHER SIDE.
SPREAD
'EM.
I--I
GO TO
SCHOOL
WITH...
OW!
LISTEN,
I'M--I'M
TELLING
YOU.
I-I'M
ON YOUR
SIDE.

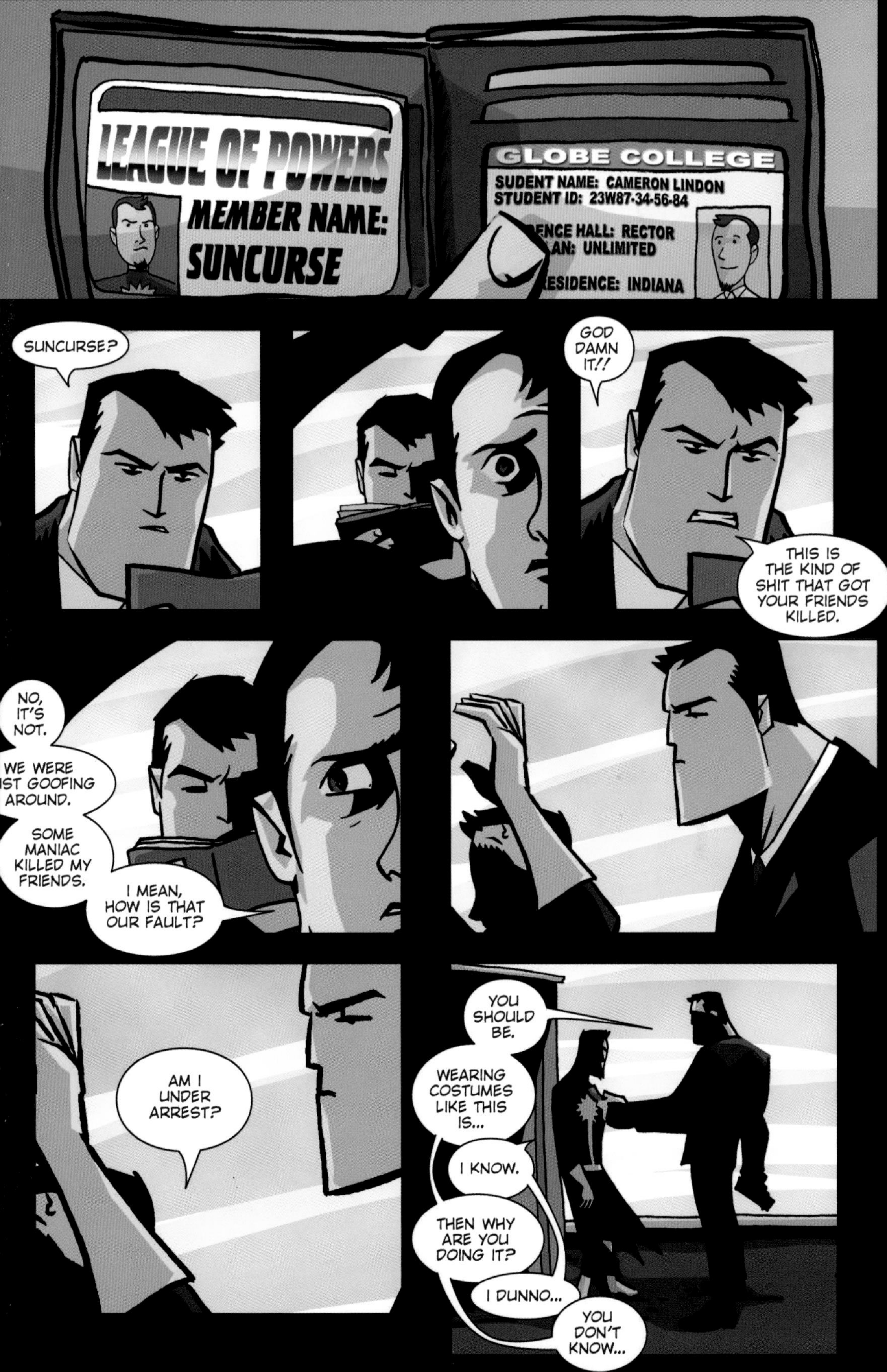
LEAGUE OF POWERS
MEMBER NAME:
SUNCURSE
GLOBE COLLEGE
SUDENT NAME: CAMERON LINDON
STUDENT ID: 23W87-34-56-84
ENCE HALL: RECTOR
AN: UNLIMITED
ESIDENCE: INDIANA
SUNCURSE?
GOD DAMN IT!!
THIS IS THE KIND OF SHIT THAT GOT YOUR FRIENDS KILLED.
NO, IT'S NOT.
WE WERE IST GOOFING AROUND.
SOME MANIAC KILLED MY FRIENDS.
I MEAN, HOW IS THAT OUR FAULT?
AM I UNDER ARREST?
YOU SHOULD BE.
WEARING COSTUMES LIKE THIS IS...
I KNOW.
THEN WHY ARE YOU DOING IT?
I DUNNO...
YOU DON'T KNOW...

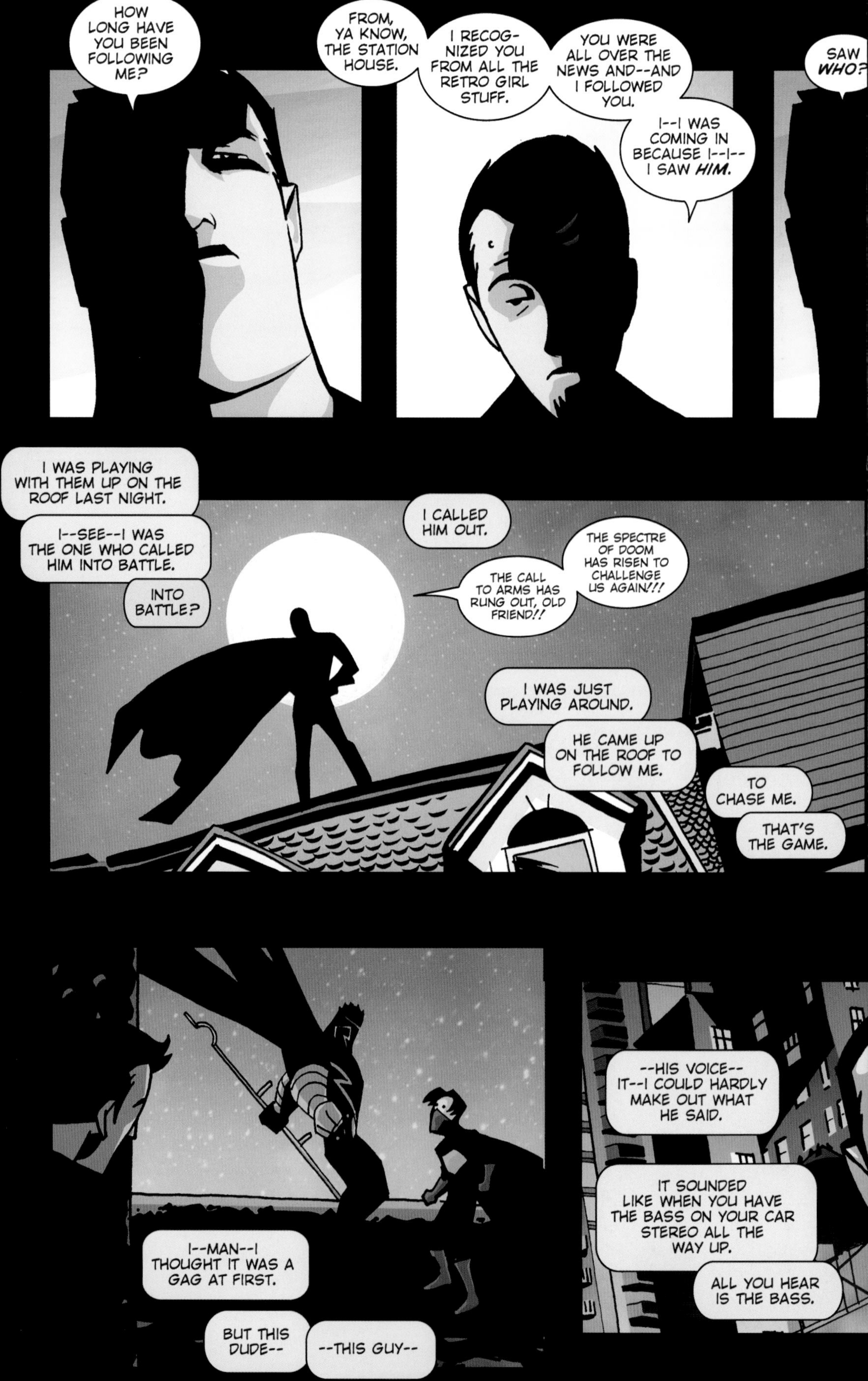
HOW LONG HAVE YOU BEEN FOLLOWING ME?
FROM, YA KNOW, THE STATION HOUSE.
I RECOGNIZED YOU FROM ALL THE RETRO GIRL STUFF.
YOU WERE ALL OVER THE NEWS AND--AND I FOLLOWED YOU.
I--I WAS COMING IN BECAUSE I--I-- I SAW *HIM.*
SAW *WHO?*
I WAS PLAYING WITH THEM UP ON THE ROOF LAST NIGHT.
I--SEE--I WAS THE ONE WHO CALLED HIM INTO BATTLE.
INTO BATTLE?
I CALLED HIM OUT.
THE SPECTRE OF DOOM HAS RISEN TO CHALLENGE US AGAIN!!!
THE CALL TO ARMS HAS RUNG OUT, OLD FRIEND!!
I WAS JUST PLAYING AROUND.
HE CAME UP ON THE ROOF TO FOLLOW ME.
TO CHASE ME.
THAT'S THE GAME.
I--MAN--I THOUGHT IT WAS A GAG AT FIRST.
BUT THIS DUDE--
--THIS GUY--
--HIS VOICE-- IT--I COULD HARDLY MAKE OUT WHAT HE SAID.
IT SOUNDED LIKE WHEN YOU HAVE THE BASS ON YOUR CAR STEREO ALL THE WAY UP.
ALL YOU HEAR IS THE BASS.

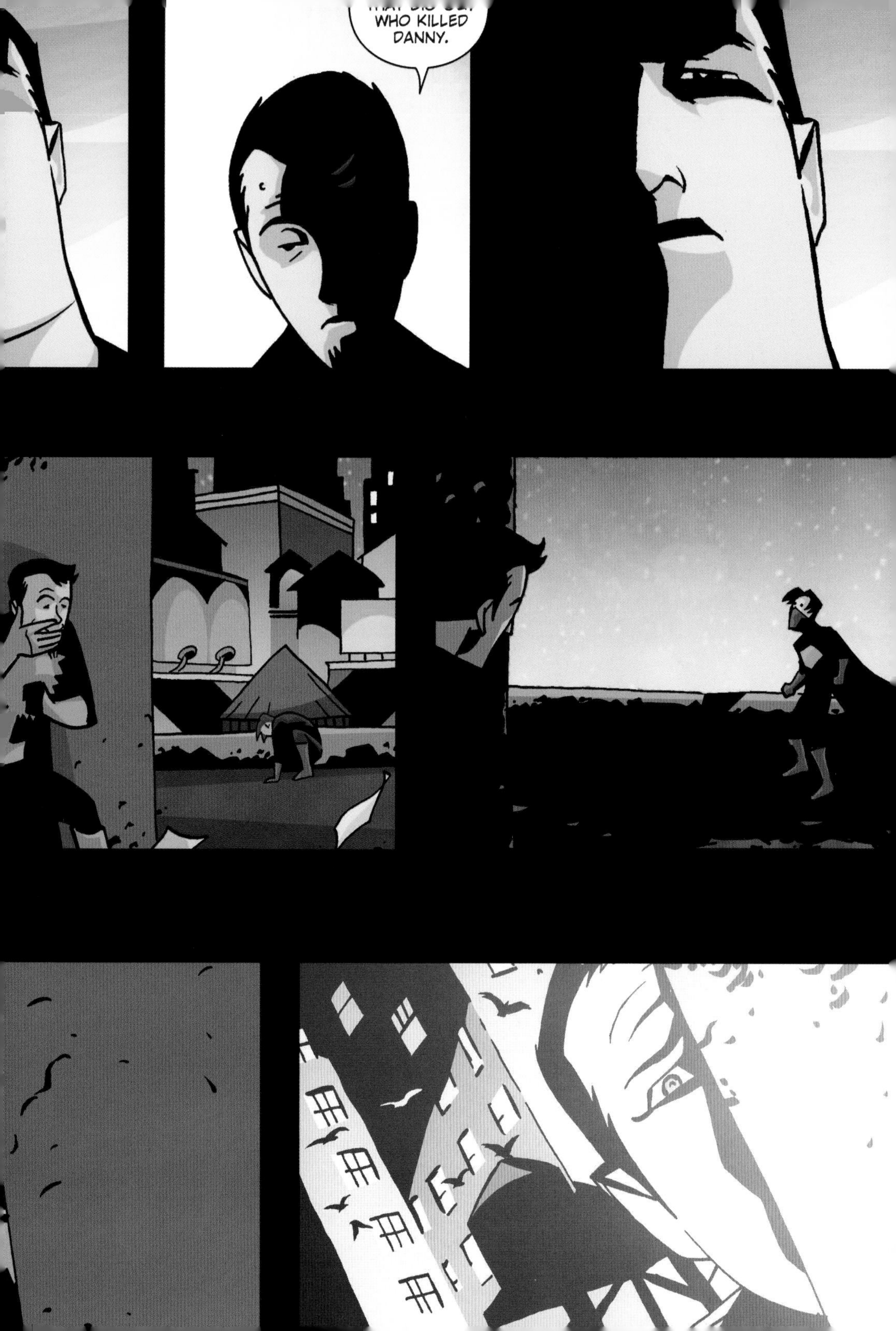
WHO KILLED DANNY.

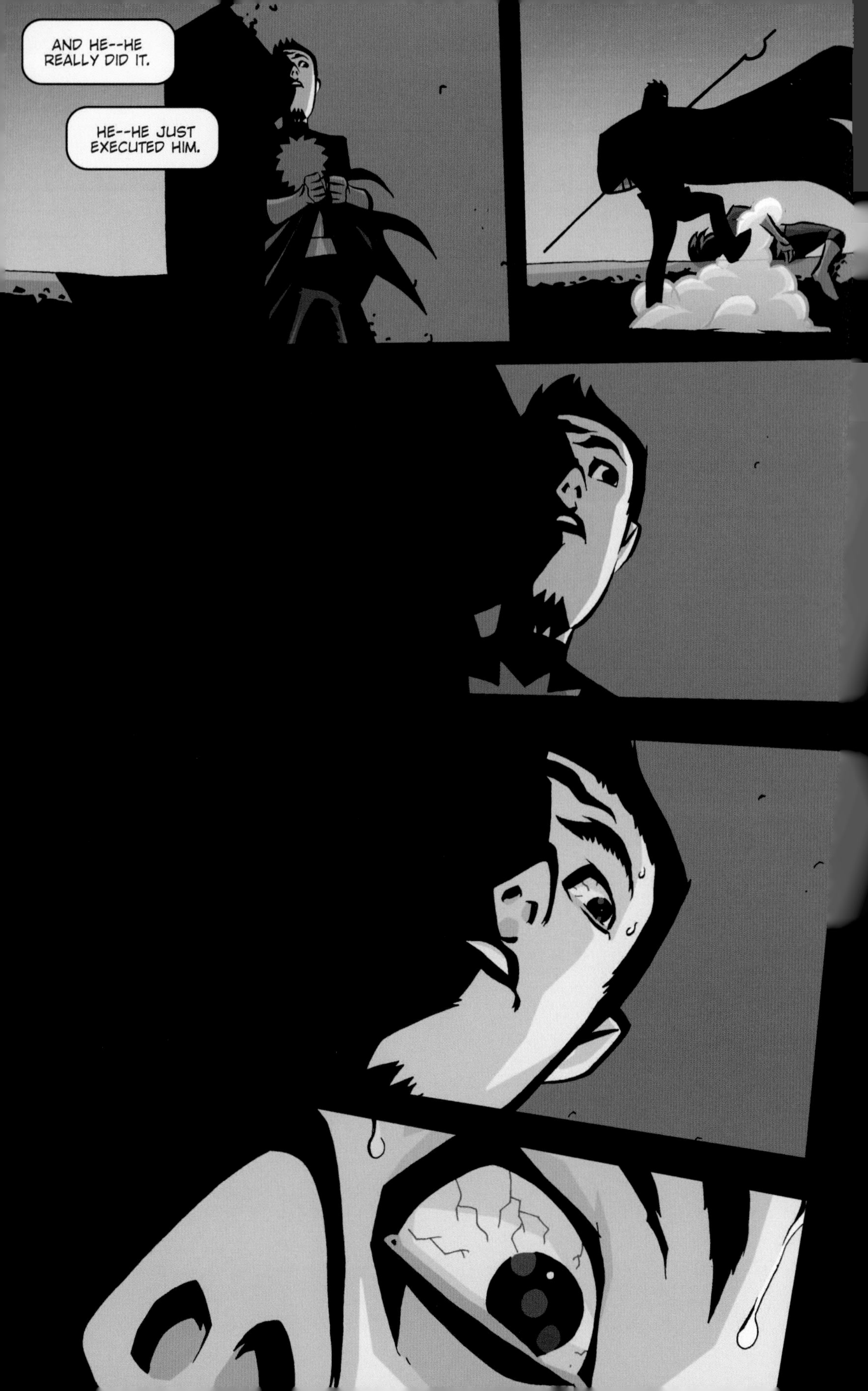
AND HE--HE REALLY DID IT.
HE--HE JUST EXECUTED HIM.

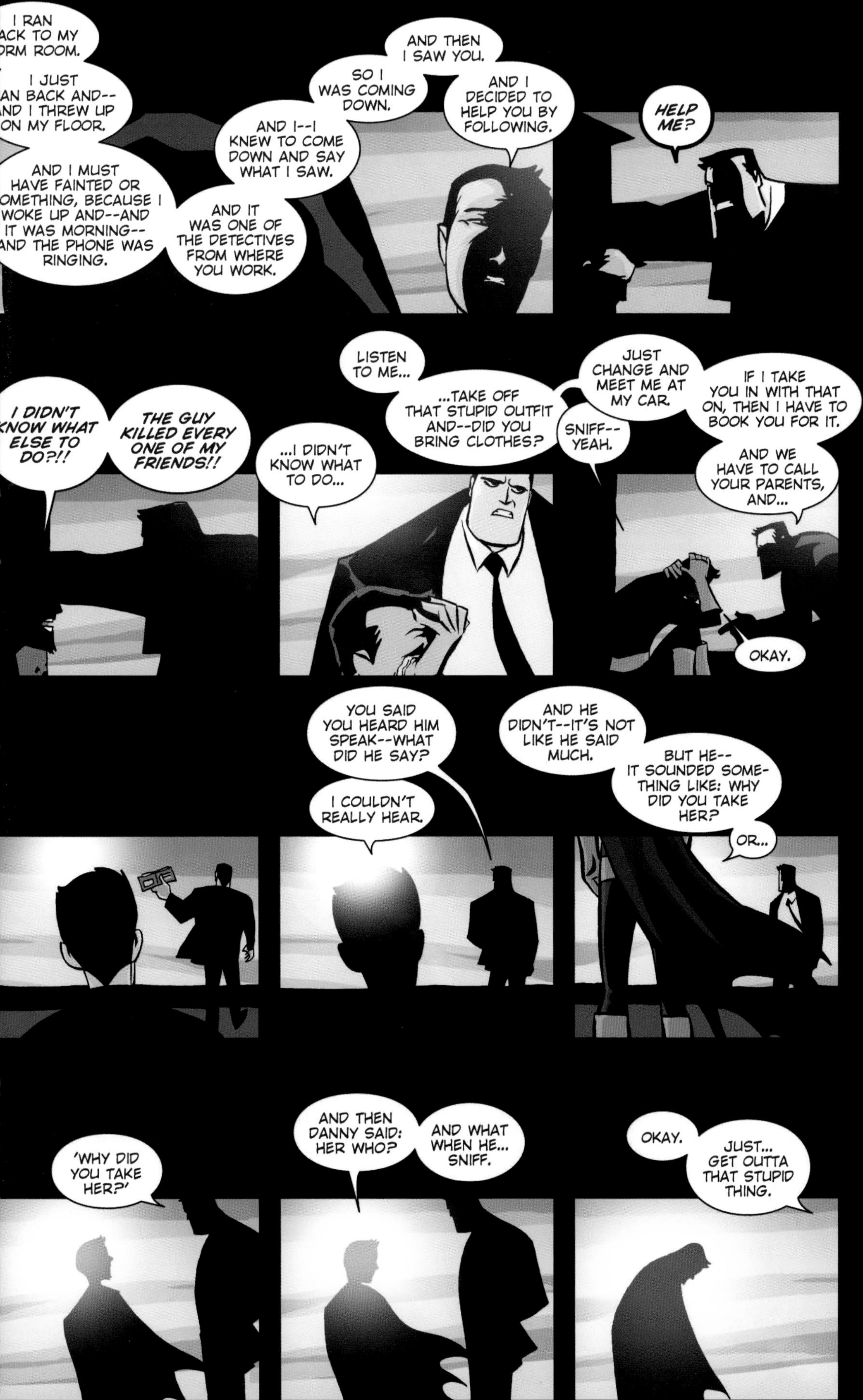
I RAN
ACK TO MY
ORM ROOM.
I JUST
AN BACK AND--
ND I THREW UP
ON MY FLOOR.
AND I MUST
HAVE FAINTED OR
OMETHING, BECAUSE I
WOKE UP AND--AND
IT WAS MORNING--
AND THE PHONE WAS
RINGING.
AND IT
WAS ONE OF
THE DETECTIVES
FROM WHERE
YOU WORK.
AND I--I
KNEW TO COME
DOWN AND SAY
WHAT I SAW.
SO I
WAS COMING
DOWN.
AND THEN
I SAW YOU.
AND I
DECIDED TO
HELP YOU BY
FOLLOWING.
HELP
ME?
I DIDN'T
KNOW WHAT
ELSE TO
DO?!!
THE GUY
KILLED EVERY
ONE OF MY
FRIENDS!!
...I DIDN'T
KNOW WHAT
TO DO...
LISTEN
TO ME...
...TAKE OFF
THAT STUPID OUTFIT
AND--DID YOU
BRING CLOTHES?
SNIFF--
YEAH.
JUST
CHANGE AND
MEET ME AT
MY CAR.
IF I TAKE
YOU IN WITH THAT
ON, THEN I HAVE TO
BOOK YOU FOR IT.
AND WE
HAVE TO CALL
YOUR PARENTS,
AND...
OKAY.
YOU SAID
YOU HEARD HIM
SPEAK--WHAT
DID HE SAY?
I COULDN'T
REALLY HEAR.
AND HE
DIDN'T--IT'S NOT
LIKE HE SAID
MUCH.
BUT HE--
IT SOUNDED SOME-
THING LIKE: WHY
DID YOU TAKE
HER?
OR...
'WHY DID
YOU TAKE
HER?'
AND THEN
DANNY SAID:
HER WHO?
AND WHAT
WHEN HE...
SNIFF.
OKAY.
JUST...
GET OUTTA
THAT STUPID
THING.

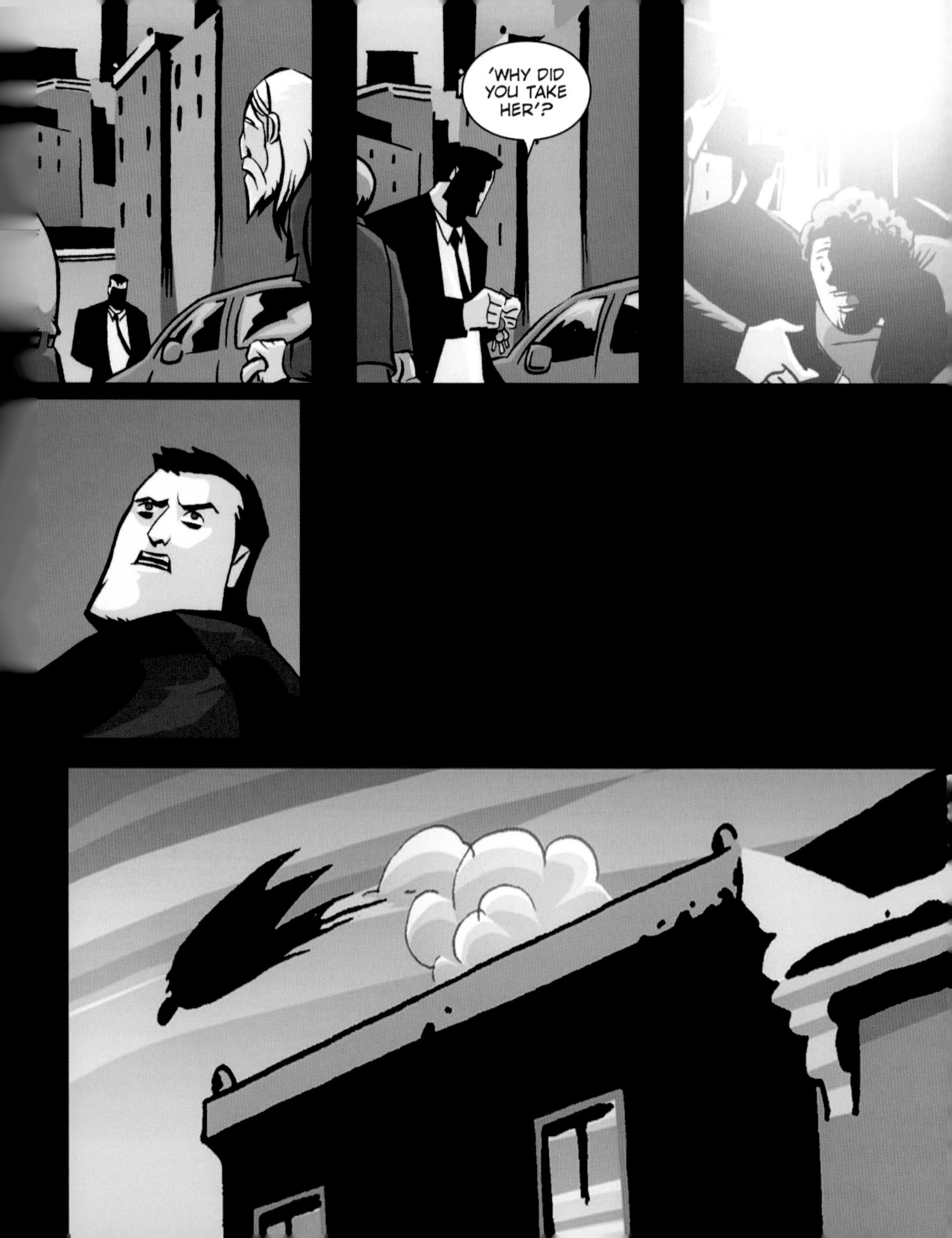
'WHY DID YOU TAKE HER'?

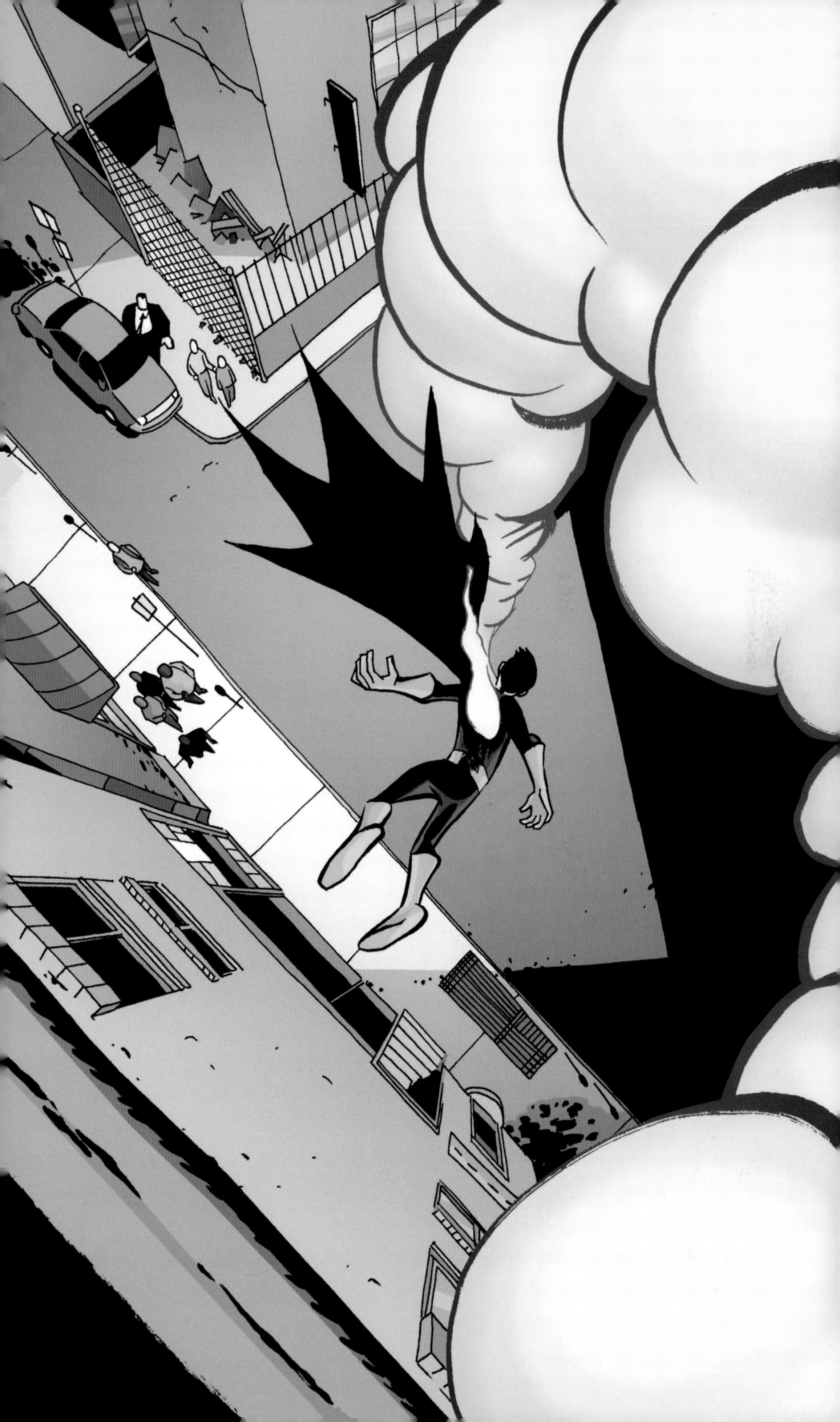

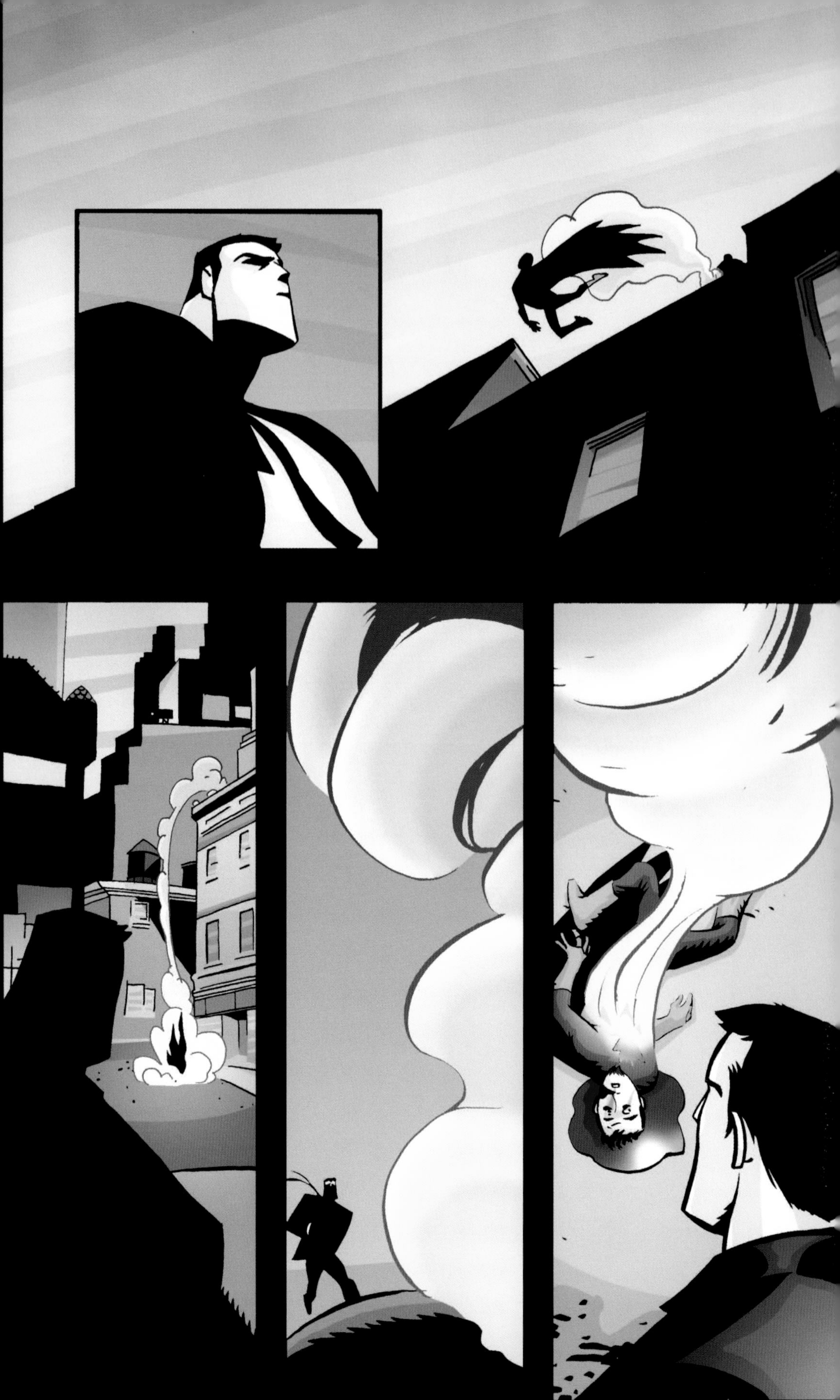

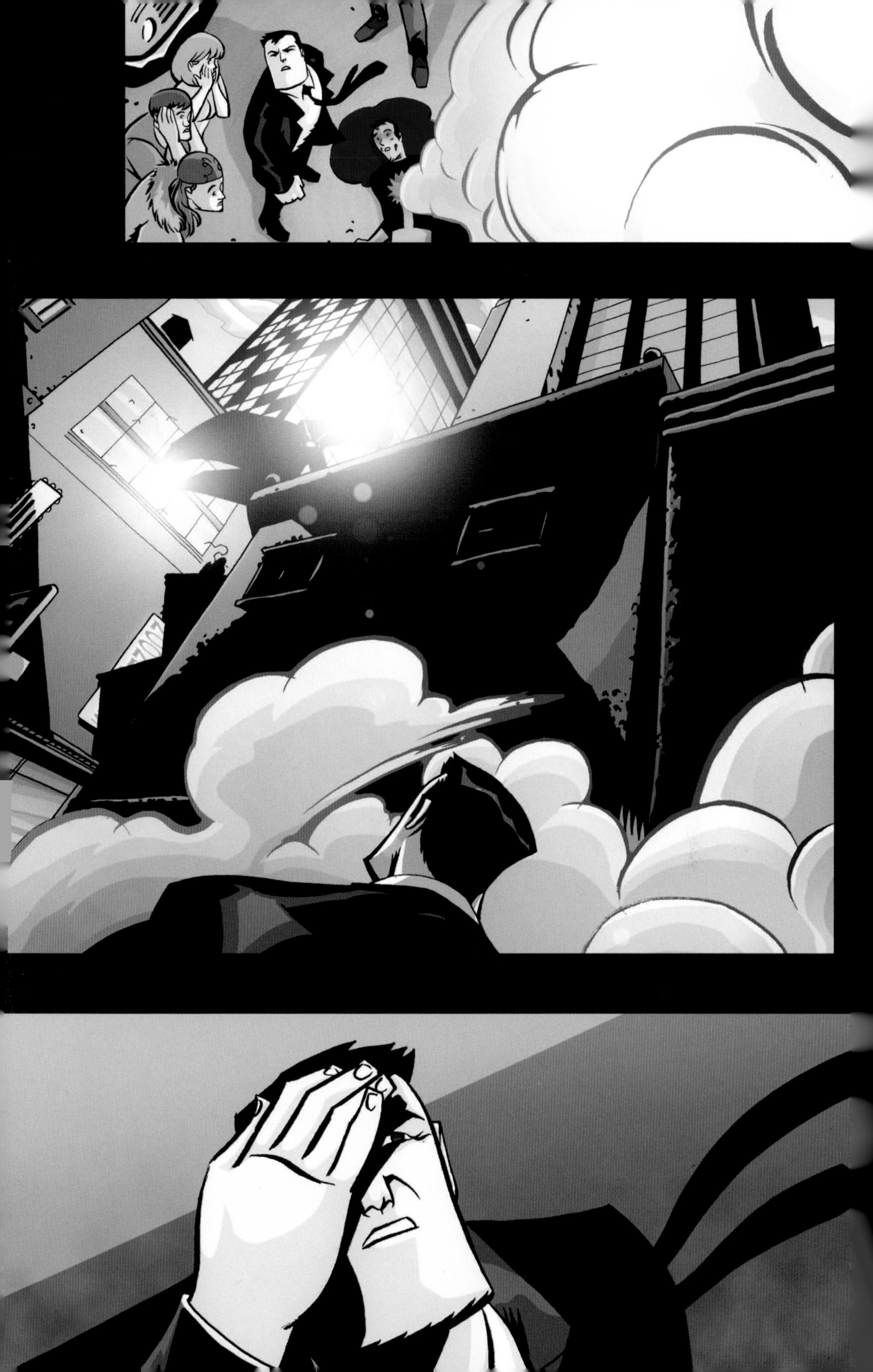

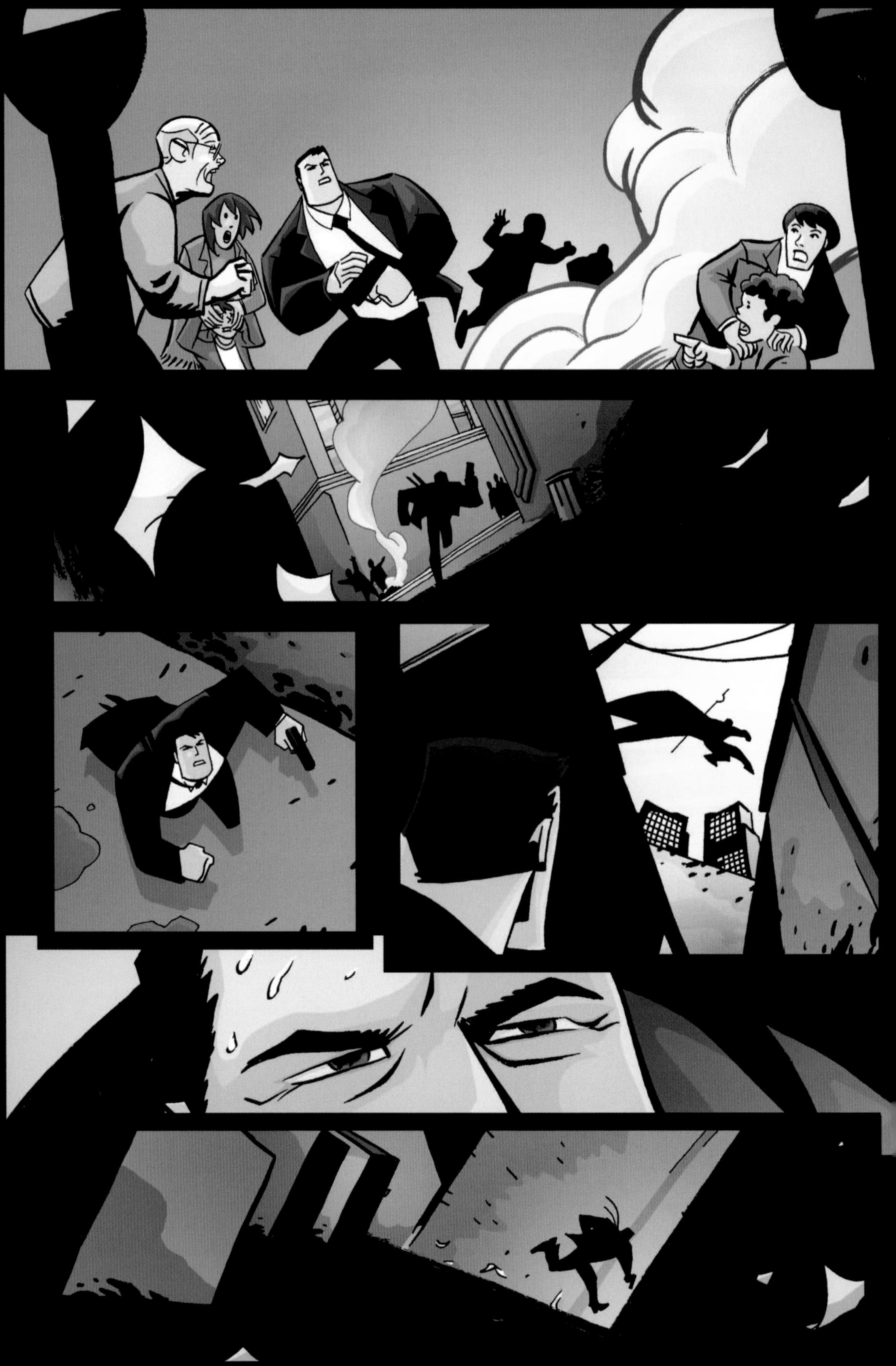

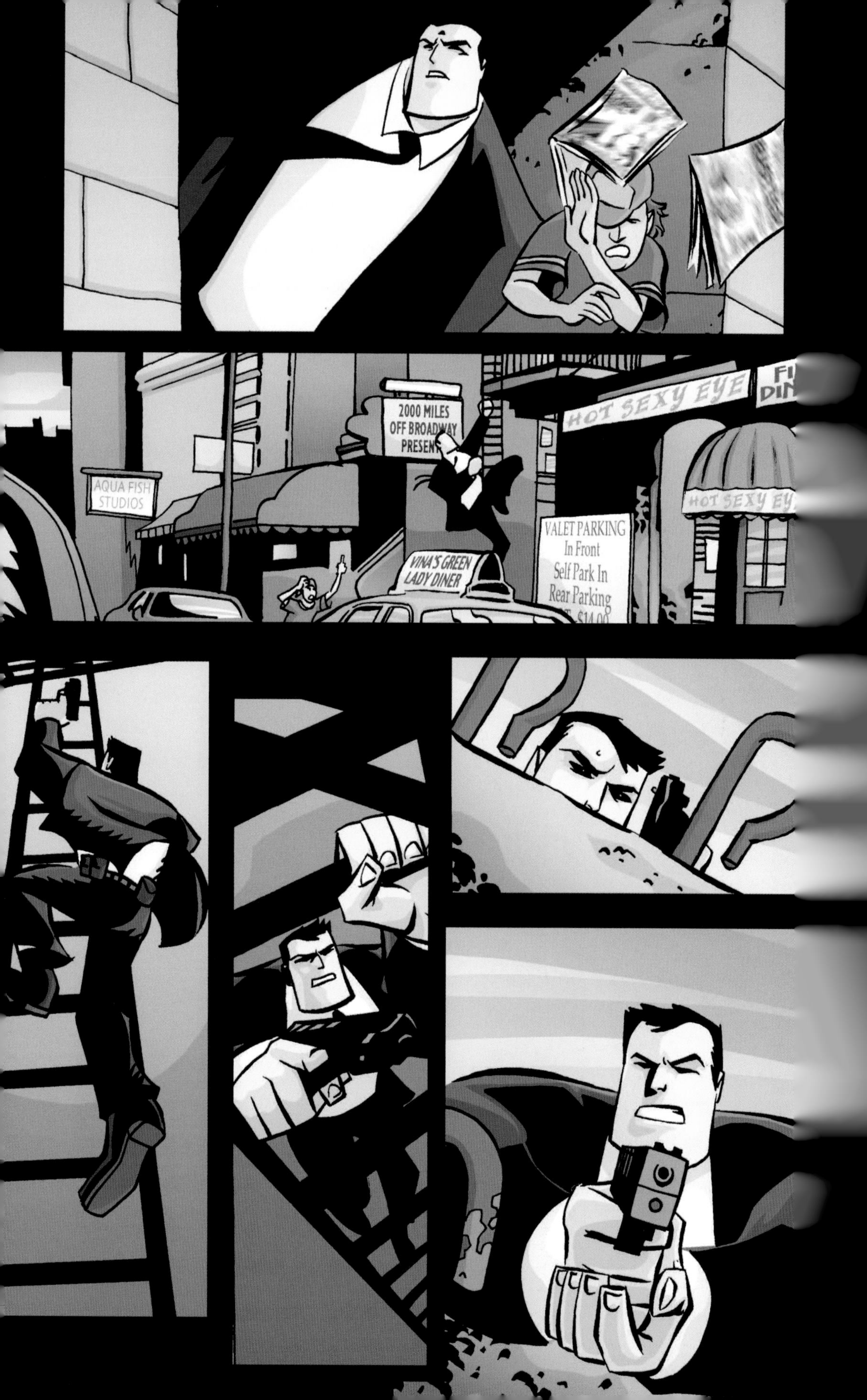
2000 MILES
OFF BROADWAY
PRESENT
AQUA FISH
STUDIOS
HOT SEXY EYE
VINA'S GREEN
LADY DINER
VALET PARKING
In Front
Self Park In
Rear Parking

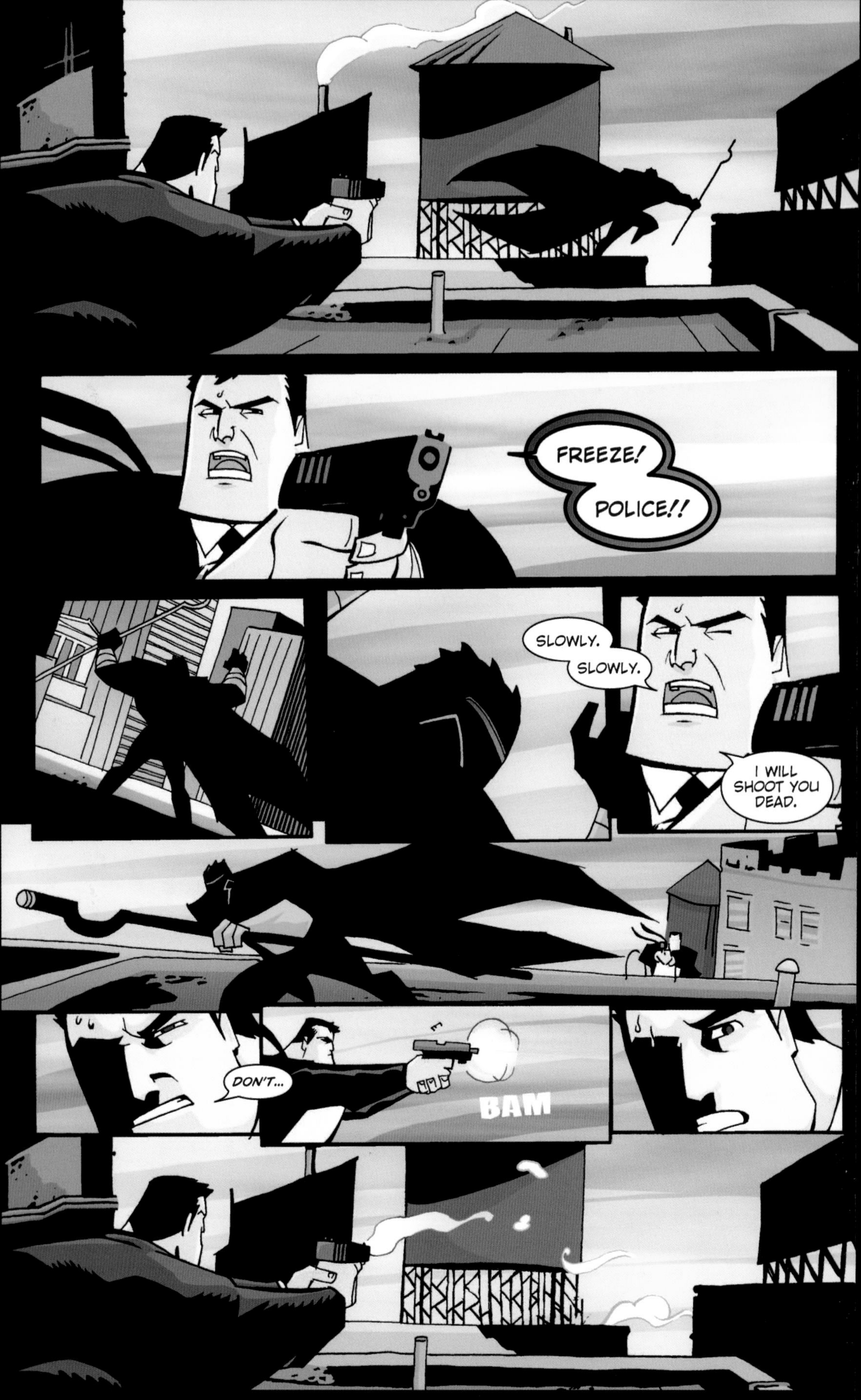
FREEZE!
POLICE!!
SLOWLY.
SLOWLY.
I WILL SHOOT YOU DEAD.
DON'T...
BAM

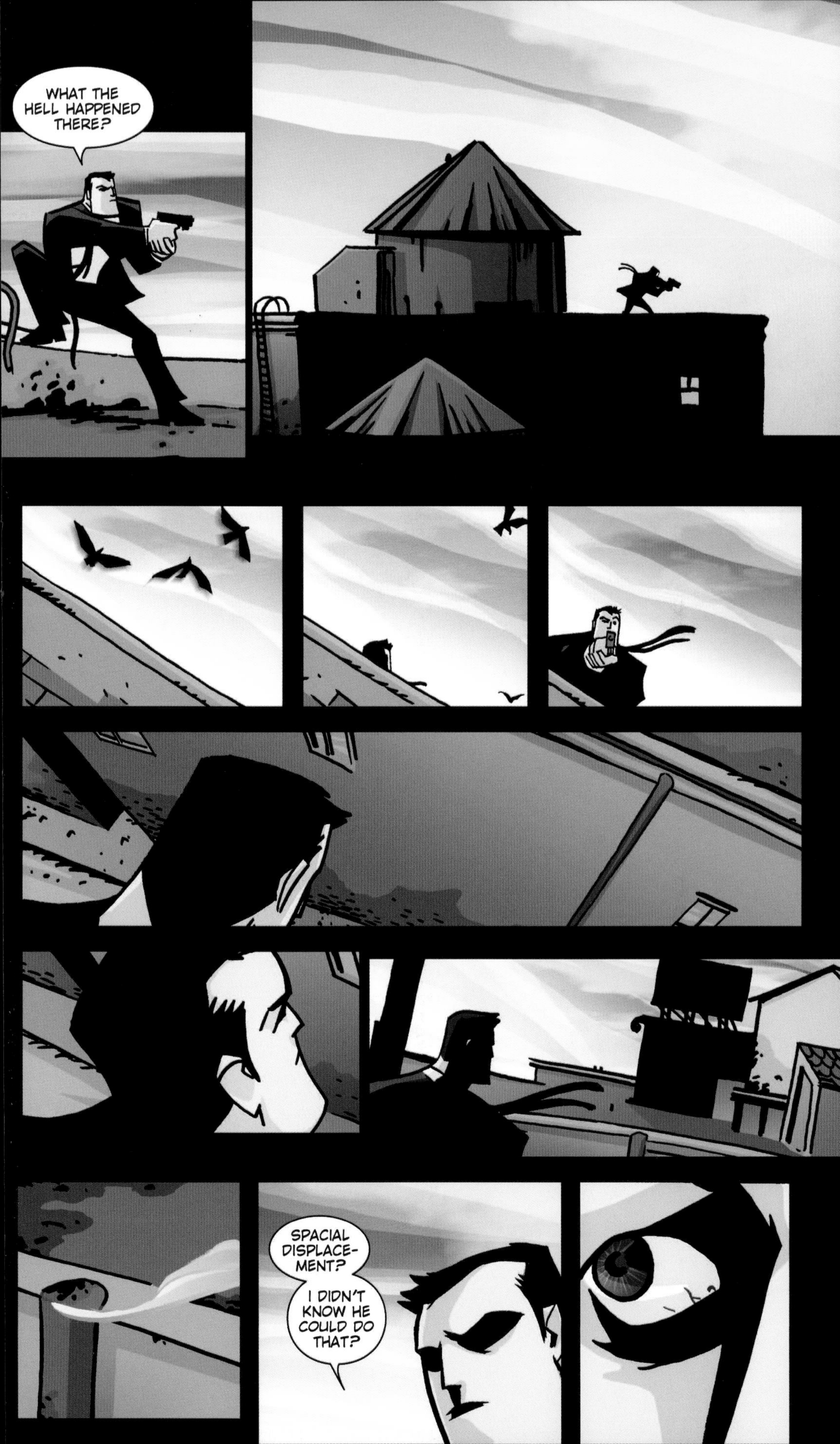
WHAT THE HELL HAPPENED THERE?
SPACIAL DISPLACE- MENT?
I DIDN'T KNOW HE COULD DO THAT?

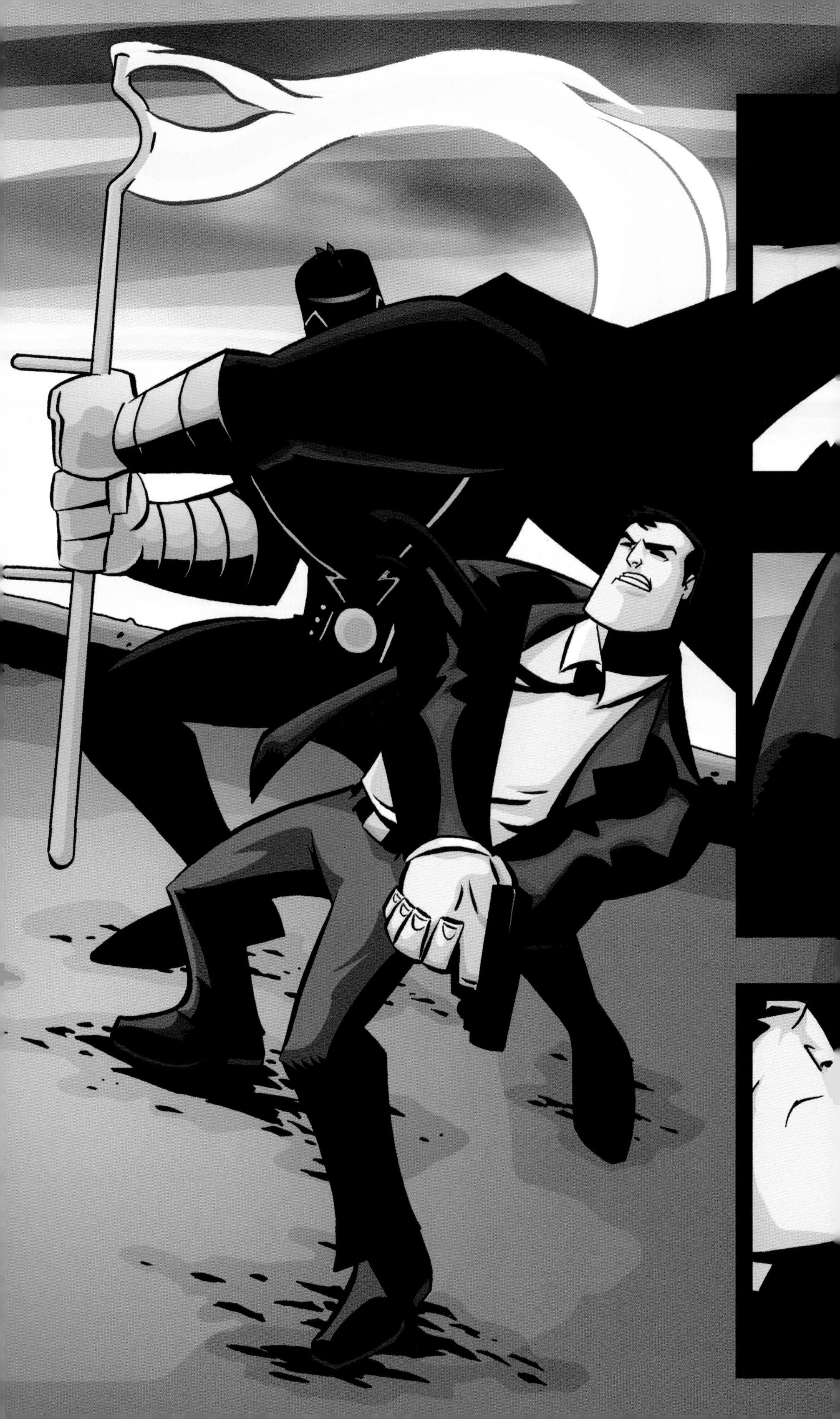

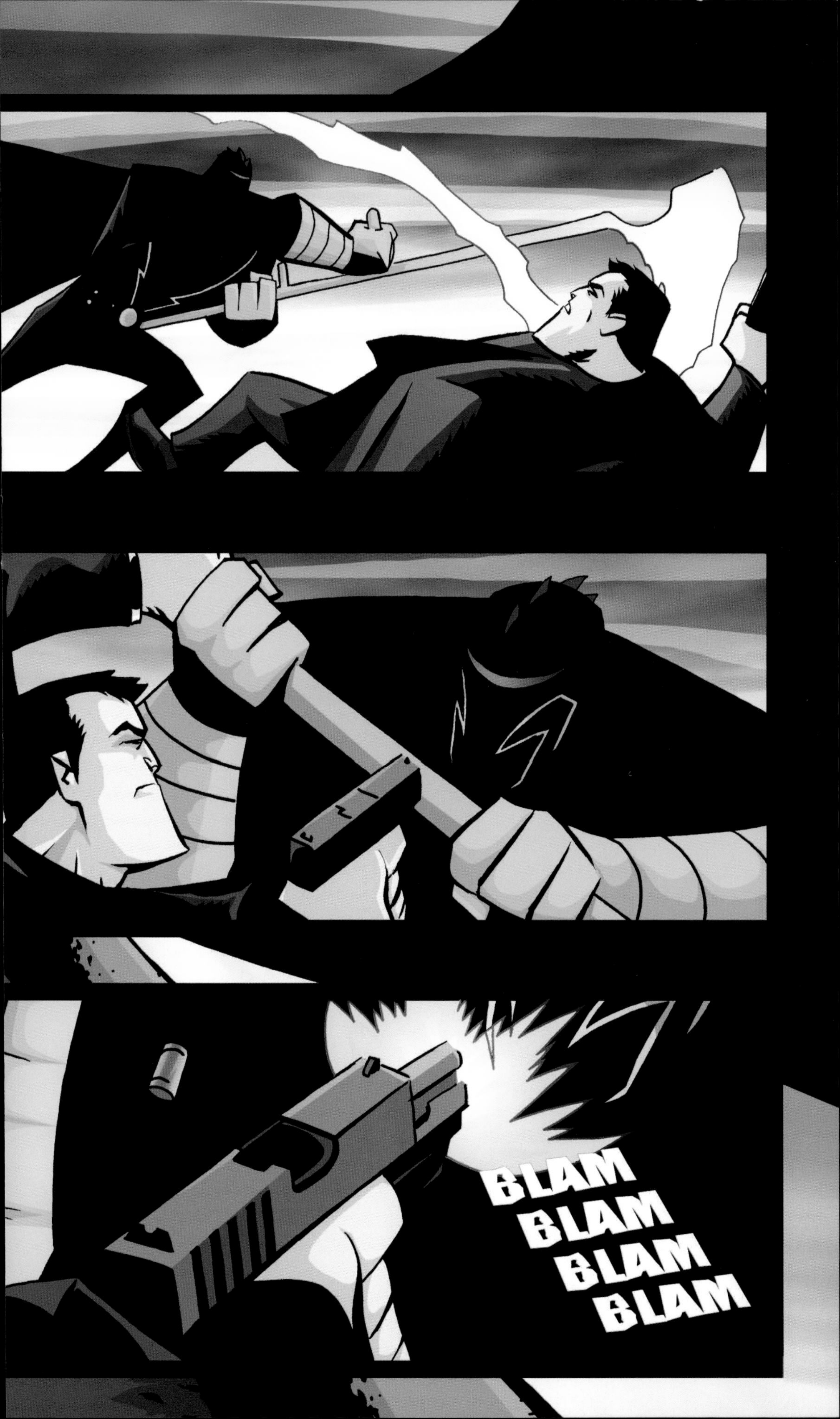
BLAM
BLAM
BLAM
BLAM

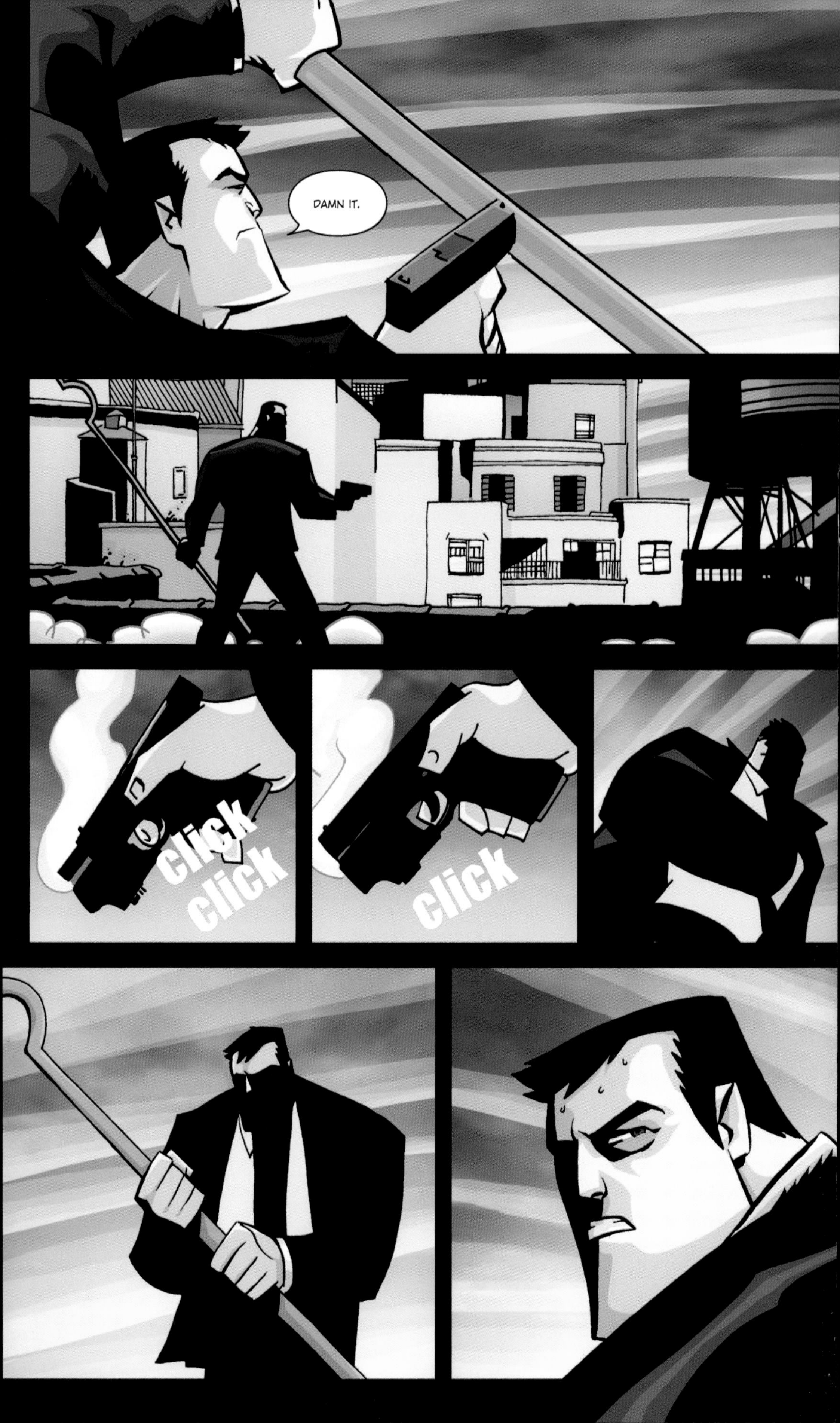
DAMN IT.
click
click
click

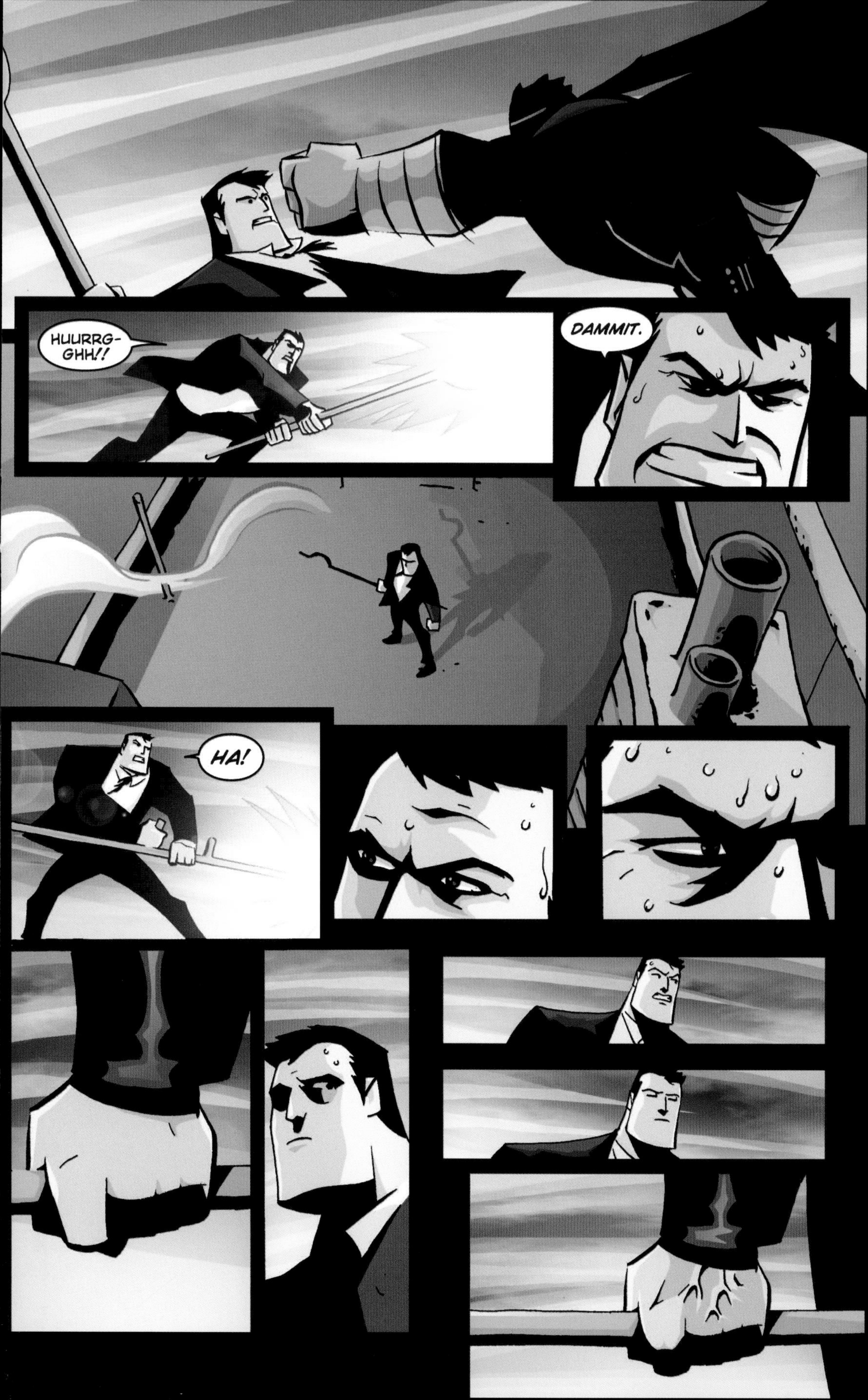
HUURRG-GHH!!
DAMMIT.
HA!

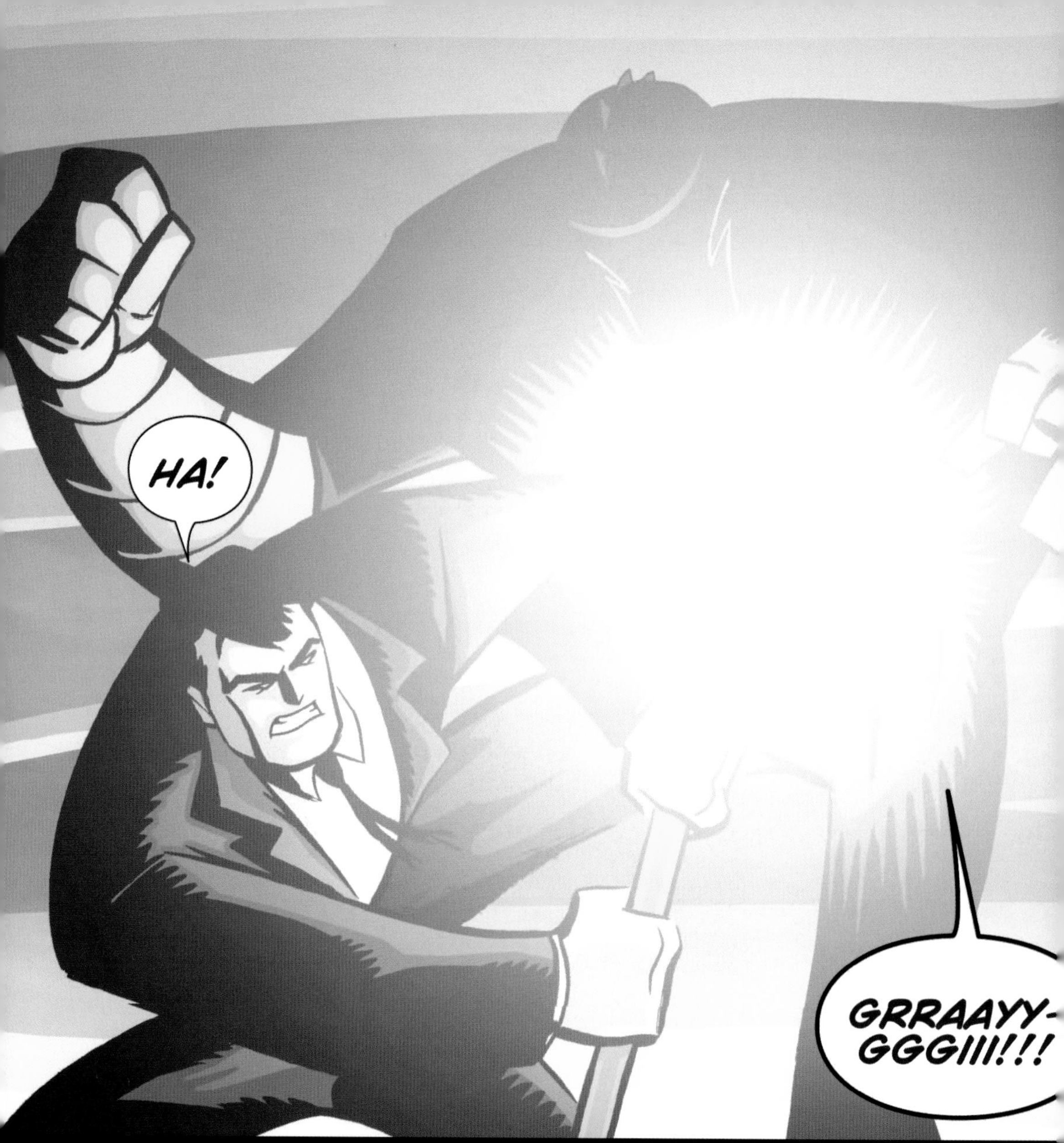
HA!
GRRAAYY-
GGGIII!!!
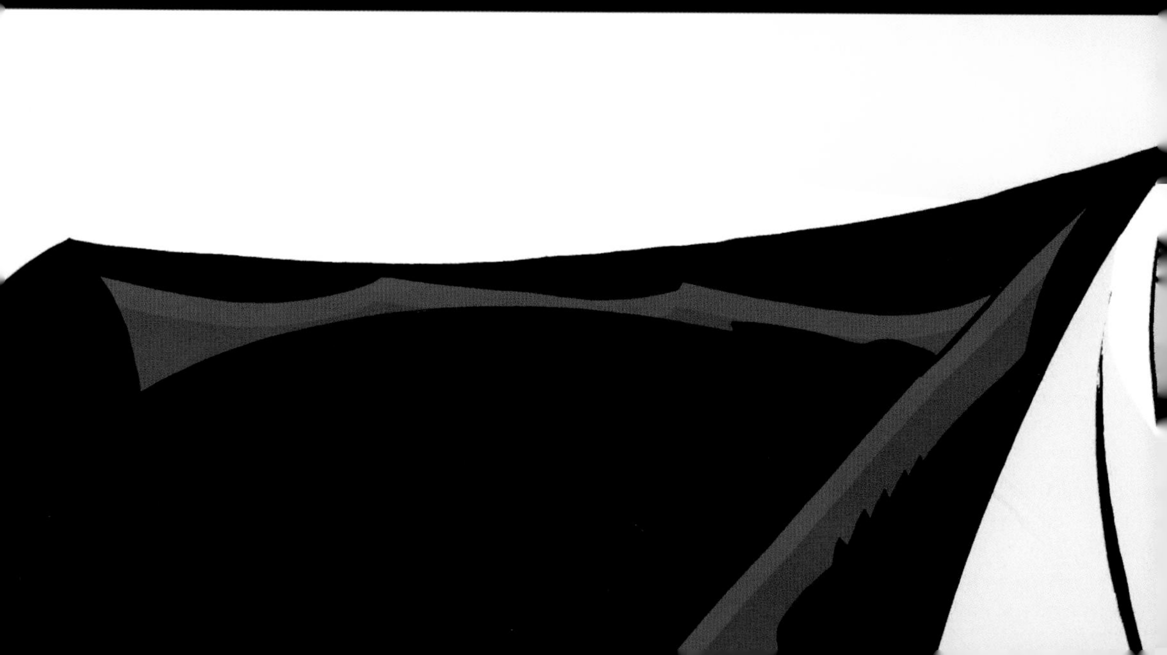

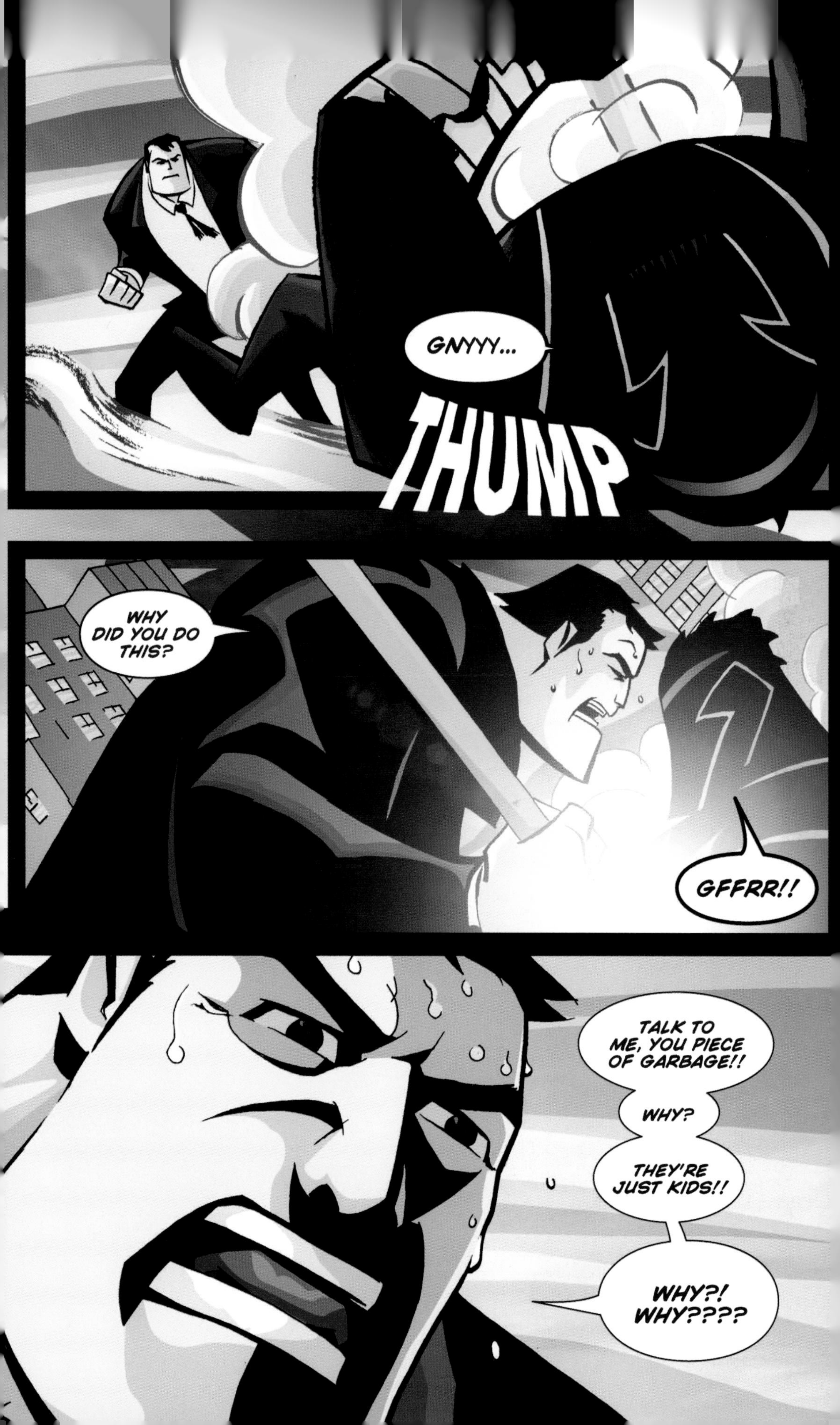
GNYYY...
THUMP
WHY DID YOU DO THIS?
GFFRR!!
TALK TO ME, YOU PIECE OF GARBAGE!!
WHY?
THEY'RE JUST KIDS!!
WHY?! WHY????

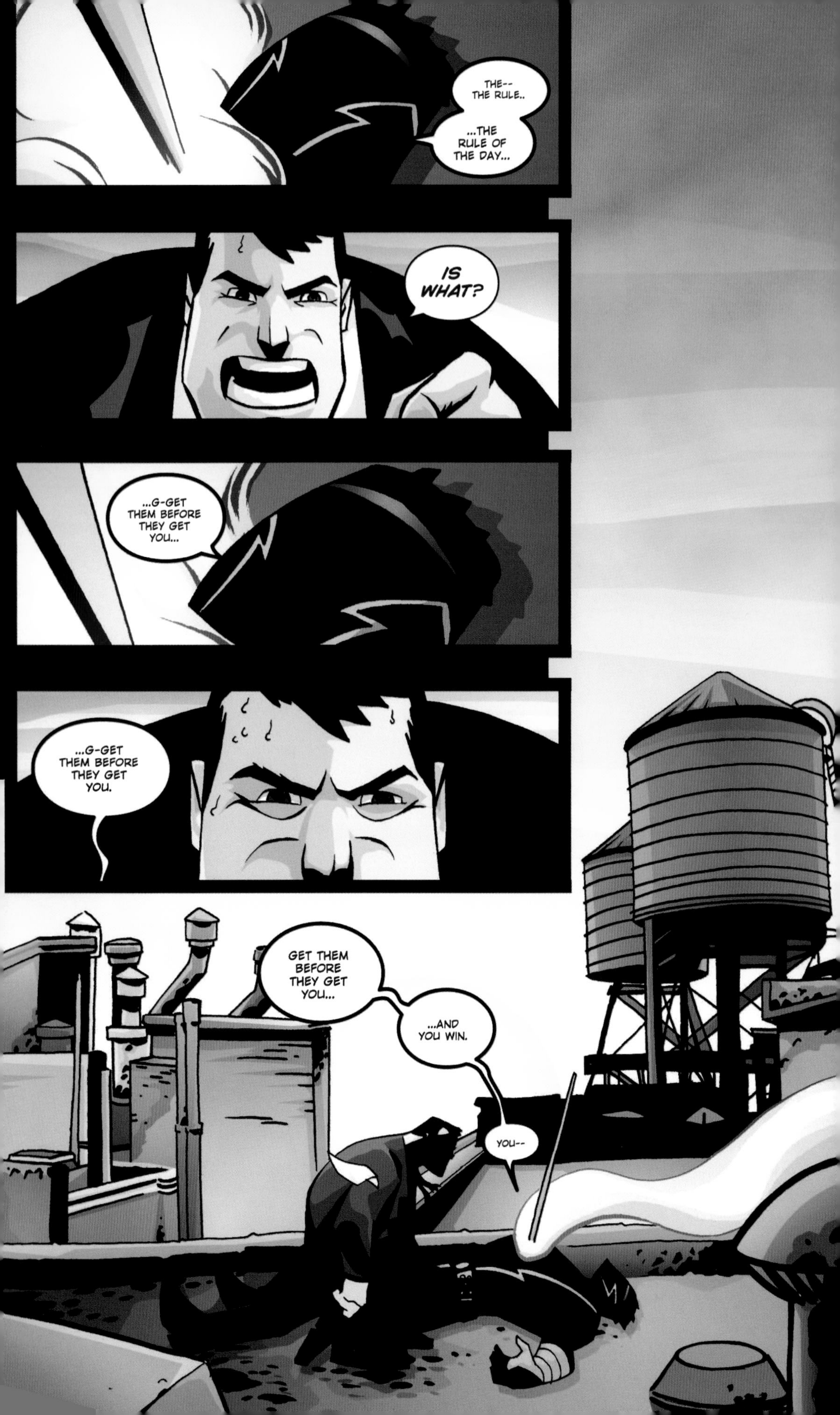

THE--
THE RULE..
...THE RULE OF THE DAY...
IS WHAT?
...G-GET THEM BEFORE THEY GET YOU...
...G-GET THEM BEFORE THEY GET YOU.
GET THEM BEFORE THEY GET YOU...
...AND YOU WIN.
YOU--

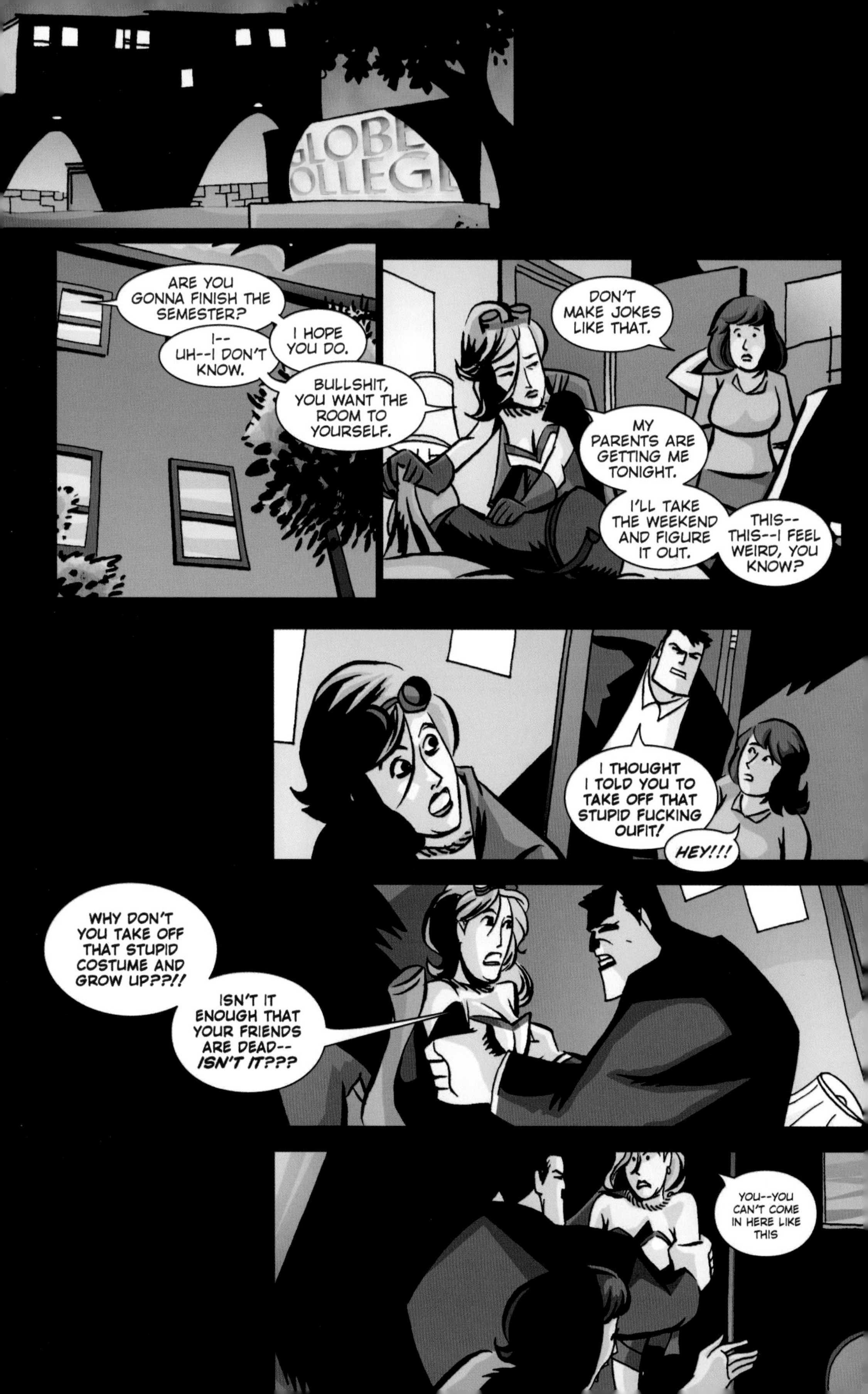

GLOBE COLLEGE
ARE YOU GONNA FINISH THE SEMESTER?
I HOPE YOU DO.
I-- UH--I DON'T KNOW.
BULLSHIT, YOU WANT THE ROOM TO YOURSELF.
DON'T MAKE JOKES LIKE THAT.
MY PARENTS ARE GETTING ME TONIGHT.
I'LL TAKE THE WEEKEND AND FIGURE IT OUT.
THIS-- THIS--I FEEL WEIRD, YOU KNOW?
I THOUGHT I TOLD YOU TO TAKE OFF THAT STUPID FUCKING OUFIT!
HEY!!!
WHY DON'T YOU TAKE OFF THAT STUPID COSTUME AND GROW UP??!!
ISN'T IT ENOUGH THAT YOUR FRIENDS ARE DEAD-- ISN'T IT???
YOU--YOU CAN'T COME IN HERE LIKE THIS

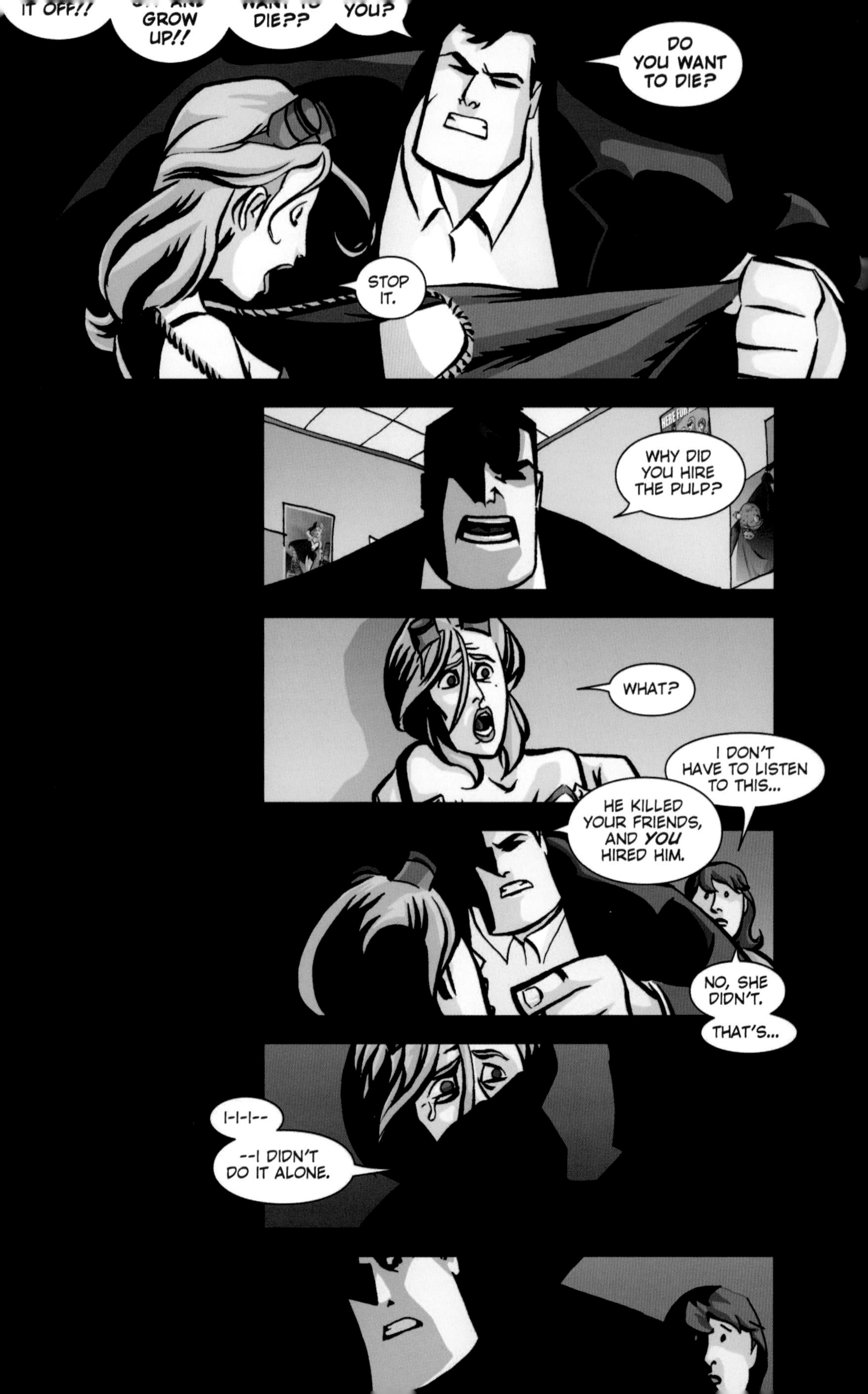
IT OFF!!
GROW UP!!
DIE??
YOU?
DO YOU WANT TO DIE?
STOP IT.
WHY DID YOU HIRE THE PULP?
WHAT?
I DON'T HAVE TO LISTEN TO THIS...
HE KILLED YOUR FRIENDS, AND *YOU* HIRED HIM.
NO, SHE DIDN'T.
THAT'S...
I-I-I--
--I DIDN'T DO IT ALONE.

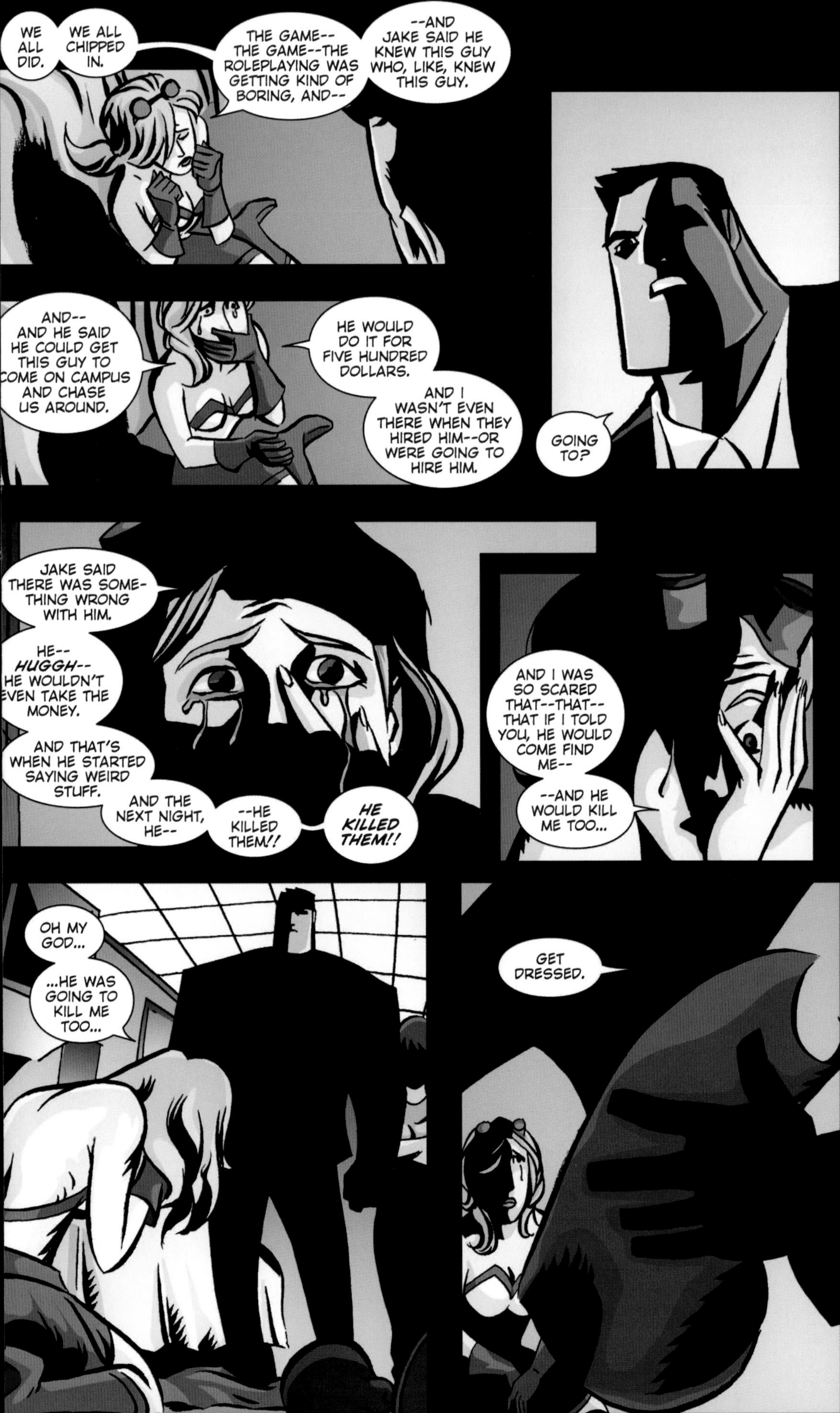
WE ALL DID.
WE ALL CHIPPED IN.
THE GAME-- THE GAME--THE ROLEPLAYING WAS GETTING KIND OF BORING, AND--
--AND JAKE SAID HE KNEW THIS GUY WHO, LIKE, KNEW THIS GUY.
AND-- AND HE SAID HE COULD GET THIS GUY TO COME ON CAMPUS AND CHASE US AROUND.
HE WOULD DO IT FOR FIVE HUNDRED DOLLARS.
AND I WASN'T EVEN THERE WHEN THEY HIRED HIM--OR WERE GOING TO HIRE HIM.
GOING TO?
JAKE SAID THERE WAS SOME-THING WRONG WITH HIM.
HE-- HUGGH-- HE WOULDN'T EVEN TAKE THE MONEY.
AND THAT'S WHEN HE STARTED SAYING WEIRD STUFF.
AND THE NEXT NIGHT, HE--
--HE KILLED THEM!!
HE KILLED THEM!!
AND I WAS SO SCARED THAT--THAT-- THAT IF I TOLD YOU, HE WOULD COME FIND ME--
--AND HE WOULD KILL ME TOO...
OH MY GOD...
...HE WAS GOING TO KILL ME TOO...
GET DRESSED.

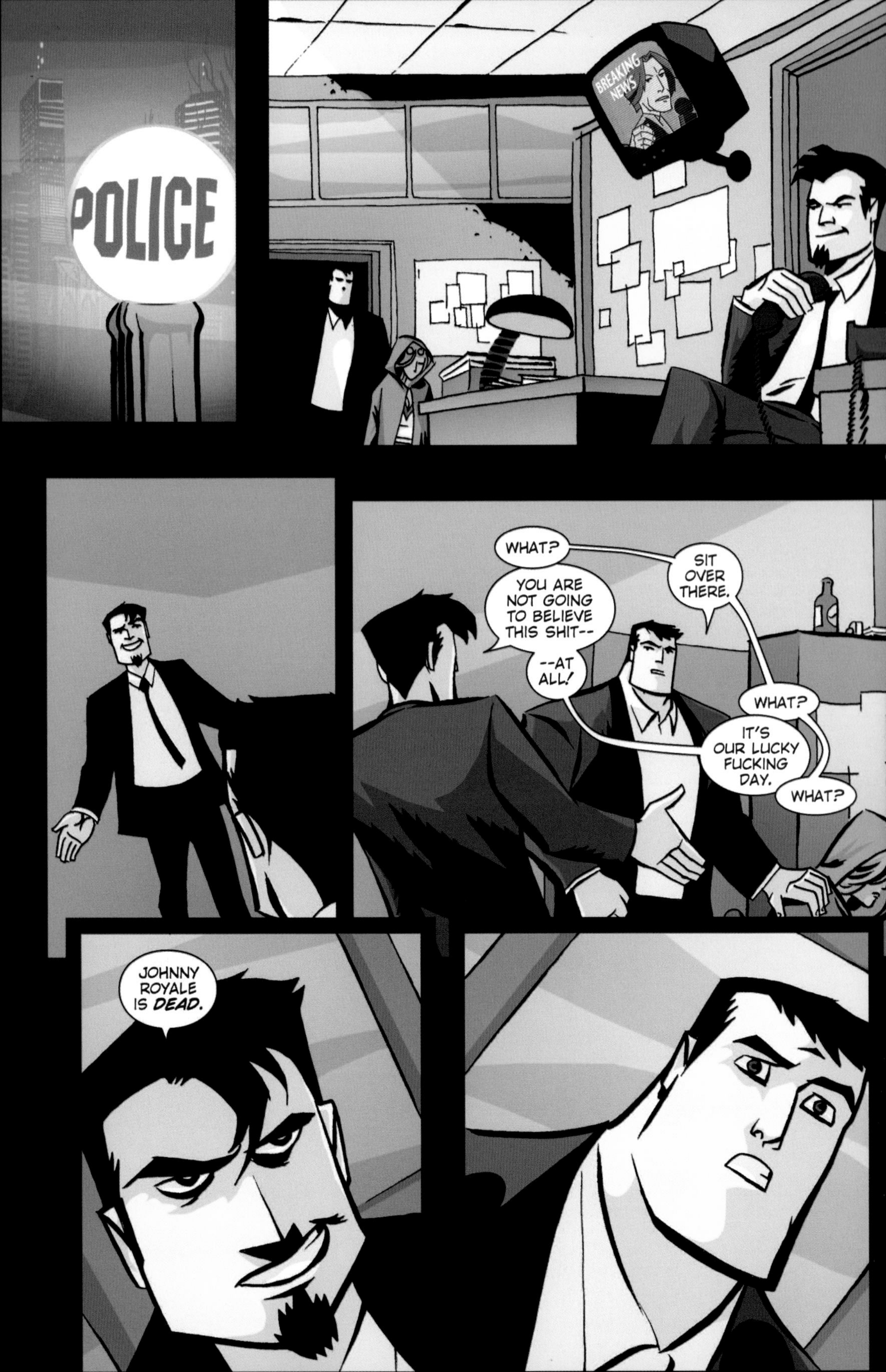
POLICE
BREAKING NEWS
WHAT?
SIT OVER THERE.
YOU ARE NOT GOING TO BELIEVE THIS SHIT--
--AT ALL!
WHAT?
IT'S OUR LUCKY FUCKING DAY.
WHAT?
JOHNNY ROYALE IS *DEAD*.

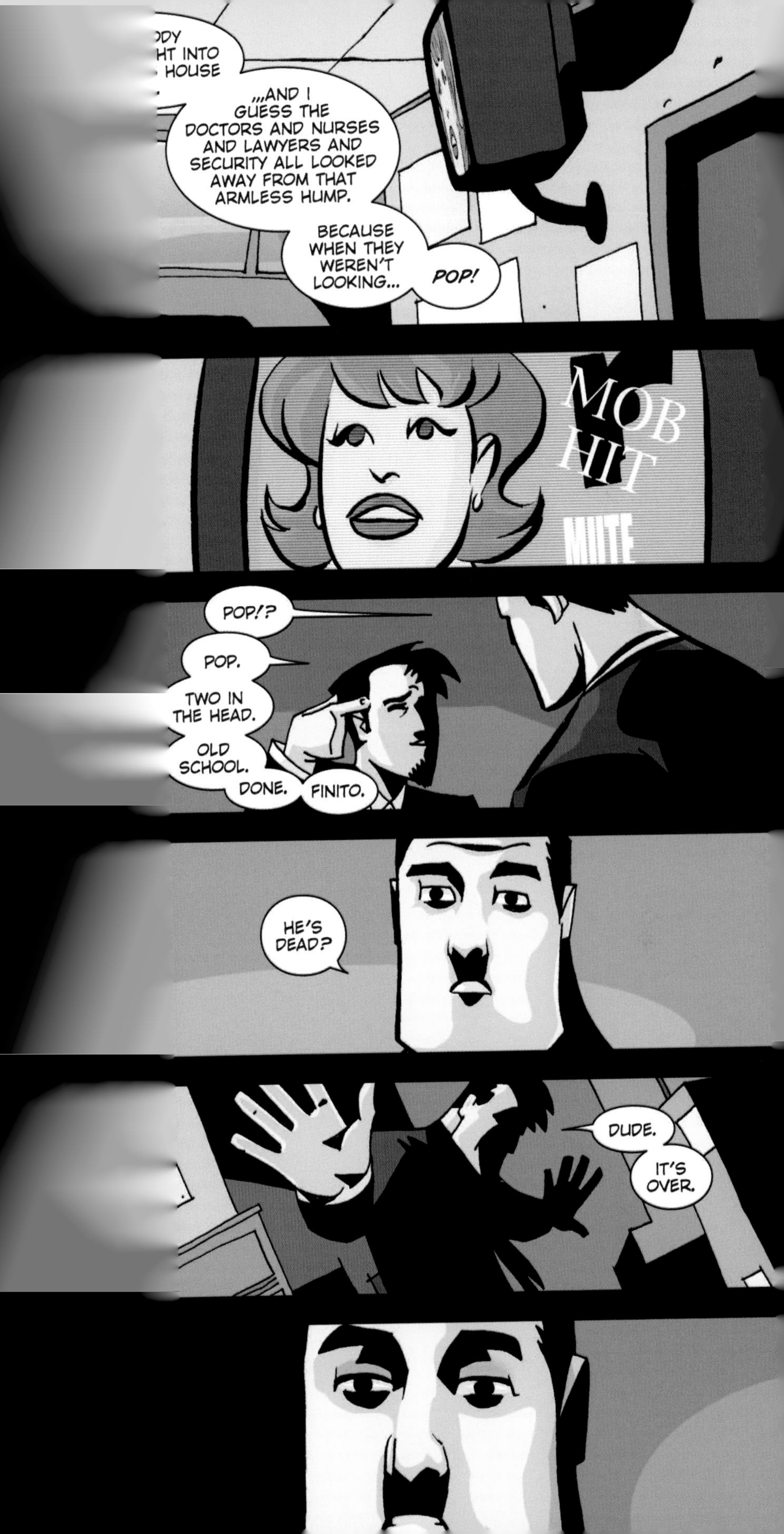

...DDY
...HT INTO
... HOUSE
...AND I GUESS THE DOCTORS AND NURSES AND LAWYERS AND SECURITY ALL LOOKED AWAY FROM THAT ARMLESS HUMP.
BECAUSE WHEN THEY WEREN'T LOOKING...
POP!
MOB HIT
MUTE
POP!?
POP.
TWO IN THE HEAD.
OLD SCHOOL.
DONE.
FINITO.
HE'S DEAD?
DUDE.
IT'S OVER.

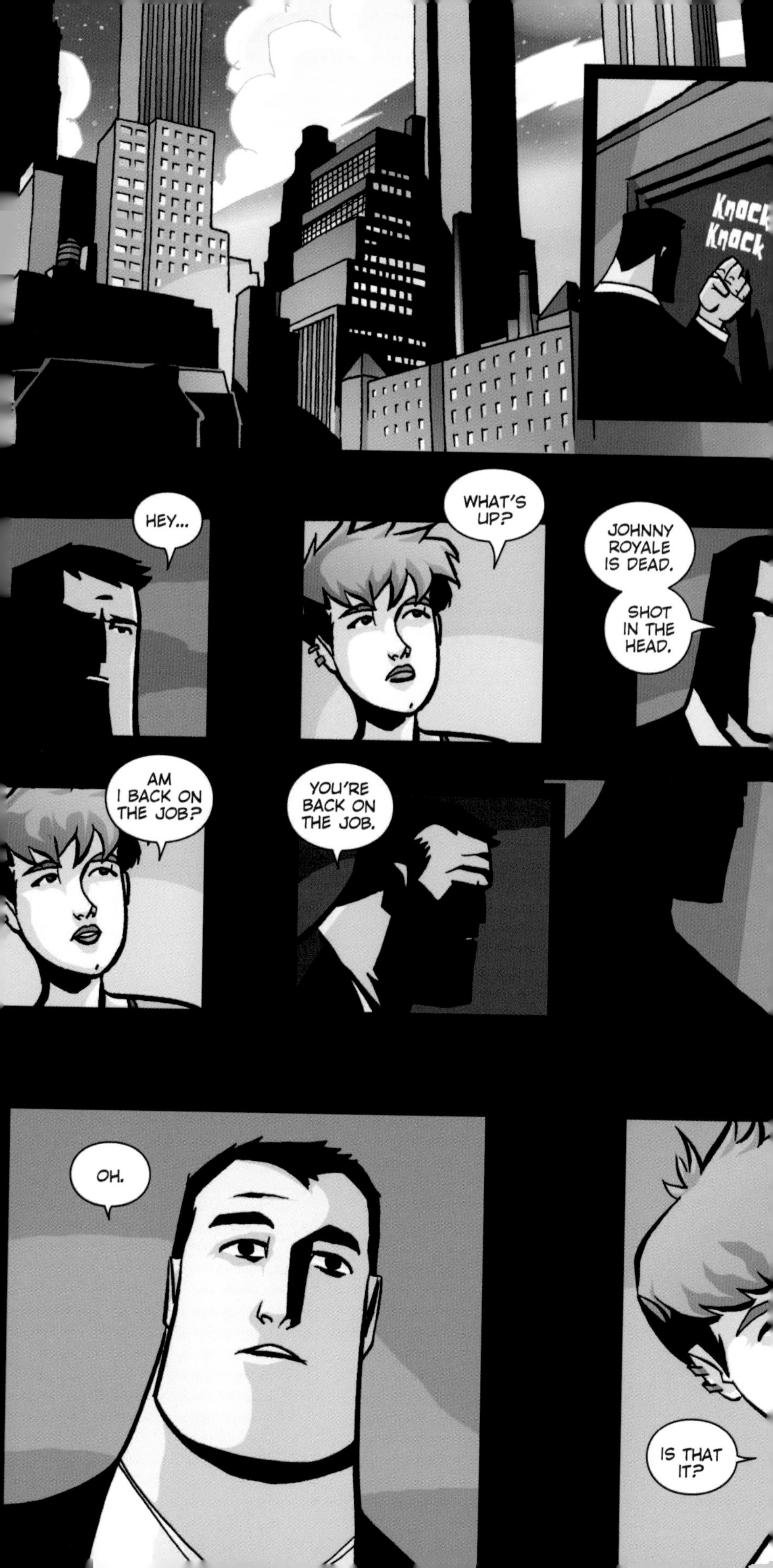
Knock Knock
HEY...
WHAT'S UP?
JOHNNY ROYALE IS DEAD.
SHOT IN THE HEAD.
AM I BACK ON THE JOB?
YOU'RE BACK ON THE JOB.
OH.
IS THAT IT?

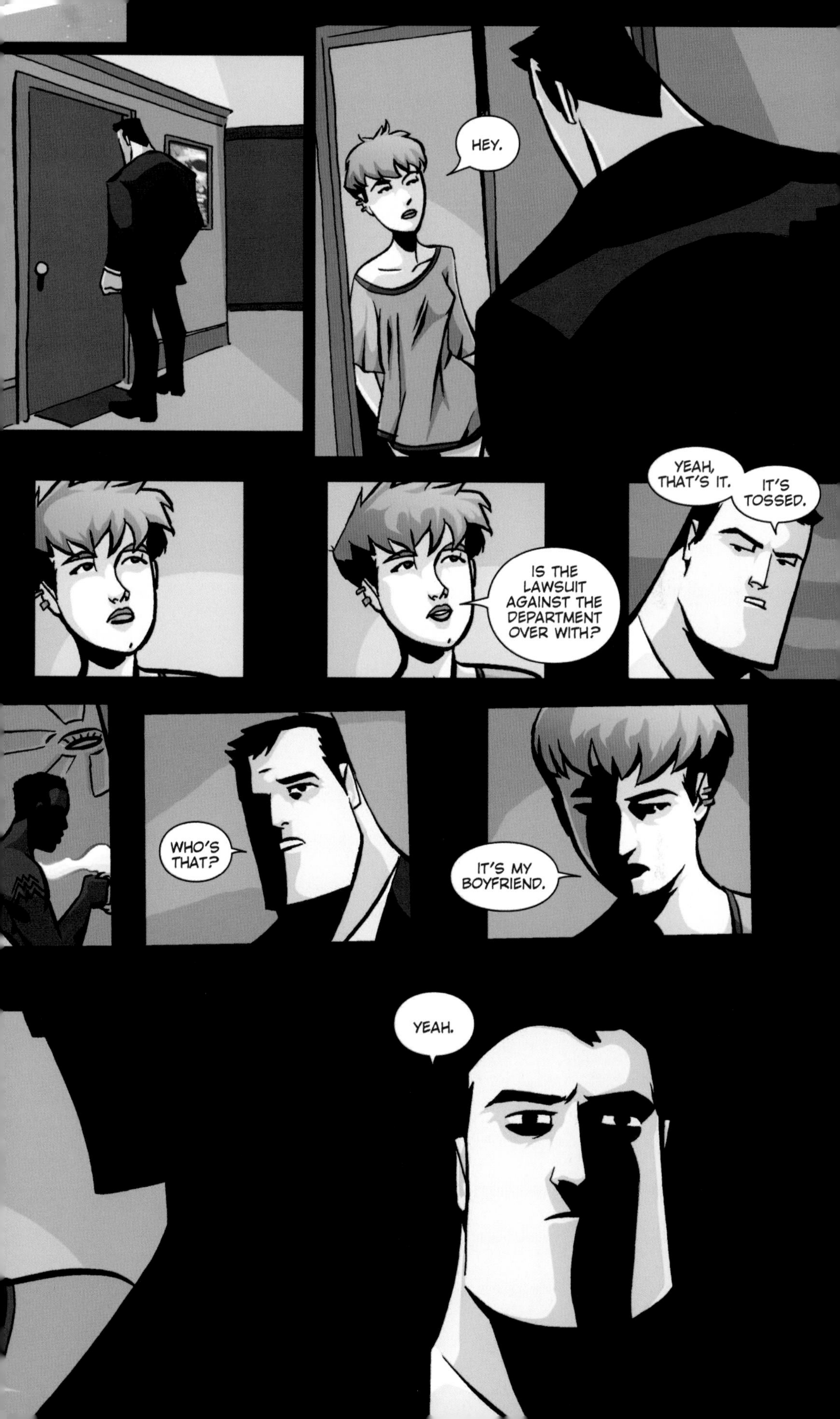
HEY.
IS THE LAWSUIT AGAINST THE DEPARTMENT OVER WITH?
YEAH, THAT'S IT.
IT'S TOSSED.
WHO'S THAT?
IT'S MY BOYFRIEND.
YEAH.

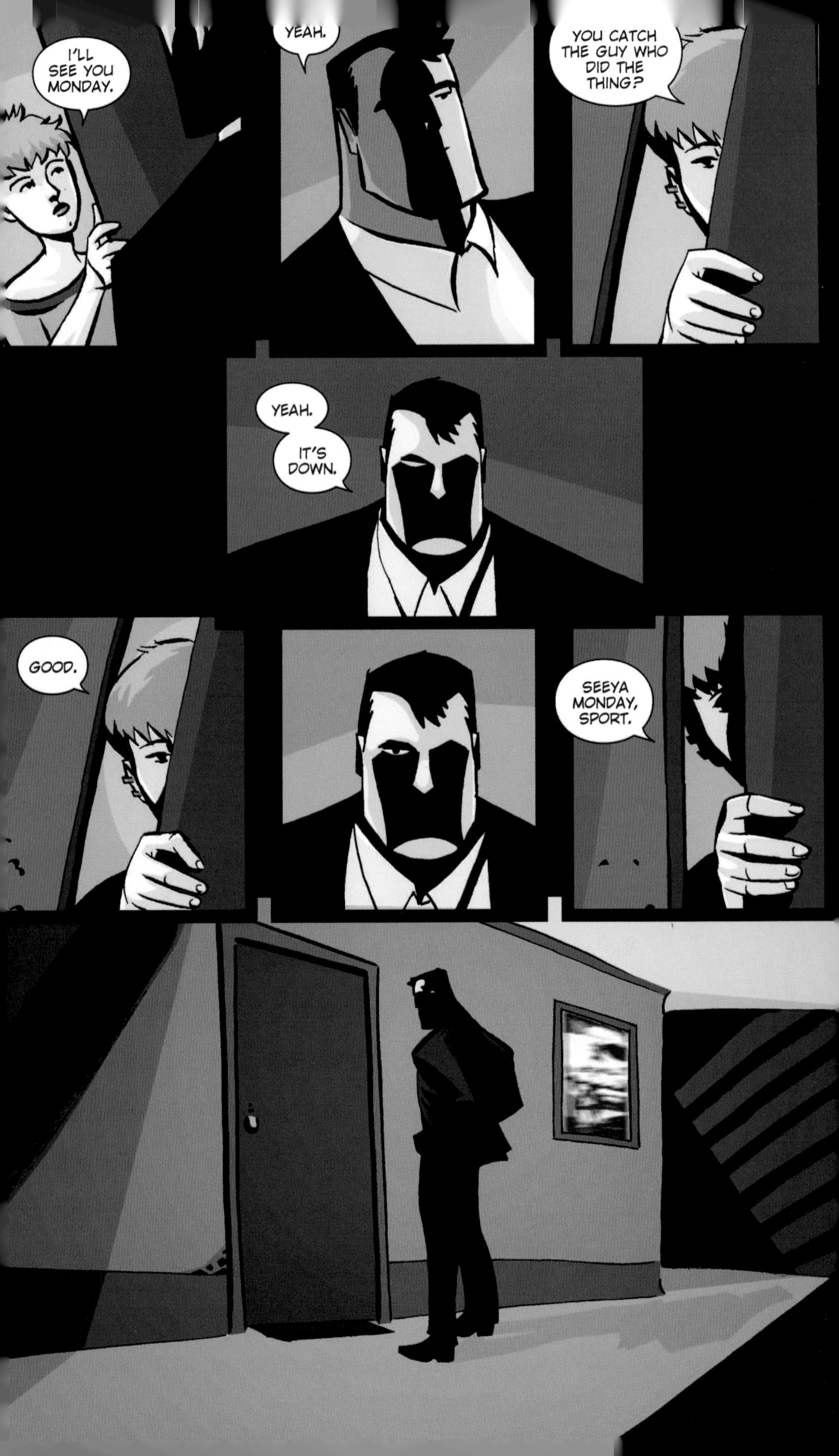
I'LL SEE YOU MONDAY.
YEAH.
YOU CATCH THE GUY WHO DID THE THING?
YEAH.
IT'S DOWN.
GOOD.
SEEYA MONDAY, SPORT.

POWERS

COVER GALLERY

Ever notice how there's about five basic mainstream comic book cover designs? You know them:

1. The hero leaping at you, readying for battle.
2. The close-up of the hero grimacing at you, with the shadow of whatever villain he is facing cast half over his face.
3. The logo of the comic smashing from the force of the great battle going on underneath it.
4. The big maniacally laughing villain close-up.
5. Let's not forget, the ever-popular giant boobs smushed together in the middle of the cover with a couple of spots of blood on them that, at first glace, somewhat resemble nipplage.

These are what we call in the business: Comic Book Cliches. And if I am ever responsible for purposefully executing one here in Powers, I will kill myself, but then make it look like Mike Oeming did it. Mike and I decided very early on to create theme covers for each story arc. And for this storyline we ended up using album cover designs from albums you would find in a collage dorm room.

But the road to a good idea is not always smooth. There's a lot of really bad ideas pursued, or as Mike likes to call them: ideas forced down the artist's throat from a know-it-all writer. And then there are the cover designs created by an artist hopped up on paint fumes.

Join us now as we take you on a trip through the cover gallery, then onto the abandoned cover concepts and sketches. We hope that you will find it interesting, and by that I mean I hope the extra effort gets us nominated for something.

POWERS

8 2.95
4.75
CANADA

POWERS

AVON FROM CRUMB

A BRAND NEW STORY ARC!

BRIAN MICHAEL BENDIS
MICHAEL AVON OEMING
PAT GARRAHY

ROLE PLAY PART ONE

Based on Janis Joplin and Big Brother & the Holding Company's *Cheap Thrills* designed by Robert Crumb.

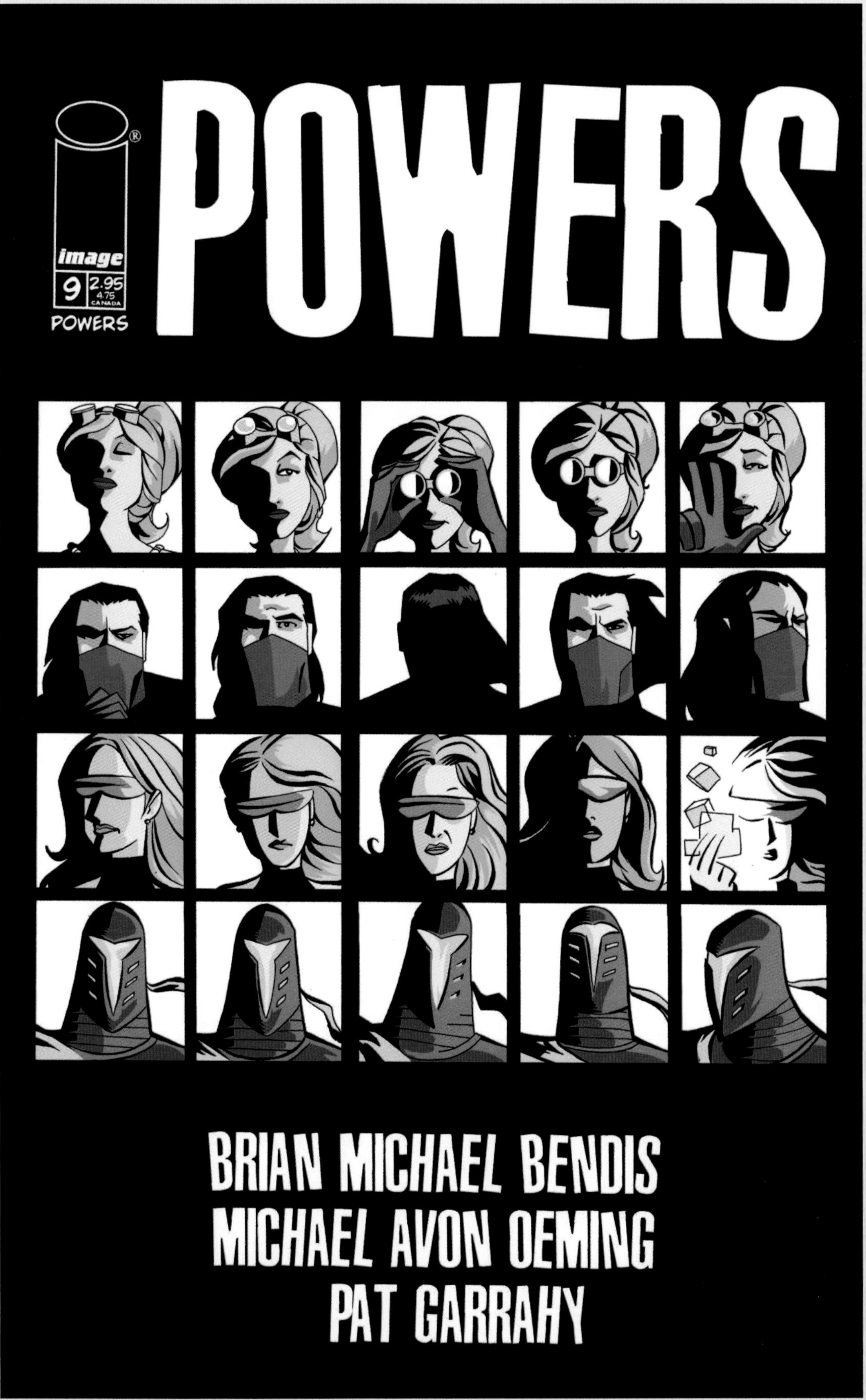
POWERS
image
9
2.95
4.75 CANADA
POWERS
BRIAN MICHAEL BENDIS
MICHAEL AVON OEMING
PAT GARRAHY

Based on the Beatles' "A Hard Days Night" British import single cover.

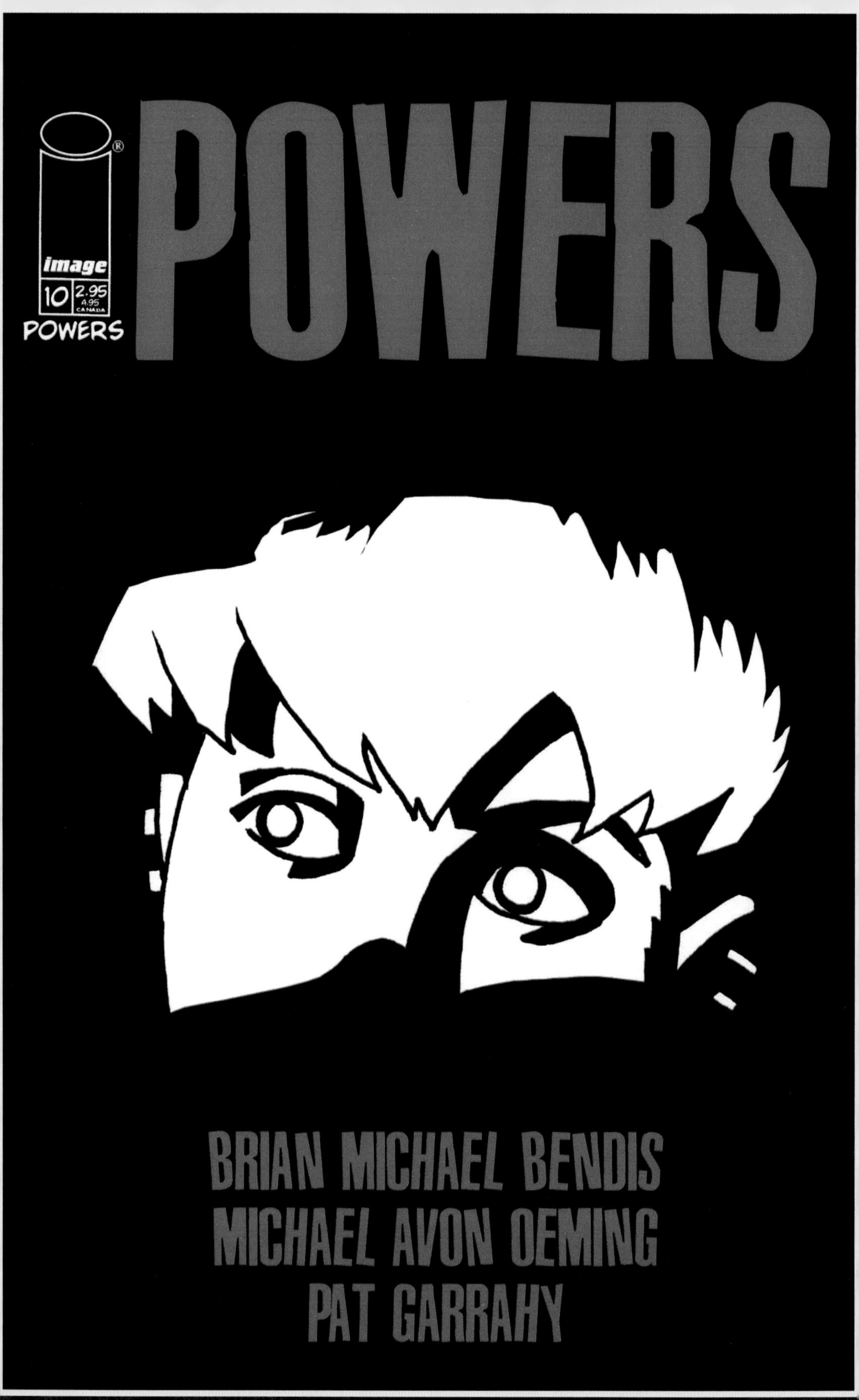
POWERS
image
10
2.95
4.95 CANADA
POWERS
BRIAN MICHAEL BENDIS
MICHAEL AVON OEMING
PAT GARRAHY

Based on Sinead O'Connor's *I Do Not Want What I Haven't Got.*

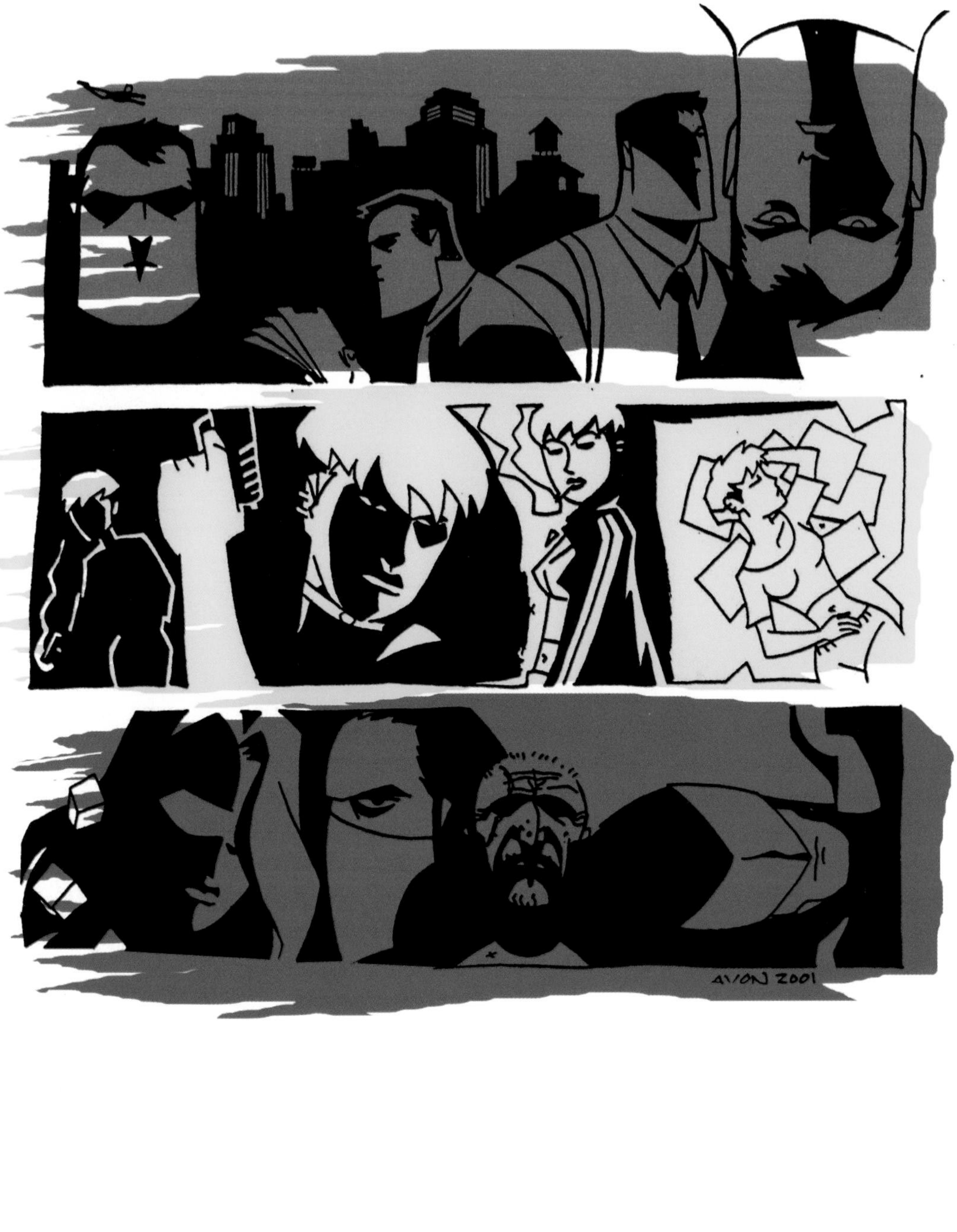
AVON 2001

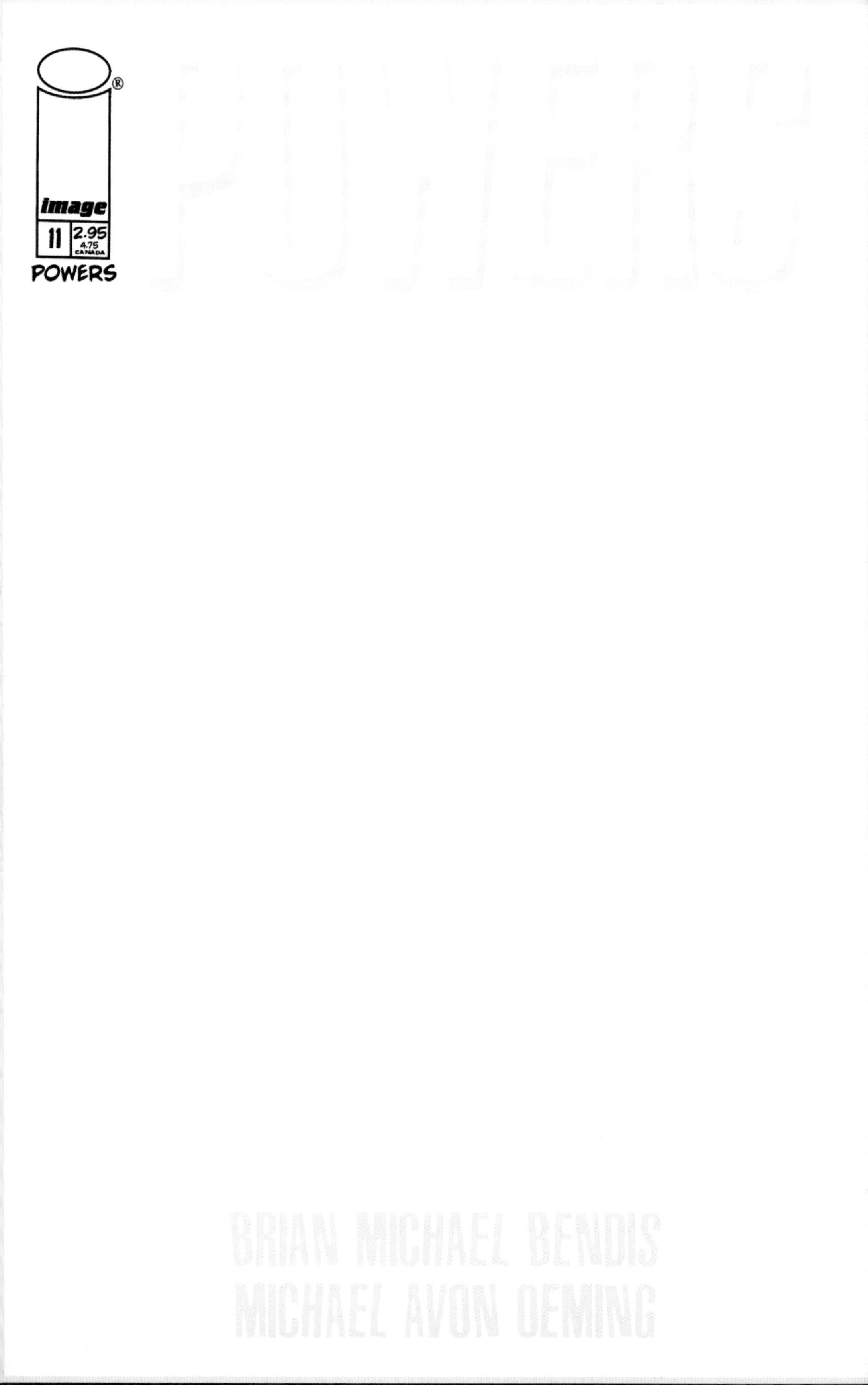
image
11
2.95
4.75 CANADA
POWERS
POWERS
BRIAN MICHAEL BENDIS
MICHAEL AVON OEMING

Based on the Beatles's *White Album.* (Duh...)

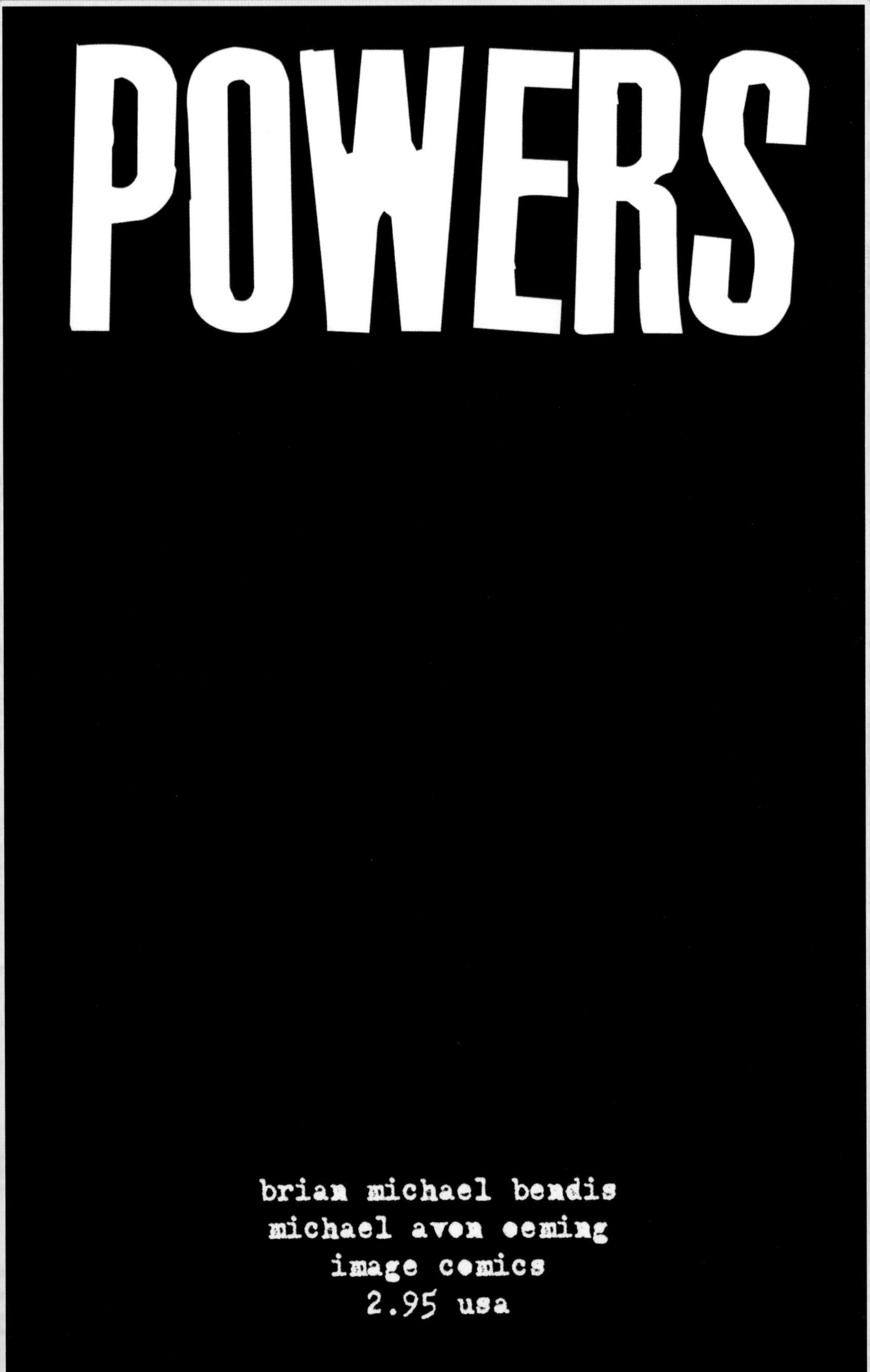
POWERS
brian michael bendis
michael avon oeming
image comics
2.95 usa

Abandoned alternate cover for *Powers* #11 based on Spinal Tap's *Smell the Glove*.
(It felt like we just stole the joke...because we did.)

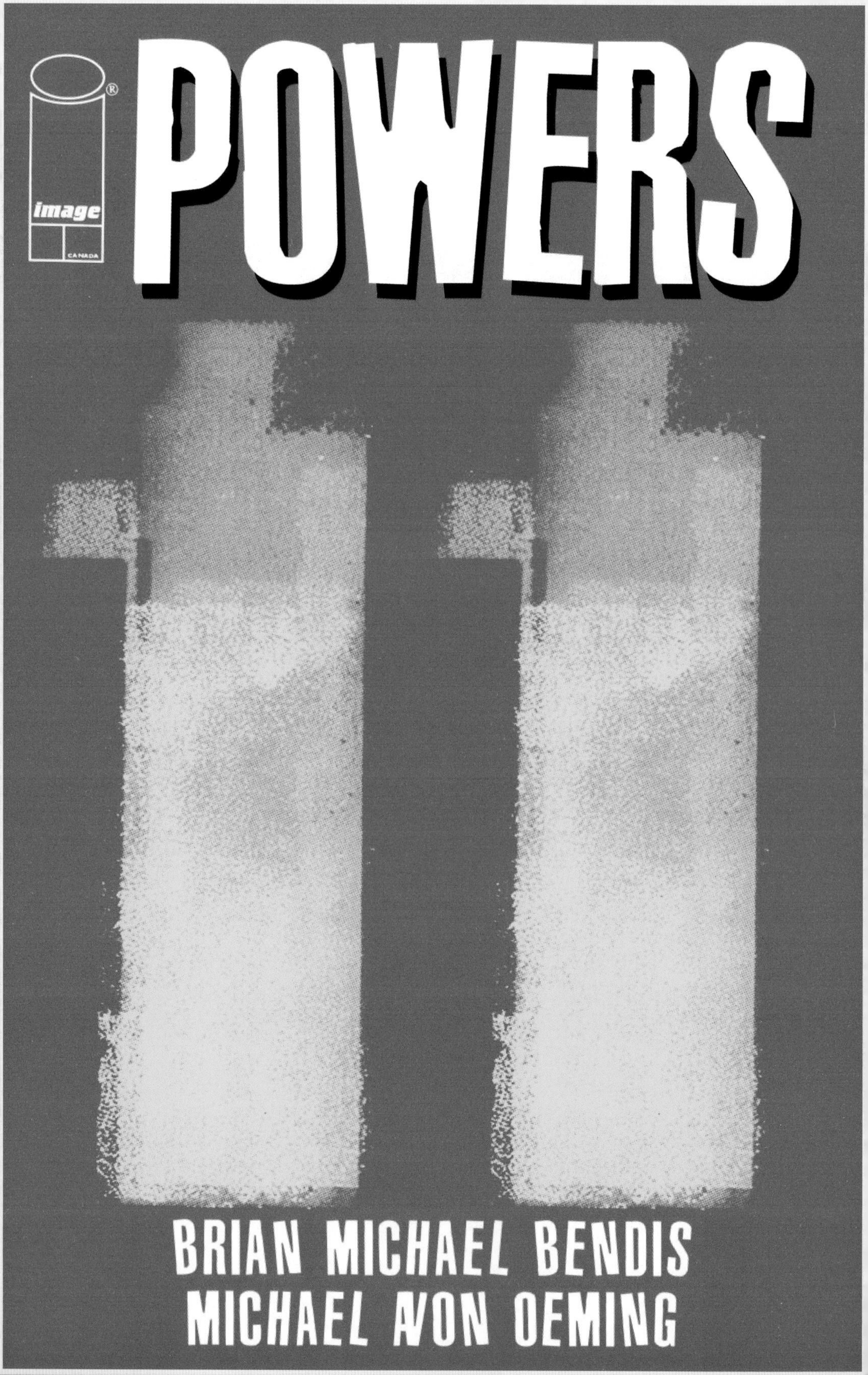
POWERS
image
CANADA
BRIAN MICHAEL BENDIS
MICHAEL AVON OEMING

Abandoned cover for *Powers* #11 based on the Beatles' *One* album.
(It felt like we just stole the artwork and altered it...because we did.)

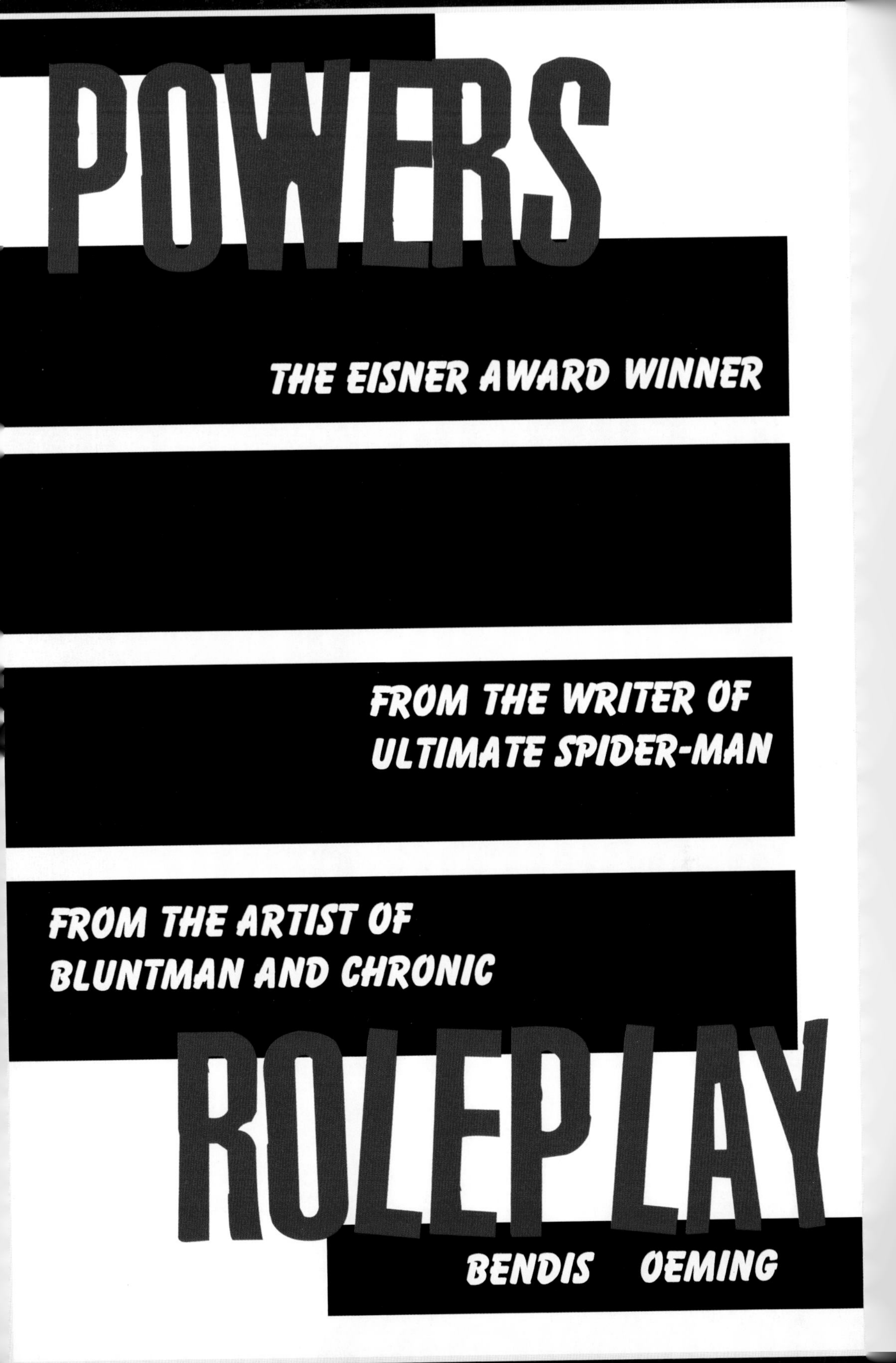
POWERS
THE EISNER AWARD WINNER
FROM THE WRITER OF
ULTIMATE SPIDER-MAN
FROM THE ARTIST OF
BLUNTMAN AND CHRONIC
ROLEPLAY
BENDIS
OEMING

Abandoned cover designs for *Powers* using graphics instead of an image.

POWERS POWERS POWE

POWERS POWERS

POWERS POWERS POWE

ERS POWERS

POW

POWERS POWERS POWE

ERS POWERS POWERS

POWERS POWE

ERS POWERS POWERS

POWERS POWERS

BENDIS
OEMING
GARRAHY

POWERS POWERS

POWERS

WWW.
JINX
WORLD.
COM

POWERS

image

P

ERS POWERS POWERS

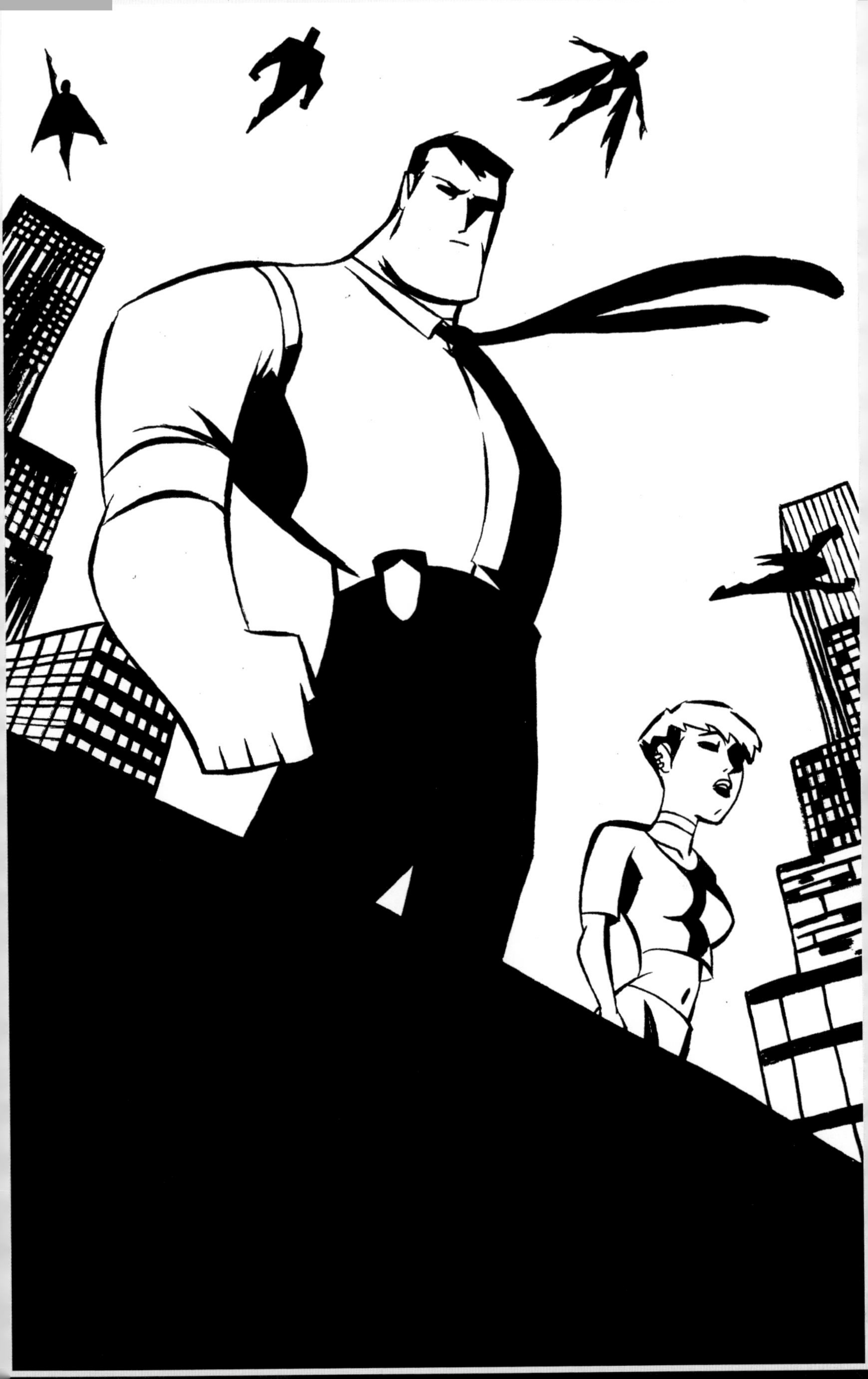

Abandoned cover illustrations for *Powers*. Good drawings that we may use some day, but wrong for the story in this collection.

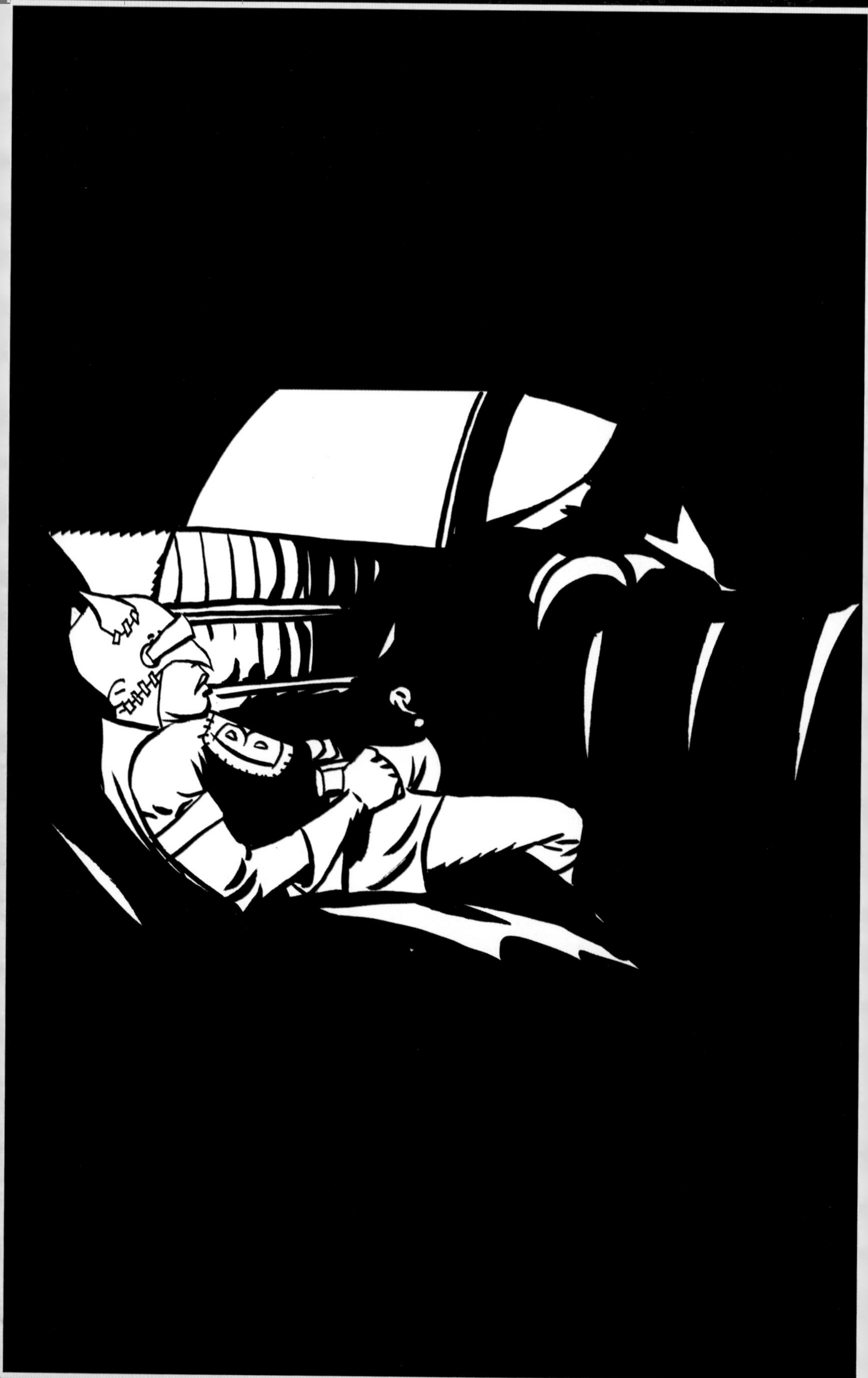

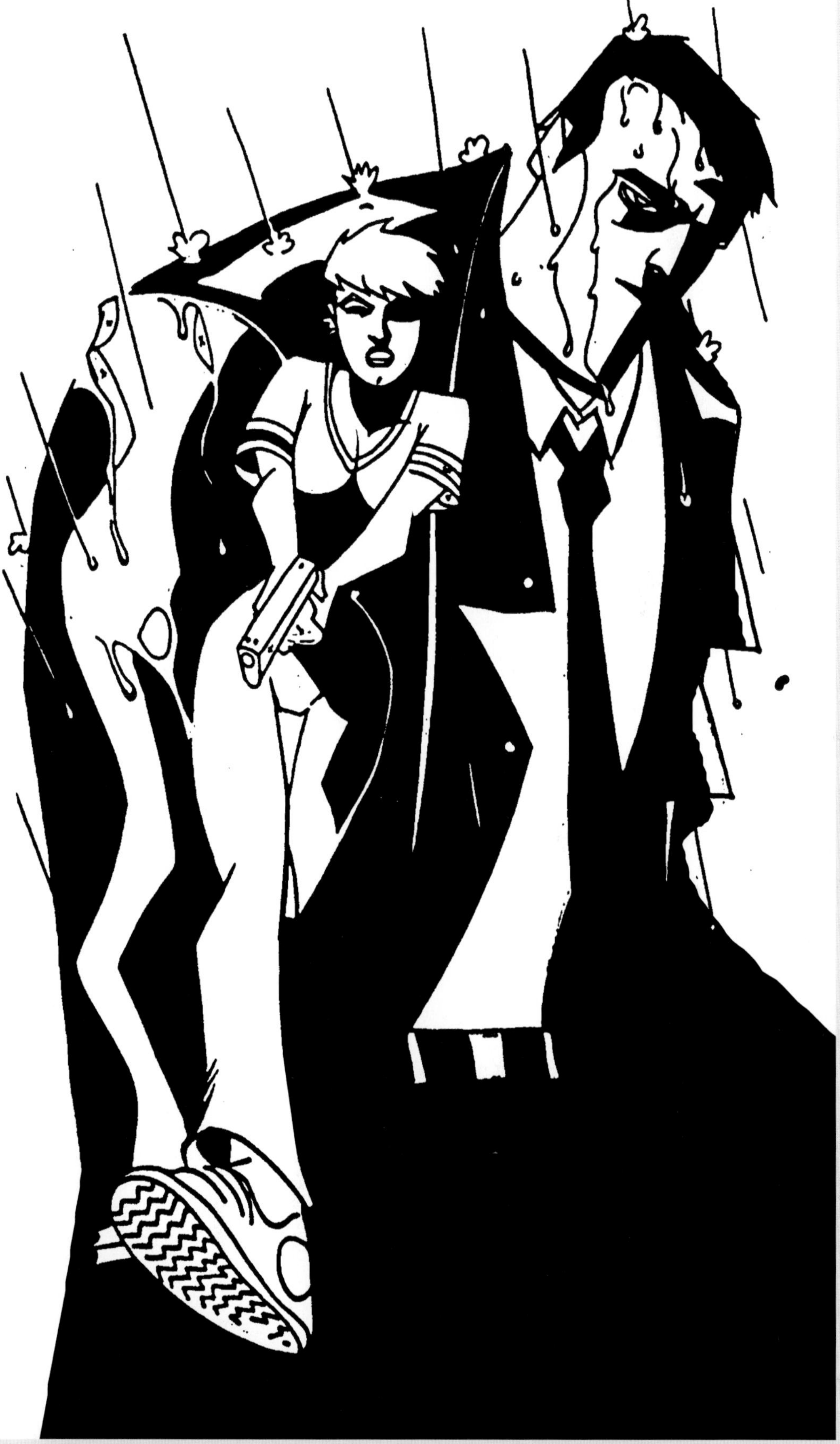

POWERS THAT BE
FIVE MINUTES WITH MICHAEL AVON OEMING

One of the hottest, most intriguing comics out there right now is *Powers*, a book that's taken the industry by storm. Following the beat of two human detectives investigating "powers-related" crimes in their superhuman world, *Powers* escaped from the minds of writer Brian Michael Bendis, who has had his own success as writer/artist with *a.k.a. Goldfish* and *Jinx*, and artist Michael Avon Oeming, whose work on *Ship of Fools* caught him more attention after his work on books like *Judge Dredd* and his superhero work.

The stylistic approach to *Powers* is very specific; in fact, Mike Oeming notes it was the impetus behind getting together with Brian Michael Bendis and specifically creating a crime comic.

"I met Brian Bendis years ago when he was doing store signings for *a.k.a. Goldfish*. We just clicked right away," Oeming relates. "We stayed in touch and talked about working together. After different projects came and went, I was looking for something new to do. I called Brian and was like, 'I want to do a crime book and I want to use this particular kind of style' — this Bruce Timm-ish/Alex Toth kind of animated stuff. And I really wanted to use it in a crime thing."

The artist explains the development of the realistic animated look of *Powers*. "The style developed from my trying to get work on the *Batman Adventures* stuff. I liked that style, but I couldn't stay on model, because I saw other things it had potential for that the series wasn't quite allowing. I really like stuff Timm was influenced by, specifically Alex Toth who was a huge influence on me. I just wanted to do some crime stuff using a combination of their two styles."

"That's basically what I told Brian," as Oeming affects a begging tone to his voice and says, "'I want to do a crime book with you 'cause you're a good writer.' And he was like, 'Absolutely!' We mulled over things. I faxed him some ideas. I didn't care what it was; I knew that we would just have fun on it. I assumed that it would be one issue or a couple of issues that would be released through Image central as a black and white. At the time, I had been doing *Ship of Fools*. So that's all we thought: little, tiny black and white book.

"It just kind of blossomed from there," Oeming explains. "Brian basically had *Powers* in its nutshell. He showed me the thing and I was hesitant at first. I wanted to do a straightforward crime thing. And I was like, 'What's this?' And he said, "No, no, it's not about the heroes!' So even I took some convincing and thank God I saw his way!"

Of course, as everyone is well aware — or if you're not, you are now — that little, tiny black and white book is a bit bigger. Oeming for one is taken by surprise by the success.

"I'm not sure why it happened," Oeming admits of the sudden hit. "I think a lot of it had to do with Bendis' fans. He's been doing these crime books for many years now. First it was *a.k.a. Goldfish*, which ran into *Jinx*, which ran into *Torso*, and then he started getting picked up for other companies to do books, like *Sam & Twitch*. So he really started building his fan base. So that and the commerciality of my artwork, it was what people were looking for, or at least people who hadn't read his stuff before. I think that's what I brought into the fold really, a certain amount of commerciality. My work's very iconic, you look at it and immediately know what it is, it's so simple. That's what I like about it. Brian's artwork is more realistic but both show the same elements of the noir, the use of blacks and lighting. Even though physically, the artwork *looks* very different, if you look at the pacing, the lighting, we're working in the same way, just in slightly different elements."

Bendis as a writer/artist has a unique way of telling his stories for Oeming, and that system works out very well. "His scripts are completely visual which works because we're on the same page, no pun intended," the artist says. "We know exactly what the other is thinking. Originally, for the first issue, he supplied me with layouts, with the grids and stuff because he had a specific way, a very cinematic way of presenting the panel-to-panel work. Once I got a hold of that, we've come up with out own secret language where he'll just call me and say, 'Change the so-and-so with blah-blah-blah' and I'll *know* what he means! And I'll change the so-and-so with the blah-blah-blah so we're definitely on the same wavelength. His sense of visuals comes through very clearly."

The newest news in regards to *Powers* is the recently announced movie deal at Sony with Mace Neufeld, producers of "Men in Black." Oeming is excited by it all, but keeps calm about it, because no matter how cool a *Powers* movie could be "I haven't seen it yet," so he's withholding a certain level of enthusiasm. "What really happens when you make a deal — and we have a really good deal, and when I say 'good deal' I mean we're well respected by the company. We're being treated very fairly, but the movie is out of our hands, so we just sit back and hope they make a good film. They have a good track record, Mace Neufeld is just widely known for doing quality stuff, so that's on our side."

But while the comic awaits Hollywood treatment, the book itself continues to work its magic on the public. In fact, in most outlets, issues can't be found. Oeming explains that "the reason we're going to trade paperback so quickly is because we basically sold out of the book. We *way* overprinted, but the reorders were so high, there's not enough to go around anymore!"

In fact, something completely new will be coming out in the near future. As Oeming describes: "Brian and I do a lot of research for our projects and before I actually started *Powers*, I went to the local police station and introduced myself. I got to do ride-alongs, I met the captain, I took extensive photo reference of all their equipment, they let me shoot a couple of rounds off at some criminals... wait, what was the original question? I got distracted and all excited about shooting people," he laughs.

Back on topic, Oeming tells the origin of what will be the *Powers Superhero Safety Coloring Book*. "So hanging around at the police station, you start noticing all the little knickknacks they have laying around. And one of those things is something for kids...safety coloring books! Big cartoony cops saying, 'Hey kids, if you see power lines down, don't touch them!' I sent Brian some as kind of a joke and he said, 'This is a great idea!' So the *Powers* coloring book will be a variation of this. You'll have safety tips like 'If you're walking down the street and you see two superhero beings fighting this guy and fire is blasting out of their eyes, immediately duck and cover. Do not touch flame retardant superheroes..' It's safety tips for the Powers universe. Kind of like kids during the A-bomb scare, but there's superheroes flying out of the sky! We're going to be making some pretty good jokes about ourselves in the process of doing the book. It'll be fun."

A big jump from what they normally do, when you think about it. And Oeming laughs and agrees, "In between dead people, we get to do a coloring book!"

— *Maureen McTigue*

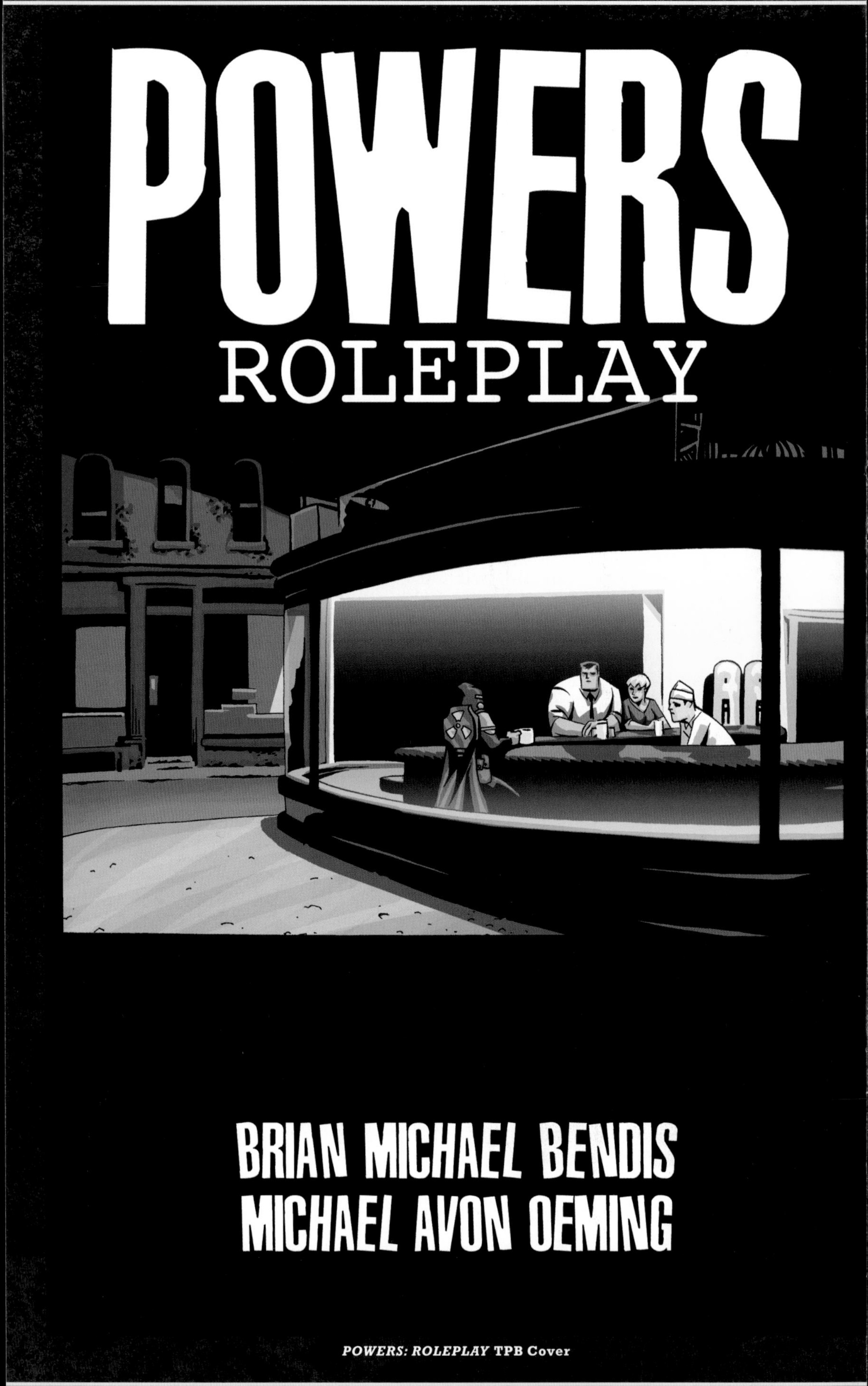
POWERS
ROLEPLAY
BRIAN MICHAEL BENDIS
MICHAEL AVON OEMING

***POWERS: ROLEPLAY* TPB Cover**